CREDIT NATION

The Princeton Economic History of the Western World

Joel Mokyr, Series Editor

A list of titles in this series appears in the back of the book.

Credit Nation

Property Laws and Legal Institutions in Early America

Claire Priest

PRINCETON UNIVERSITY PRESS

PRINCETON AND OXFORD

Published by Princeton University Press
41 William Street, Princeton, New Jersey 08540
6 Oxford Street, Woodstock, Oxfordshire OX20 1TR

press.princeton.edu

ISBN 978-0-691-15876-1
ISBN (e-book) 978-0-691-18565-1

British Library Cataloging-in-Publication Data is available

Editorial: Joe Jackson and Jacqueline Delaney
Production Editorial: Brigitte Pelner
Jacket/Cover Design: Karl Spurzem
Production: Erin Suydam
Publicity: Kate Hensley (US) and Kathryn Stevens (UK)
Copyeditor: Karen Verde

Jacket Image: Reverse of $40 colonial currency from the Province of Georgia, 1778. Courtesy of National Numismatic Collection, National Museum of American History, Smithsonian Institution

This book has been composed in Adobe Text and Gotham

Printed on acid-free paper ∞

Printed in the United States of America

10 9 8 7 6 5 4 3 2 1

To my parents, George and Kathy, and to Neal and Rohan

CONTENTS

ACKNOWLEDGMENTS

The debts for this project run deep, and none involve collateral. I am deeply grateful for the privilege of studying and working with wonderful scholars who serve as a constant inspiration. A series of fortunate events led me to feel welcome in the field of early American history as a junior professor: meeting Edmund Morgan, whose greatness as a scholar was matched by his magnanimity and kindness; an invitation by Bernard Bailyn to his Atlantic seminar, a remarkable group of scholars; meeting Gordon Wood, with whom I had the privilege of teaching at Northwestern while having a baby mid-semester; and attending Joel Mokyr's economic history workshop, a step toward publishing this book in Joel's series at Princeton University Press. Other strokes of good luck: taking inspiring classes unknowingly filled with future colleagues and friends, such as a junior seminar on slavery and antislavery with David Brion Davis and a legal history seminar with Reva Siegel and Bob Gordon. More recently, the mentors whose scholarship I greatly admire—Naomi Lamoreaux, Carol Rose, and Bob Gordon—have become colleagues.

I am very grateful to Joel Mokyr and everyone at Princeton University Press for bringing this book to print, especially Joe Jackson and Seth Ditchik, Jacqueline Delaney, the anonymous reviewers, and Brigitte Pelner and copyeditor Karen Verde for their detailed work.

Yale Law School is a tremendous institution to be a part of, and it is an honor to be associated with the legal history group of John Langbein, Sam Moyn, Nick Parrillo, Reva Siegel, Jim Whitman, John Witt, and Taisu Zhang. In the broader faculty, I am especially grateful for the support of the Deans Harold Koh, Robert Post, and Heather Gerken, and for professional camaraderie to Bruce Ackerman, Muneer Ahmad, Emily Bazelon, Sharon Brooks, Stephen Carter, Fiona Doherty, Bob Ellickson, Owen Fiss, James Forman, Abbe Gluck, Miriam Gohara, Henry Hansmann, Oona Hathaway, Brad Hayes, Christine Jolls, Paul Kahn, Al Klevorick, Tony Kronman, Yair Listokin, Jon Macey, Daniel Markovits, Tracey Meares, John Morley, Doug NeJaime,

George Priest, Cristina Rodriguez, Roberta Romano, Vicki Schultz, Scott Shapiro, Reva Siegel, Kate Stith, Mike Wishnie, and Gideon Yaffe.

Karen Crocco and Kelly Mangs-Hernandez have given me wonderful help at Yale Law School. I also thank the Yale Law students who have served as research assistants: Caroline Harkins, Enrique Pasquel, Leah Carter, and especially Brent Salter, whose assistance with the footnotes of this book was invaluable. During a two-week fellowship at PERC in Montana, I first compiled the statutes on colonial title recording that form the basis of chapter 2.

Northwestern Law School was a terrific place to start my academic career and I thank Steve Calabresi, Charlotte Crane, David Dana, David Haddock, Heidi Kitrosser, Andy Koppelman, Janice Nadler, Jide Nzelibe, Dorothy Roberts, Max Schanzenbach, and Kim Yuracko for their support and friendship. A special thanks goes to Jim McMasters who helped me find documents relating to the Debt Recovery Act.

My professional friendships mean a great deal and I would like to thank Steve Pincus for bringing together a community of early Americanists, and Holly Brewer, Sally Gordon, Emma Rothschild, Chris Tomlins, John Wallis, and Gavin Wright for their encouragement. Outside of the world of early American studies, I thank Bernadette Atuahene, Kenworthey Bilz, Susanna Blumenthal, Eleanor Brown, Daniela Cammack, Kris Collins, Noah Feldman, David Grewal, Jill Hasday, Amalia Kessler, Alison LaCroix, Carlton Larson, Dan Sharfstein, and Tico Taussig-Rubbo for being great friends and colleagues.

I am also grateful to my friends Ashlie Beringer, Nina Bhatt, Sarah Bilston, Jonah Blank, Anjanine Bonet, Rick and Heidi Brooks, Belinda Chan, Sue Chan, Judy Chevalier and Steve Podos, Navtej Dhillon, Barbara Endres and Bill Butler, Jacob Hacker, Sheila Hayre and Pericles Lewis, Jim and Leslie Huffman, Alison and Christopher Illick, Binnie Klein, Alison MacKeen, Charity McNabb, Talbot and Tom Mason, Maria Morodo and Patrick Lindley, Kaivan Munshi and Soenje Reiche, Ify Nwokoye, Polly and John Sather, Leslie Stone and Michael Sloan, Marcy Stovall and Jim Farnam, Joe Child and Mary Nell Wegner, Nina Scherago and George Jones, Sara Sullivan and Zachariah Hickman, Amy Vatner, Jason Vincz, and Annie Wareck. And to my family: all the Kiefers and Battles, Shannon, JL, my siblings and their spouses, my nieces and nephews, as well as the Shivakumars, the Rajagopalans, and the entire extended family of Danny Shivakumar who have been so supportive of me, Neal, and Rohan.

Marcus Rhinelander and I were in Peru with my sons in the spring of 2020 when we learned that instead of working on a project together, we had to leave the country immediately due to the new pandemic. Not able to pursue documentary photography, Marcus read every word of this book (almost), twice, and gave invaluable suggestions throughout. But far more important, I thank Marcus for all of the amazing adventures we have had these past few years and I look forward to many more.

This book is dedicated to my parents, Kathy and George Priest, and my sons, Neal and Rohan. My parents helped me raise Neal and Rohan and are inspiring role models in their professional life and their love of adventures large and small. Neal and Rohan, thank you for being excellent fellow travelers.

Excerpts from the book were published as: Claire Priest, "Creating an American Property Law: Alienability and Its Limits in American History," *Harvard Law Review* 120 (2006): 385–458; Claire Priest, "Law and Commerce, 1580–1815," in *The Cambridge History of Law in America*, ed. M. Grossberg and C. Tomlins (Cambridge: Cambridge University Press, 2008): vol. 1, 400–446; Claire Priest, "The End of Entail: Information, Institutions, and Slavery in the American Revolutionary Period," in *Law and History Review* 33 (2015): 277–319; Justin duRivage and Claire Priest, "The Stamp Act and the Political Origins of American Legal and Economic Institutions," in *Southern California Law Review* 88 (2015): 875–912.

CREDIT NATION

Introduction

In the United States today, there is a vast credit economy that almost anyone who owns property or who has a steady income can access by obtaining home mortgages and car loans, by financing a home business, or by running up credit card debt. On a larger scale, corporations rely on institutional credit markets to raise billions of dollars for investments every year. This world of credit, with its many advantages, but also with risks of over-leveraging, real estate bubbles, and widespread foreclosures, rests on a structure of laws and legal institutions that is often obscure in our day-to-day lives. At the most basic level, obtaining credit requires having property, and taking on debt implies the risk of losing that property. Two centuries of American economic prosperity have been based on the laws governing credit and property. We take access to credit for granted but, in fact, decisions made centuries ago set the stage for our modern economy. *Credit Nation* examines the early origins of property rights and the formal legal institutions serving as a foundation for the market economy and political system of the United States.

The legal origins of our credit economy were shaped in the British colonial era and the American founding period, from roughly the 1620s to the 1790s. The book describes how British laws relating to property and credit were imported to the colonies and adapted for the colonial context. Laws and legal institutions surrounding property were at the heart of the entire, slowly emerging colonial enterprise. It emphasizes how, in creating an "American" property law prior to Independence, the colonial legislatures, regulated by Parliament in England, were focused on matters relating to expanding collateral and credit. The expansion of slavery, a labor system based on property rights in human beings, coincided with the reform of legal institutions to encourage slaveholders to obtain credit on the basis of slaves as collateral. A second theme of the book asks how the legal history of credit relates to the political history of the United States. How were property laws shaped by the context of British colonial rule? How are property laws and institutions linked to representative government in American history? The book illustrates the central role of collateral and credit in the rule of Britain over the colonies, the American Revolution, and the reform of legal institutions in the founding era.

———

At the Constitutional Convention in 1787, Alexander Hamilton described "the security of Property" as one of the "great obj[ects] of Gov[ernment]."[1] Despite gaining independence from Britain, the founding era was a period in which landed wealth still framed conceptions of the economic, social, and political order. At the time of the Revolution, every state but one required freehold land ownership for participation in the franchise, meaning that the voting public was a small minority of the population.[2] And yet, an idealized view emerged that the country was defined by its relative equality. To Thomas Paine (who immigrated from England to America in 1774), for example, a central difference between English and American society was that "[i]n America, almost every farmer lives on his own lands, and in England not one in a hundred does."[3]

Whiggish commentators of the founding era and early nineteenth century created narratives of the American Revolution in which property served as a central connection linking the political system, the economy, and the society. Prominent legal treatises emphasized that, in the process of settling British America, the colonists built institutions and reformed the property laws of England in ways that reinforced the republican political and ideological revolution of the times. In his famous Plymouth Oration commemorating the two-hundred-year anniversary of the pilgrims' arrival, Daniel Webster focused on the exceptional nature of property in America and its relation to republican government. He remarked that "[t]he history of other nations may teach us how favourable to public liberty is the division of the soil into small freeholds."[4] He continued that "[A] multitude of small proprietors . . . constitute not only a formidable, but an invincible power." It followed that, "In this country we have actually existing systems of government, in the maintenance of which, it should seem, a great majority, . . . must see their interest."[5] Many shared Webster's belief that the widespread ownership of land across the American states was the linchpin of the republican political system.

Political leaders of the founding era defined the new American political world by its rejection of hereditary privilege, the core of the European aristocratic political order. In England, from the late medieval period through the modern era, ownership of landed estates was associated with political privileges ranging from, at the highest levels, membership in the House of Lords, to local political offices and social influence.[6] English law was characterized by a preference for maintaining the integrity and cohesiveness of estates over the generations, securing political power within families.[7] The English legal scholar William Blackstone's *Commentaries on the Laws of England*, published in the years 1765–1769, for example, describes "the principal object of the laws of real property in England" as the law of inheritance.[8]

In the American founding era, the prevalence of land ownership in the United States dispersed political power throughout the population. In Europe, one justification for the political power of a landed aristocracy was that it served as an essential counterweight to the tyranny posed by monarchy. In contrast, in a republican America, any political tyranny would be warded off by the masses of freehold property owners who participated in government. Landowners were celebrated as fiercely protective of their civil liberties. As Noah Webster stated in 1787, for example, "[a]n equality of property, with a necessity of alienation, constantly operating to destroy combinations of powerful families, is the very *soul of a republic*."[9]

Widespread ownership of property was assumed to flow from easy circulation of land in the marketplace. The dominant ideological framework of the founding era equated large consolidated landholdings with aristocratic property law that privileged inheritance and inalienability. Aristocracies were believed to exist, in part, because property law protected land from the dynamism of the market. Land markets, in contrast, were predicted to break down aristocracy. To many legal thinkers, property laws allowing landowners to sell or devise land out of the family line, in property parlance, the *alienability* of land, was a defining feature of the American property system.

Security of title was the foundation upon which the purported political and economic virtues of landowning rested. In England, the legal technicalities of land conveyancing, such as buying, selling, and mortgaging land, and placing land in trusts, often took place in private homes and lawyers' offices.[10] The transfer of an ownership interest in land was formalized in a public ceremony, but mortgages and other claims against the land were not generally publicized or required to be recorded by the local government or in the courts. Instead, the parties and their lawyers pored over documents relating to the status of title of a particular parcel. In a celebrated treatise in the 1830s, the legal authority James Kent attributes the "very limited" practice of recording deeds in England to "the general and natural disposition to withdraw settlements, and the domestic arrangements, from the idle curiosity of the public."[11]

The private English system, however functional, privileged large land-owners whose family reputations, political influence, and large income streams provided access to credit unavailable to those with smaller estates. Smaller landowners were excluded from the credit lines available to the elites because of the costs of title authentication under the private system. There were popular movements to introduce public registries in the seventeenth and eighteenth centuries in England to expand access to credit, but large landowners consistently opposed the proposals.[12]

Supreme Court Justice Joseph Story, explaining the sources of the American Revolution in his 1833 *Commentaries on the Constitution*, emphasized the role of property as an underpinning of the American political order. Story notes that in the United States, "few agricultural estates in the whole country have at any time been held on lease . . . The tenants and occupiers are almost universally the [owners] of the soil." To Justice Story, the widespread ownership of land and the strength of colonial property rights had made citizens fiercely protective of their civil liberties. He stated, "The yeomanry are absolute owners of the soil, on which they tread; and their character has from this circumstance been marked by a more jealous watchfulness of their rights, and by a more steady spirit of resistance against every encroachment, than can be found among any other people."[13] Perhaps surprisingly from the modern vantage point, Story continued by linking the property rights underlying landowners' "jealous watchfulness of their rights" and "spirit of resistance" in the American Revolution with the history of legal institutions that clarified title and expanded land markets. In Story's words, "Connected with this state of things, and, indeed, as a natural consequence flowing from it, is the simplicity of the system of conveyances, by which the titles to estates are passed, and the notoriety of the transfers made."[14] After describing the system of land title recording, Story continued that "It is hardly possible to measure the beneficial influences upon our titles arising from this source, in point of security, facility of transfer, and marketable value."[15] Story described how colonial laws had made land "a substitute for money," which he explained as "a natural result of the condition of the people in a new country, who possessed little monied capital; whose wants were numerous; and whose desire of credit was correspondingly great." He added, "the growth of the respective colonies was in no small degree affected by" this legal transformation.[16]

Similarly, Zaphaniah Swift's 1795 treatise celebrated that "our conveyancing can boast of a simplicity, conciseness, facility, and cheapness, superior to any other country."[17] Webster's Plymouth Oration emphasized as one of many important aspects of property in America that "[t]he establishment of public registries, and the simplicity of our forms of conveyance, have greatly facilitated the change of real estate, from one proprietor to another."[18] James Kent's 1830 treatise remarked in a section on conveyancing law that "In no other part of the civilized world is land made such an article of commerce, and of such incessant circulation."[19]

The simplicity and relative inexpensiveness of American conveyancing allowed landowners to buy and sell property as a liquid asset, and supported the vast colonial credit system. Title registries were a quintessentially "republican" institution in the sense that, by publicizing titles and by prioritizing creditors' claims at a low cost, they allowed smaller landowners and slaveholders access to credit. The institutional infrastructure developed in colonial America was the formal mechanism for protecting property rights, and essential foundation underlying the credit system and republican government.

Institutions

In examining the legal history of colonial British America through the lens of credit, this book traces three themes. First, it examines colonial legal institutions relating to property and credit. Scholars define the term "institutions" in many different ways. The focus here is on the "ground-level" legal institutions, such as courts and title recording measures that protected property titles, supported mortgage markets, and processed debt claims. Colonists settling in America brought with them familiarity with British laws, customs, and legal institutions. Building a new society from the ground up, however, offered the opportunity for modifications of British legal traditions, which led sometimes, in aggregate, to dramatic changes. Already in the 1600s, colonial administrations began establishing county-level common law courts where debts could be litigated and enforced and where disputes over land titles could be resolved and publicized. Moreover, each of the colonies enacted laws instituting local title recording that often expressly promoted the security of mortgages. These recording offices or registries allowed for simple conveyances by deed, publicly accessible records, and the extension of credit on the basis of a multiplicity of assets.

One of the most novel and important features of American property law is centrally linked to American political history: property law and legal institutions were shaped by means of the statutory enactments of representative assemblies in collaboration with the crown-appointed governors. In the American colonies, the colonial administrations defined the problems to be addressed, shaped law, modified it, built institutions, controlled their costs, and regulated their operation in response to local conditions. The creation of property law and institutions by colonial statutes was quite in contrast to the property law of England, which reflected centuries of customary practice, political negotiation between kings and elites, and the legacy of feudalism, in addition to parliamentary and local law. In hindsight, founding era commentators recognized that the legislative creation of property law during the colonial era was a special phenomenon: the colonial legislatures had initiated a process of representative involvement and input into their institutions and laws that reflected a political transformation toward a republican form of government. One of the colonial lawmakers' tremendously important innovations was the use of local legal institutions in the colonial credit economy. The ease of access to credit that this created was key to the explosive growth of capitalism in nineteenth-century America.

A major complexity in interpreting the political conception of landownership in the founding era is that commentators avoided the topic of slavery and how their theories of republicanism accommodated property rights in slaves.[20] Slavery was a system of labor rooted in the starkest inequality one can imagine: where the laborers are owned as property and their owners capture any profits they generate. Moreover, in colonies relying on slave labor, there was often greater inequality within the free White population, compounding the obvious inequality between owners and slaves.[21] The liquidity of slave property and the institutional reforms to protect property rights directly promoted the expansion of slavery and the use of slaves as collateral in the credit economy.

Slaves were among the most valuable of the "assets" used as collateral in the colonial era and in the early republic. Slaves were valued highly as collateral because of their mobility.[22] Having both land and slaves serve as collateral expanded slavery because it expanded access to credit that could be used to finance the purchase of more slaves. It is estimated that by 1770,

467,000 Black people lived as slaves in the North American colonies.[23] Alice Hanson Jones's study of probate records reveals that, at the time of the American Revolution, in the South, slaves constituted 35.6% of total wealth.[24] The use of slaves as collateral for debts was one of the great evils of American slavery. Being sold or auctioned off to pay the slaveholders' debts tore slaves from their families and communities. The constant threat of such a sale in the context of highly liquid slave markets was coercive and cruel, even by the appalling standards of slavery itself.

Legal institutions played a central role in advancing this form of cruelty in slavery. Colonial legal institutions offered a centralized location to record mortgages with slaves as the collateral, to enforce debt judgments involving the seizure of slaves, and to administer slave auctions. Free colonists relied on these institutions while treating slaves as a central commodity and form of collateral in the economy.

Commodification

A second major development involved the scope and process relating to creditors' remedies. Traditional English laws and procedures stabilized the society by shielding landed estates against creditors' claims. Land markets were active in England, but land was primarily treated by the law as a source of wealth that, like an endowment, would persist through the generations. Notably, prior to 1732, the British colonial regime operated under principles of federalism with regard to debtor/creditor and property law: the legal definition of property and the scope of creditors' remedies were within the discretion of each colonial administration to repeal or amend. Although each colony had its own policies and culture, the British emphasis on protecting stable landownership gave way to a more commercial view: one where, more often, land served as a monetary asset in credit agreements.

The New England colonial governments initiated the transformation of the legal definition of land. Starting in the seventeenth century, the New England colonies redefined land to be a "chattel" or commodity when it came to creditors' claims. When the New England colonies legally defined land as a chattel, even unsecured creditors (for example, merchants who gave goods to shopkeepers on credit, or shopkeepers recording debts of farmers in book accounts) could have courts order that debtors' land be taken to satisfy their debts if the debtors' other property was insufficient. In contrast to New England, the colonies in the South initially were more likely to retain English law and protect land against unsecured creditors' claims. Initially, colonies adopted a variety of policies regarding slaves: they defined slaves either as "land" (protected from unsecured creditors under English law) or as "chattel" (available to satisfy the claims of creditors).

THE DEBT RECOVERY ACT

In 1732, Parliament acted to push colonial property law farther from the model of English landowning. In 1731, British merchants who had extended credit to planters in the colonies lobbied aggressively for Parliament to pass sweeping legislation regulating the status of colonial property rights. In August 1731, a group of thirty-two merchants in London submitted a petition to the Board of Trade complaining that they had no "Remedy for the recovery of their just Debts" in some of the colonies due to the laws in place, to court processes, and to currency manipulation.[25] Their attention at that moment was focused on Jamaica, where the legislature had passed a law holding that unsecured creditors could not use legal process to seize their debtors' land.

In 1732, Parliament responded by enacting the sweeping Debt Recovery Act, which required that, throughout all of the British colonies in America, all land, houses, and slaves were assets available to satisfy creditors' claims against debtors.[26] The Debt Recovery Act was a landmark: English society had long privileged land as a unique form of property that warranted shielding from creditors. Land conferred on its owners political and social status. Legal protections on land from creditors' claims reduced widespread financial risk, promoted social stability through the inheritance of estates, and stabilized the political system. In contrast, Parliament's Debt Recovery Act mandated that throughout the British colonies in America and the West Indies, property held in landed estates—as well as slaves—would be mere chattels, or things, when creditors pursued their claims.

Parliament's Debt Recovery Act was a law for the colonies only, starkly differentiating the colonial property regime from that of the mother country. Why a separate law for the colonies? According to the Whig agenda of Sir Robert Walpole, the role of the colonies was to benefit the British economy. British authorities prioritized the interests of the English and Scottish creditors who lent extensively to the colonies over any interest in replicating English law and political society. As Joseph Story later described, this law made colonial "land, in some degree, a substitute for money, by giving it all the facilities of transfer, and all the prompt applicability of personal property."[27] Although not mentioned by Story, in reality slaves, even more so than land, were the primary collateral and liquid asset in many areas.

Slaves had been used as collateral and had been sold in judicially super-vised auctions long before Parliament enacted the Debt Recovery Act. The Act, however, transformed local practice, determined colony by colony, into a parliamentary mandate. The Debt Recovery Act's enforcement of slave auctions was recognized by the early nineteenth-century abolitionists in Britain. In 1806, in the first known pamphlet on slave auctions, Bryan Edwards, a Member of the House of Commons, describes the practice of auctioning slaves to satisfy the slaveholder's secured and unsecured debts as a grievance "so remorseless and tyrannical in its principle, and so dread-ful in its effects," which, "though not originally created, is now upheld and confirmed by a British act of parliament."[28] Edwards says of the Debt Recov-ery Act: "It was an act procured by, and passed for the benefit of British creditors; and I blush to add, that its motive and origin have sanctioned the measure, even in the opinion of men who are among the loudest of the declaimers against slavery and the slave trade."[29] After describing the horrors of the slave auction and the fact that the practice of selling slaves at auction to satisfy debts "unhappily . . . occurs every day," Edwards states: "Let this statute then be totally repealed. It is injurious to the national character; it is disgraceful to humanity."[30] In 1797, Parliament repealed the Debt Recovery Act with respect to slaves in the remaining British colonies.[31] In the United States, slaves would continue to be used as collateral until emancipation sixty-five years later.

What emerged as a result of these wholesale changes to English law was a truly colonial property law: a body of law and institutions developed to encourage liquid markets and the extension of credit on the basis of land and slaves in the British colonies, societies with social, political, and eco-nomic structures entirely different from that of the mother country. For the remainder of the eighteenth century in Europe, land might still secure the political, economic, and social status of nobility and other elites. In contrast, in the British colonies and later in the United States, the legal structure made land more liquid, more extendable as collateral, and more readily available as a source of investment capital. This legal shift fundamentally transformed the economic, political, and social structure of the colonies.

COLONIAL MEASURES TO RESPOND TO ECONOMIC RISK

Extending property as collateral for a loan means that there is a risk of losing the property. The contradictory desires for available credit and security of property led to a range of solutions that varied between the colonies and over time. A legal regime that prioritized the claims of creditors and expanded access to credit infused the economy with greater financial risk. In times of economic downturn, creditors sued for repayment of debts, increasing the threat to debtors of losing their property in the courts.

Within this context of expanding collateral and credit, in some colonies, most notably Virginia, property owners made use of an aspect of English property law to shelter their assets from creditors' claims. Like in England, colonists drafted wills that stated that one or more of their children would inherit property in a form called the "fee tail." Fee tail property passed directly to the named devisee and could not be seized by creditors. The fee tail came to be seen after Independence as a hallmark of aristocracy. Aristocracies were rooted in illiquid estates in land that passed through generations and were linked to positions of political power. The use of the fee tail in the colonial era has been treated by historians as a grasp for aristocracy overturned by the American Revolution. The abolition of the practice in Virginia in 1776, coinciding with the Independence movement, was celebrated as the centerpiece of the transformation to a republican form of government.

This book diverges from the focus on aristocracy by examining the fee tail through an economic lens. It suggests that colonists used the fee tail strategically to protect their assets from financial risk. Today, the wealthy often shelter assets in trusts, and many states offer homestead protections exempting a certain amount of money invested in the family's primary residence from creditors' claims. The fee tail was the colonial analogue. The Debt Recovery Act of 1732 imposed a law on the colonies requiring that land and slaves be available to be seized by creditors, but did not ban the practice of fee tail. Virginians who put their land in the form of fee tail created protected islands of wealth within a broader world where the traditional English protections for land had been repealed by the Debt Recovery Act (again, under English law, debtors' title to land could be taken when they mortgaged property but not for unsecured debts). Fee tail played a special, countervailing role in a context where the legal regime expanded access to credit and collateral, and where property was defined as a commodity in credit markets.

Colonial Rule

Third, this book focuses on the central role of laws and legal institutions related to credit in the history of British rule and the tensions leading to the American Revolution. Colonial legislatures' responsibility for crafting property law and local economic policy empowered them to become powerful forces within the British governing structure. In the 1760s, after the Seven

Years' War, British authorities expanded oversight of colonial laws and institutions. One pivotal moment was Parliament's Stamp Act of 1765—which many historians view as the act that triggered the American Revolution. This book highlights the fact that colonists objected to the Stamp Act because it imposed taxes on the legal institutions that were central to the colonial credit economy: the Stamp Act taxed legal documents involved in obtaining title deeds and mortgages, and securing and enforcing credit agreements.

During the Stamp Act crisis, British officials thought that the economic benefits of the Debt Recovery Act's property regime would keep colonists aligned with the Crown. William Knox, who served as British undersecretary of state from 1770 to 1782, was a central strategist in policy-making relating to the American colonies throughout the Revolutionary Era. In reaction to the Stamp Act protests, Knox vehemently defended parliamentary authority over the colonies. To Knox, the primary advantage the British colonies held over other European colonies was the "superior credit given to the planters by the English merchants." And, "if we inquire into the cause of this unbounded confidence and credit given by the English merchants to the Colonies, from which the Colonies have reaped so great advantage," it was *the security which they have for their property by the operation of the laws of England in the Colonies.*" There were countries where the English merchants might have found "greater profit" than the British colonies, "but in foreign countries they cannot be certain of a legal security for their property, or a fair and effectual means of recovering it; whereas in the British Colonies they know the laws of England follow their property, and secures it for them in the deepest recesses of the woods."[32] Later Knox emphasized the importance of the Debt Recovery Act in particular, which he describes as "subjecting lands and negroes in the Colonies to the payment of English book debts." To Knox, it "may truly be called the Palladium of Colony credit, and the English merchants' grand security." If they gained Independence, the colonial legislatures would likely enact laws that brought an "end of their confidence" and that would check "the prosperity of the Colonies."[33] To Knox, parliamentary authority was best defended by its legal regulations that expanded colonists' access to credit. Yet, to colonists convinced that legal institutions were central to their economic life, the Stamp Act's taxes reflected the Crown's hostility to colonial legislatures' authority over policies relating to commerce.

After Independence, the property laws and legal institutions developed in the colonial era to promote the expansion of credit were maintained and reformed. In the founding era, many state legislatures extended the Debt

Recovery Act and reformed ground-level legal institutions to bring greater transparency to property titles, further advancing credit markets. A profoundly important colonial legacy was a deep commitment to the institutions that would inexpensively publicize property interests for the purpose of market exchanges and credit markets.

This is not to say there was not opposition to the property regime of expanded collateral and credit. For example, Thomas Jefferson's writings show his opposition to the policy of taking land to satisfy debts. Virginia failed to extend the Debt Recovery Act and returned to the English law protecting land from unsecured creditors. More dramatically, Shays's Rebellion in the 1780s involved hundreds of mostly former soldiers shutting down courthouses in Western Massachusetts, where their debts were being foreclosed upon and where they felt saddled with court fees. Starting in the 1820s, and increasing after the economic crisis of 1837, states enacted laws that protected debtors by allowing individuals to shield property from creditors and by introducing procedural hurdles to foreclosure.

The fact that it was the British Parliament that imposed the Debt Recovery Act on the colonies weighed on the issue of federal oversight of state law in the new republic. Alexander Hamilton reflected in the 1780s that the Debt Recovery Act "Admitted more then our Legislature ought to have assented to; it was one of the Highest Acts of Legislature that one Country could exercise over another."[34] But, however reluctantly, many in the founding era recognized the value of federal oversight of local economic policies relating to collateral and credit. The framers of the US Constitution inserted parliamentary-style control in its text by prohibiting state legislatures from passing legislation that would "impair the obligations of contracts," from coining money, and from making anything but gold and silver legal tender. The states maintained local control over laws pertaining to property and credit, receiving only indirect forms of oversight from the federal government.

Despite the wide variation between the states on the laws regulating debt, access to credit underlies the modern US economy and its culture of entrepreneurialism. Today, virtually any sort of property can be used as collateral for a loan. Many countries still do not recognize chattel mortgages and have far more limited credit markets.[35] In the United States, over-leveraging in housing markets and putting too many assets in financial risk is often a greater concern than a lack of credit. The complex legacy of the colonial laws and institutions expanding collateral and credit is still with us.

At one time leading historians characterized the colonial era as a pre-market world of small, largely self-reliant communities, described as "peaceable kingdoms" insulated from today's economic culture.[36] Their assumption fed into the field of legal history, where scholars emphasized that the legal transformations associated with the market revolution of nineteenth century reflected a dramatic departure from the values and the society of the colonial era.[37] Over subsequent decades, however, colonial historians and legal historians advanced the understanding by showing, in contrast, how colonial communities evolved and interacted with labor markets, production for profit, and legal institutions.[38]

Property laws feature centrally in scholarship on the American Revolution: historians have long emphasized that the founding generation of political leaders placed property law at the heart of the ideology they advanced in the new nation. With regard to theories of the American Revolution itself, the path-breaking work of Bernard Bailyn and Gordon S. Wood established the central ideological origins of colonists' movement for independence.[39] One of the great symbols of early republicanism in the dominant historiography is the rejection of the English inheritance policies of primogeniture and the fee tail that kept estates intact over the generations.[40] As Gordon S. Wood has described, the English landed elite based its political authority on the stable rental income gained from owning large estates. The reform of inheritance laws in the founding era came to symbolize the dominance of new ideological principles and the rejection of aristocracy.[41] This account adds to the existing narrative by emphasizing the extent to which a "commercial republican" ideology in the founding era celebrated land as a marketable commodity, with titles that could be transferred easily, and that was a foundation for a world of credit, collateral, and capitalism.[42]

This book differs from those that center exclusively on the American Revolution as the time period when colonial society rejected English property law and its emphasis on inheritance. It asserts that by the 1730s, colonial and parliamentary law had substantially dismantled the English inheritance system by permitting unsecured creditors to use legal process to take title to land and priority over heirs in inheritance proceedings. The founding era was a time of ideological revolution, of course; however, this book shows that both local colonial legislation and Parliament's Debt Recovery Act laid the underpinnings of this revolution decades earlier.

The British American colonial credit economy must be understood as part of the broader financial revolution of the seventeenth and eighteenth centuries. In this period, governments and banks adopted novel ways to expand liquidity and credit, such as debt instruments and currencies. The landmark event of the creation of the Bank of England in 1694 revolutionized public finance. The Bank of England held the government's reserves and issued stock—creating an early financial market—as well as issuing notes based on government debt.[43] Fully understanding the financial revolution of the seventeenth and eighteenth centuries, however, requires understanding the direct relationship between "top-down" measures by governments to legally authorize debt and currencies for government finance and the "bottom-up" efforts by individuals to mortgage their land and slaves to gain access to credit described here. Building legal institutions that supported property rights and creditors' claims led to vastly expanded liquidity as governments also created financial instruments to expand the society's moveable wealth.

Slavery was an integral feature of the colonial credit economy and the origins of capitalism. Edmund S. Morgan long ago described the deep connections between slavery and republicanism: as White southerners united around the ideology of equality, they simultaneously subjugated Native Americans and Black people.[44] The "commercial republican" mentality of the founding era continued on in the Southern states with the expansion of slavery in the late eighteenth and nineteenth centuries. In 1944, Eric Williams published *Capitalism and Slavery*, a groundbreaking history of slavery in the British Empire and its direct connection to the rise of British capitalism.[45] Williams focused on the profits from slavery, the production of crops like sugar, international trade flows, and how they lead to riches in Europe. Emphasizing the use of slaves as collateral, as this book does, provides a different, internal link to capitalism. The funds that were used to expand slavery and plantation agriculture were gained by adopting laws that defined slaves as chattel property and by institutions that processed legal claims against slaveholding debtors. That funds for economic expansion were raised on the basis of slaves as collateral reveals new dimensions of the atrocities of slavery and its relation to the emergence of capitalism. Slaves' vulnerability to their slaveholders went beyond violence and rape: as collateral, slaves could be seized and sold depending on markets for crops, weather conditions, and their masters' bookkeeping and finances.

Recent scholarship on the nineteenth-century history of capitalism, such as Sven Beckert's *Empire of Cotton* and Walter Johnson's *River of Dark Dreams: Slavery and Empire in the Cotton Kingdom*, examine the emergence of capitalism through the lens of power politics and forms of coercion deriving from efforts to expand production and access to markets. The history of capitalism literature suggests that ground-level institutions often played a minimal role within the broader context of domestic cultural and ideological claims on power and authority and the broader context of the politics of empire.[46] In contrast, this book emphasizes that laws and institutions did have a major impact on the emergence of capitalism.

When an English ship carrying trade goods arrived in a colonial Virginia port, the ship captain might have unloaded his cargo knowing that the goods would not be paid for until the following year. Did the legal institutions matter? When a Pennsylvania farmer bought seed from a store that he would pay for with his next harvest, did institutions matter? This account suggests that laws and legal institutions informed these transactions in the sense that (1) public recording of debt judgments, mortgages, and titles provided transparency and encouraged creditors to trust that the system would recognize their priority over subsequent creditors; (2) the background laws set the ground rules that applied when things went wrong. When a debtor had taken on too much debt, or during times of economic recession, it mattered greatly whether land and slaves were available to be seized as assets to satisfy debts. The background laws provided constant leverage for creditors seeking repayment, even if they never exercised the legal option of seizing the debtors' assets. To understand the importance of colonial laws and institutions, one need only see how litigation on debts dominated the dockets in court records of any county in the colonial era. Though most economic actors did not sue each other when commercial relations were going well, the dominance of actions based on debts and mortgages in the colonial court records shows that colonial institutions served as an essential backdrop to the entire commercial system.

There were many facets to the eighteenth-century economy: from the politics of empire, to the revolution in government finance, to the Atlantic slave trade, to legal reforms related to land. This book suggests that the legal commodification of land and slaves as collateral and the creation of legal institutions for recording property titles and foreclosing on mortgages and debts were important underpinnings of the future capitalist society.

———

Chapter 1 provides context by describing the general structure of trade and credit and Parliament's legal regulation of commerce in British America. It examines how colonial land policy, a central crown prerogative, emphasized cultivation and distributing land in relatively small parcels. In the founding era, political commentators stressed that the nation enjoyed widespread land ownership. The same policy, however, encouraged the importation of slaves. Chapter 2 describes the basic colonial legal institutions such as common pleas courts and title recording devices that served as a foundation for credit.

Chapter 3 shifts its focus away from institutions to the legal doctrines relating to credit markets and commodification, looking at the issue of assets the legal system protected from the claims of creditors. It describes how colonial legislatures reformed English law to expand the scope of creditors' remedies against land and slaves. The chapter examines the way that, prior to 1732, colonial legislatures used debtor-creditor law strategically to advance local interests vis-à-vis English creditors. Colonial legislatures were also responsible for creating the law of slavery, a foreign concept to English law. Laws were enacted throughout the colonial era defining slaves variously as "real estate" or "chattel" to achieve alternate ends.

Chapter 4 examines how parliamentary law pushed colonial property law farther from the model of English landowning through the Debt Recovery Act of 1732. In England, the property law shielded land and protected inheritance from unsecured creditors. In the colonies, creditors' claims trumped the interests of landowners and heirs and made slaves highly vulnerable to being sold when their owners faced financial distress.

Chapter 5 examines the fee tail, or entail, the principal private means by which individuals could shield wealth from creditors. This practice had particular importance in Virginia, where the current historiography suggests that a significant amount of land was entailed at the time of the American Revolution, and thus shielded from English creditors and removed from market exchanges.

Chapters 6 and 7 examine the legacy of colonial property law and the reform of laws and institutions in the Revolution and founding era. Chapter 6 begins by describing how colonial legislatures assumed authority over establishing the level of fees imposed by the county-level institutions. Moving to the Stamp Act crisis, it examines how colonial protestors found the Stamp Act taxes offensive because, in addition to usurping colonial legislatures' power over taxation, they targeted official legal documents in the course of services offered by colonial institutions, like land transfers, mortgages, and court procedures. The opposition to the Stamp Act was, in part, rooted in a profound hostility to raising the fees and costs of the institutional infrastructure that was foundational to the day-to-day workings of the colonial economy. The legislative reforms of the founding era reveal that a lasting legacy of the colonial era was an opposition to using institutional services as a source of government revenue.

Chapter 7 discusses the founding era laws relating to creditors' rights. It discusses the aftermath of Parliament's Debt Recovery Act in state law both relating to creditors' claims and in the law of slavery. Although English abolitionists mounted an attack against the commodification of slaves in the Debt Recovery Act, American Southern states moved closer to full chattel slavery, retaining slaves' liquid features with respect to creditors' claims to promote Southern labor and credit markets. The chapter discusses the reform of legal institutions toward greater transparency by state legislatures in the 1780s. It also analyzes the abolition of the fee tail estate in land through the lens of debtor/creditor relations. Chapter 8 discusses the federal structure of debtor/creditor law in the founding era. Chapter 9 places this historical work in the context of scholarship in economic history.

PART I

Foundations of Property and Credit

1

Colonial Land Distribution and the Structure of British Colonial Commerce

When Thomas Paine remarked that "[i]n America, almost every farmer lives on his own lands," and when nineteenth-century legal scholars described land ownership as the linchpin of the republican society of the United States, the question arises: what was the source of the relatively greater and more equal land ownership among free Whites in relation to other societies in the eighteenth and nineteenth centuries? This chapter uses a broad brush to describe land distribution in the British American colonies. British policy in the Americas was notable for its goal of putting land into cultivation and for offering small parcels of land to immigrants to achieve the goal. The chapter starts by describing the structure of British colonial government. It goes on to describe the role of the colonies in the broader conception of Great Britain's commerce, and the legal regulation of colonial trade and credit relationships.

Property as Prerogative

American colonial history involves an interplay between the dictates of top-down colonial rule and the on-the-ground, local operation of colonial institutions. By what source did the colonial officials get their power? The British Crown formed the colonies in America by means of charters that conveyed land and that granted lawmaking authority. Some colonies began as incorporated trading companies funded by investors, such as the early Virginia Company, the Plymouth Company of 1609, and the Massachusetts Bay Company of 1629.[1] Other colonies were proprietorships, which were grants from the Crown to an individual or a group of individuals, such as the charters to William Penn and Lord Baltimore, creating Pennsylvania and Maryland.[2] A third type of colony, the royal or provincial colonies, were directly ruled by the Crown.[3]

In each case, a governor or proprietor appointed by the King served as the top executive official.[4] An appointed council (an advisory board or cabinet) typically consisting of twelve "councilors" or "assistants" as well as other lower-level officials, advised and assisted the colonial governors and their lieutenant governors.[5] Assemblies, constituted by elected representatives, quickly assumed the role of enacting laws in association with the governors' offices. In each of the colonies, the originating documents (charters, proprietorships) granted colonial governments lawmaking powers as long as the laws were not "repugnant" to the laws of England.[6] The question whether colonial laws were "repugnant" at times worked its way from the colonial legislatures by appeal to the English Privy Council, which had judicial authority to review colonial laws.[7]

The British also exercised oversight of colonial lawmaking through the Board of Trade (officially, the Lords Commissioners of Trade and Plantations), an English governmental body formed to supervise colonial matters. The Board of Trade typically had the power to disallow colonial laws that were in conflict with English trade policies, to nominate governors and other appointed officials, and to advise Parliament on laws to enact for the colonies. Often the Board of Trade would issue its instructions, or guidance, to the colonial governors, who would then appeal to the colonial assembly to enact a law consistent with the Board of Trade's request. The Board of Trade might require that a colony's laws include suspending clauses: clauses that suspended the operation of an act until it received approval and confirmation in England, often by the Board of Trade.

Yet, ultimately the Board of Trade's powers were merely advisory and its instructions were routinely ignored. As the historian Edmund S. Morgan describes, "The Board of Trade told the Secretary (of State) what to do; he told the royal governors; the governors told the colonists; and the colonists did what they pleased."[8] The assemblies controlled appropriations, including for the governors' salaries. Colonial governors were often in a bind: they were pressured to comply with instructions coming from Britain, but knew the assemblies had the power of appropriations and could hold back their pay. This dialog between the colonial assemblies and crown-appointed government officials was a persistent feature of colonial governance.

LAND DISTRIBUTION IN BRITISH AMERICA: AN EMPHASIS ON CULTIVATION

Under the constitution of the English monarchy, land policy was a central prerogative of the King and his deputies, the colonial governors. Policies relating to land distribution were therefore determined at the highest levels of government, by Parliament and the Board of Trade, and implemented by the proprietors' and governors' offices of the various colonies. From the perspective of authorities in London, the colonies' role was to generate revenue for the Crown. Toward that end, British colonial land distribution policies encouraged immigration and settlement in North America by people who would actually inhabit the land and work the soil.[9] Rather than granting land in vast parcels to a small group of elites, which was more typical in Spanish American colonies, in British America, the policy was to grant land directly to cultivators in small quantities.

Labor, and therefore immigration, was desperately needed to achieve the crown goal of land cultivation. In several colonies (Virginia, New York, Maryland, Pennsylvania, Delaware, New Jersey, the Carolinas, and Georgia), the British initially encouraged immigration by granting a "headright," a free fifty-acre parcel of land per laborer. Robert Beverley's 1705 account of Virginia defined a headright as "the Title any one hath by the Royal Charter, to fifty Acres of land, in Consideration of his Personal Transportation into that Country, to settle and remain there."[10] A Virginia law of 1705 clarified that "all and every person, male or female" coming to the colony "has a right to fifty acres of land."[11] The policy encouraged individuals to import laborers, such as slaves, indentured servants, wives, or children, because a petitioner would obtain fifty additional acres for each laborer the petitioner could prove would work the land. The servants had a right to their fifty acres "after he or she becomes free, or time of servitude is expired." According to the contemporary understanding, this policy promoted slavery because slaves, unlike servants paying off their transport, would have no future claims to land of their own from their employer. The most one person could obtain was 4,000 acres per patent.[12] By the time Beverley's book was published, however, land was so inexpensive that it was typically purchased outside of the headright system from the crown authorities directly or from larger landowners.[13]

Many colonial titles were founded in conveyances from Native Americans. To give one of many examples, according to the historian Edmund S. Morgan, Roger Williams, founder of Rhode Island, "warned the settlers that they could not really acquire land in Massachusetts by a grant from an English king: 'they could have no title . . . except they compounded with the natives.'"[14] There is much more work to be done by historians on how land was taken and purchased from Native Americans and distributed to immigrants. It is beyond the scope of this book to address land acquisition from Native Americans, which is worthy of its own book. The legal historian Stuart Banner has documented the pervasiveness of colonial purchases of land from Native Americans. Banner revealed that although seventeenth-century legal theories of discovery and conquest "assumed . . . that a patent from the Crown was all that was necessary for an English settler to claim property in North America," experience ran counter to these conceptions. Banner emphasizes that "[p]urchasing land from the Indians became common almost from the beginning of English settlement," and describes the extent of the practice in Massachusetts, Virginia, Carolina, Pennsylvania, New York, and other colonies.[15] The historian Colin G. Calloway has similarly described land sales as elements of the extensive body of treaties executed between Native American tribes and government officials.[16] Both Banner and Calloway describe in detail the questionable features of the purchases, ranging from the fact that the Native Americans and colonists often had differing conceptions of the substance of the transactions, to inadequate pricing, to questionable authority in the party selling the land, in addition to more blatant fraudulent acts on the part of the settlers. Nonetheless, the colonists were eager to prove that they had good title and would therefore customarily trace the root of title to a formal purchase from Native Americans.

After the acquisition of land, often with both the force of a royal grant and an explicit purchase from Native Americans, the question became how to distribute it. With regard to official British policy, the basic principle underlying the headright system and similar government programs was to allocate land according to the landowner's ability to improve it. Indeed, headrights and many other colonial land titles were made contingent upon cultivation. According to Beverley, Virginia's headright policy gave landowners three years "to clear, plant, and tend an Acre of Ground with Corn, or to build an House, and keep a stock of Cattle, for one whole year together upon the Land; after which 'tis presum'd they will continue the Settlement." Land that was not cultivated in the three-year time frame, according to Beverley, "is said to be Lapsed, and any Man is at liberty to obtain a new Patent of it in his own Name" by petitioning the General Court.[17]

The policy of granting land to petitioners in small parcels according to their ability to cultivate was a pillar of British colonial regulation that was surprisingly consistent throughout the colonial era. For example, as late as the 1760s, the English Board of Trade lamented that some of the colonies were "granting excessive quantities of land to particular persons who have never cultivated or settled it and have thereby prevented others more industrious from improving the same." The colonies were to "take especial care that in all grants . . . the quantity be in proportion to their ability to cultivate." The instruction stated that no more than one hundred acres be given to a master or mistress of a family for himself or herself, and fifty acres for every white or black man, woman, or child of which such person's family shall consist." However, those that could prove they were in a "condition and intention to cultivate" could obtain a greater amount of acreage.[18] Requiring cultivation limited the size of the parcels granted to individuals and spread titles widely across the population.

In contrast to the headright system, high-level officials were recruited into colonial administration with the promise of amassing large landed estates. Land was the principal asset that could be doled out to incentivize crown officials to immigrate to the colonies. It was universally accepted, for example, that colonial administrators such as the governor and his appointed council would receive large grants of land and be in a position to work through local channels to augment their land holdings.[19] There was often little or haphazard oversight regarding how that land would be used or subdivided in the future. Throughout the colonial era, a segment of the elites connected to government was able to amass large land parcels.

These higher-level officials, proprietors, royal governors, and council members also received patronage-related benefits from controlling land distribution, managing records of property titles, and appointing judges and controlling courts and other institutions. When dealing with the representative assemblies, as the historian Marshall Harris has noted, they "maintained with few exceptions exclusive executive prerogatives, appointed judicial officers, and convened or dismissed the assemblies at will."[20] A 1754 pamphlet supporting the governors' land-granting prerogative in Virginia, expressed the power clearly:

> [T]he King has an absolute property in all the Lands in this Colony, not already granted out; . . . He may dispose of them upon what Terms he pleases; that the Governor, as his Substitute, may, with his Majesty's leave, make what Reservations he shall judge convenient; the Governor may take any fee with his Majesty's leave.[21]

George Clarke, who administered grants of property in New York as a member of the council, wrote to England in 1731 to alert others that petitions were arriving "thick for lands if they should all be granted what will there be for the new Governour to Grant; this I thought fit to hint to you in confidence, it being in your power singly to prevent their going too far."[22] Similarly, the appointment of lower executive officials and judicial officers was the backbone of a patronage system that had political and financial implications for all involved. As stated by Gordon S. Wood in reference to the American colonies, "Patronage was most evident in politics, and there its use was instinctive. . . . The appointing to governmental offices, the awarding of military commissions or judgeships, the granting of land or contracts for provisions—all these were only the visible political expressions of the underlying system of personal obligations and reciprocity that ran through the whole society."[23]

The early colonial officials who acquired large parcels expected to achieve profits from increasing land values and land sales. The primary way to increase land prices was to encourage rapid settlement and cultivation. Rental income that supported the landed elite in England was not available because the land was uncultivated. Therefore, even in an atmosphere where well-connected officials and British subjects sought to acquire vast estates, there was always a competing pressure to allocate land titles in smaller parcels to develop the land and to increase land prices.

Important in this effort was another pool of individuals who played a major role in land distribution in the American colonies: entrepreneurs and land speculators who spearheaded the process of founding and settling the towns. John Frederick Martin's *Profits in the Wilderness* shows that the town founders were often closely connected to the colonial government, and indeed frequently had appointments on the committees or offices in charge of granting land or founding towns.[24] They obtained permission from the General Court to purchase land from Native Americans. They regularly used their government positions to advocate for the confirmation of questionable titles.[25] They invested their own personal assets in establishing the rudiments of town surveying.[26] They directly recruited settlers to new areas. By examining the probate records of the major land speculators in New England, Martin found that town promoters tended to hold smaller parcels in several different areas (an average of 8.7 different parcels) rather than accumulating larger estates that could serve as the basis of local political and economic power.[27]

In sum, the headright policy and widespread granting of land on the basis of actual cultivation were great equalizers. Elites with connections to government were of course able to amass large estates in the colonial era. Nonetheless, the Board of Trade's goal of granting free land to immigrants and putting it into actual cultivation likely contributed to the fact that, in relation to Europe, the United States in the founding era enjoyed wider distribution of land ownership among free Whites.

LAND TENURE IN THE BRITISH AMERICAN COLONIAL CHARTERS

The colonial charters defined the form of tenure in which land was held in the colonies. With some variation, the charters and grants from the King conveyed land in a form that was free of most feudal dependencies. The charters typically expressed the lack of feudal obligations by specifying that the land will be held "as of his Mannor of East Greenewich in the County of Kent, in free and common Soccage, and not in Capite or by Knight's Service," with the requirement that one-fifth of any gold or silver mined would be paid to the Crown.[28] Understanding the significance of this form of conveyance on land tenure requires some background on feudalism.

In the early modern era, title to land in England was often dependent upon the performance of feudal obligations that involved personal responsibilities and military obligations to local lords and the king. The king was the ultimate owner of all of the lands he ruled.[29] Those receiving their land directly from the King held it *ut de corona* or "as of the crown" or *ut de manore*, "as of the manor," in honor of the King.[30] With regard to land held *ut de corona*, the land holdings carried the obligations of fealty and often homage and knight service. Knight service originally meant an obligation to provide knights "to attend his lord to the wars for forty days in every year, if called upon," with lesser numbers of days owed if the parcel had been subdivided. Over time, property owners could provide money instead of actual knights, but knight service land continued to carry with it a vulnerability to assessments for crown "emergencies," military or otherwise.³¹ As Blackstone describes, knight service land carried particularly onerous obligations because, however "honourable," the payments were "unavoidably uncertain" and "left to the arbitrary calls of the lord" as to the time and extent of the performance or monetary substitute.³²

In contrast, colonial land was held in "free and common socage," which Blackstone describes as "the most free and independent species" of landholding.³³ Landholders in "free and common socage" could be required to make payments or to perform labor for the lord, but the obligations were fixed with certainty. The colonial charters most commonly conveyed land *ut de manore* of the county of Kent.³⁴ According to Blackstone, in Kent "the socage tenures were the relicks of Saxon liberty" retained by landholders who "had never forfeited them to the king" nor had been required to submit to knight service.³⁵

According to the historian Viola Florence Barnes, in the early modern era, the Crown began to grant lands in free and common socage while chartering corporations for the purpose of expanding the quantity of taxable land and incentivizing infrastructure development. If a group of investors proposed, say, to reclaim land by drainage, or to convert waste land to farming with an irrigation project, the Crown routinely agreed that the reclaimed land would be held in free and common socage.³⁶ The practice then expanded to those forming trading companies, like the early Levant Company, whose principals might in the process acquire land and want to take possession or grant it away.³⁷ Extending "free and common socage" tenure to the British colonies directly followed from earlier practice.³⁸ The investors founding the Massachusetts Bay Company and Virginia Company had good reason to want free land tenure to encourage settlement of the colony.

As Barnes documented, the land tenure granted in colonial charters reveals three stages of British colonial policy. The first, discussed above, reflected corporate landholding, which granted land in its freest form. The next two stages granted greater authority to the colonial proprietors and founders to rule from above. The colonial charters often included a "Bishop of Durham" provision granting the various proprietors, such as Lord Baltimore, "almost regal power and authority," namely the prerogatives, royalties, liberties, rights, and franchises that any Bishop of Durham had ever enjoyed.³⁹ Nonetheless, the land tenure remained in "free and common socage" and, during the colonial era, attempts by proprietors and governors to establish feudal relations with settlers were met with resistance and, with limited exceptions (such as the Hudson in New York), ultimately failed.⁴⁰

The Foundations of Colonial Credit Markets

To understand how colonial property law was shaped by a drive for credit, some background on the structure of trade in the British American colonies is necessary. British loans to the colonial merchants in the eighteenth century typically took the form of short-term commercial credit. English or Scottish export firms financed the costs of transporting goods to the colonies. The colonies did not have banks or other financial institutions, and "credit" consisted of offering imported goods or slaves and allowing repayment at a later time.

The central problem of the trans-Atlantic trade was that the time it took to sail between England and the colonies created information disparities that complicated credit relationships. It was difficult for merchants residing in the British Isles to be familiar with current market conditions in America or the creditworthiness of colonial debtors. One solution to the problems of distance and lack of information was that transactions were structured, when possible, so that risks relating to legal enforcement were contained within England. Bills of exchange payable in London served as the basic currency in all large commercial transactions within the Atlantic trade. The ultimate liability for the bills therefore resided with an individual who had an account in London. To obtain major loans, colonists were often required to find guarantors in London. London-based insurance companies were preferred to such an extent that the colonial insurance industry never developed beyond small operations in the major cities.

In addition, English and Scottish merchants typically hired factors who resided semi-permanently in the colonies. Once English goods arrived in the colonies, factors typically sold to planters in the Southern colonies or, in the Northern colonies, to retailers or storekeepers who, in turn, sold the goods directly to consumers.[41] Merchants often hired family members or acquaintances to work as factors or worked through factorage firms, which typically charged higher rates but had better established connections. The primary responsibility of factors was to develop information and contacts and to seek out the highest prices for the goods they sold on the merchants' behalf. The "price" they received, of course, also included consideration of the terms of credit and the creditworthiness of the purchasers. British creditors typically offered a term of twelve months for repayment for goods imported from the British Isles. For the colonial importers to pay their debts on time, goods were offered locally, within colonial markets, on shorter credit terms. Customarily the terms of local credit ranged from six to twelve months, but could be less.[42] To be competitive, factors often remitted payments to the British merchants immediately, in advance of actually collecting debts from those to whom they sold goods.[43] The factors assumed the role of creditors on the ground, who could navigate the informal and formal means available to collect debts.

REGIONAL VARIATIONS IN ECONOMIC STRUCTURE

In 1759, an English clergyman visiting America doubted that the colonies would ever unite in a "voluntary association or coalition, at least a permanent one," because "fire and water are not more heterogeneous than the different colonies in North-America."[44] The Southern continental colonies and the West Indies, dominated by slave labor, conformed most closely to the model of dependent staple crop-producing colonies. The economies of Virginia and the Carolinas were highly specialized in the production of tobacco and rice, and the West Indies in the production of sugar. The relationships between planters in these colonies and their English and Scottish creditors were extremely close: Merchants in Britain typically provided planters with financing both for the production of staple crops and for imports of goods sold to the planters in advance of return shipments. The English and Scottish merchants exported the colonial crops to Europe or sold them locally under a consignment system, satisfying the colonial planters' debts with the proceeds of the sales.

Southern merchants controlled only a small local fleet of ships. Moreover, Southern planters did not fully control the internal marketing of imported goods. In the early years, "Scots peddlers" wandered the countryside selling goods and purchasing tobacco directly from small farmers. The "Glasgow system" was developed by the mid-eighteenth century, when Scottish factors had set up chains of stores throughout the Chesapeake that sold imported goods in return for payments of tobacco. This system involved, first, sending traders throughout the Chesapeake region to deal directly with small planters and farmers, and second, a willingness to accept low-quality tobacco.[45] English merchants never replicated the Glasgow system. They dealt with larger planters and dominated the market for higher quality tobacco.

In contrast, Northerners owned a large fleet of ships and invested in shipping and marketing their exports abroad. Northern merchants were exporters, importers, wholesalers, retailers, purchasing agents, bankers, insurance underwriters, and attorneys. In contrast to Southern colonists who allowed their internal markets to be dominated by Scottish importers, Northern colonists controlled the internal markets of their colonies. Transactions with English and Scottish merchants and factors relating to the importation of goods typically took place in major port towns.

In the British colonial framework, the role of colonies was to improve the mother country's balance of trade. First, the colonies provided access to natural resources or locally grown staple crops, like tobacco or sugar, which English and Scottish merchants could export at a profit to other parts of the world. Second, colonists added to Britain's wealth as consumers of manufacturing goods.[46] Because Northerners never managed to produce lucrative goods desired by the English and Scots, they were free from many of the restraints of the Navigation Acts, which will be described below. Prior to the 1760s, merchants in the Northern colonies were free to market most of their goods anywhere in the world. Great Britain imported only a small portion of their exports. In the period 1768 to 1772, for example, only 17.8% of commodity exports from New England and 22.8% of commodity exports from the mid-Atlantic colonies were exported to the British Isles. In contrast, during the same period, 81.8% of the commodity exports of Virginia and Maryland and 71.6% of the commodity exports from the Carolinas and Georgia were exported directly to Great Britain.[47]

Northern markets, however, were dominated by imported goods. To pay for the British imports, the merchants of New England and the mid-Atlantic colonies exported foodstuffs, such as wheat, corn, timber, and especially salt fish, to colonies and nations that had a favorable balance of trade with Britain. The most important markets were in the West Indies and Spain and Portugal. The Northern merchants sold their goods there in return for cash (bills of exchange payable in London) or products, such as molasses, sugar, and wine, which could be used to pay British creditors directly. The profits rising out of the slave system of labor and sugar production in the West Indies and wine production in the Iberian Peninsula meant that these areas had more liquid markets than New England and the Mid-Atlantic. Sugar was so profitable that the six sugar islands—Jamaica, St. Kitts, Barbados, Montserrat, Nevis, and Antigua—contributed almost as much (more than 9%) to Britain's external commerce as the thirteen continental colonies combined (approximately 10%).[48]

THE FRAMEWORK OF BRITISH REGULATION OF COMMERCE

The credit system in the American colonies had its roots in the history of joint-stock companies. In Britain, by the second half of the sixteenth century, the Crown began regularly granting monopolistic corporate charters to groups of private investors and individual mariners interested in trading ventures abroad. The principal purpose of these early companies was to run trading posts, delivering goods from the British Isles to sell abroad and bringing back high-demand items in return. In the late sixteenth century, the joint-stock company device was used to finance trading ventures in Russia, Turkey, the Levant, and the East Indies.[49]

As mentioned, the first English colonies in the Americas were organized as for-profit, joint-stock companies, such as the Virginia Company of London (chartered in 1606), which created the first settlement at Jamestown, and its companion Plymouth Company, which attempted to settle at Sagadahoc, Maine. Unlike the companies trading in the East, which had imported goods for which they knew a market existed, the companies operating in America had to discover and develop lucrative items for export. Finding such goods in North America proved difficult. One original economic ambition of the British colonies, as reflected in many colonial charters, was to find gold and silver mines on the scale of those that had been discovered in the Spanish colonies.[50] But the minerals were not there to be found. The types of goods that appeared to be marketable, such as tobacco and rice, required labor.

The companies' ventures thus became complicated by the need to transport laborers to the New World and establish permanent settlements with governance structures and legal institutions. Laborers were initially recruited by means of indentured servant contracts, and later coerced by slavery. Estimates suggest that indentured servants constituted possibly one-half to two-thirds of White males immigrating to the American colonies between 1630 and 1776, or approximately 300,000 to 400,000 people.[51] Slave importation to British North America—primarily an eighteenth-century phenomenon—is estimated at 264,759 by 1776.[52]

In the initial years, the Virginia Company, the Massachusetts Bay Company (chartered 1628), and the companies that created the first colonies in Bermuda (1609–10), Newfoundland (1610), and Nova Scotia (1610) were not highly profitable.[53] By mid-century, however, goods such as tobacco grown in Virginia, sugar produced in Barbados, and fish landed in the Northern colonies led to profits that justified further settlement, investment, and military support.

During Cromwell's Commonwealth period, in large part due to merchant lobbying, the government for the first time assumed responsibility for military protection of merchant vessels trading abroad. The British Navy expanded rapidly in just over a decade: from 39 vessels in 1648, to 80 in 1651, and to 287 in 1660.[54] With a far larger fleet, after prevailing over the

Netherlands in the Anglo-Dutch wars, the navy offered military protection to British merchants trading within its waters.

By 1660, the British government monopolized trade over its colonies in America. The British colonies were united by the reach of comprehensive trade regulations enacted to advance the mercantilist goal of improving England's (and Scotland's) balance of trade. The commercial regulations were enacted in piecemeal fashion and were often the product of highly contested political debate. They are, however, collectively referred to as the "Navigation Acts." As one act stated, the regulations were intended to keep the colonies "in a firmer dependance" upon England, and to render them "more beneficial and advantagious" to the mother country by furthering the "imployment and increase of English shipping and seamen," the export of "English woolen and other manufactures and commodities" to the colonies, and by making England a clearinghouse for colonial imports (the "commodities of th[e] plantations") and for "commodities of other countries and places" that English merchants could "supply" to the colonies.[55]

The 1660 Act for the Encouraging and Increasing of Shipping and Navigation was the central statute defining the regulatory framework. A 1651 ordinance had required that the produce of the English colonies be transported in English-owned ships. The 1660 act extended the 1651 ordinance and prohibited all non-English ships from entering colonial ports. It also prohibited non-English subjects from acting as factors or merchants in the British colonies and thereby promoting foreign-produced goods. The act cemented control over colonial markets by requiring that certain lucrative items—originally sugar, tobacco, cotton-wool, ginger, and various dyes produced in the New World—be exported only to ports in Britain or to another British colony prior to reexportation.[56] Later acts extended this requirement to molasses, rice, coffee, coconuts, cacao-nuts, pimento, "whalefin" (whale bone or baleen), hemp, raw silk, beaver and other pelts, hides, and skins, potash, pearl ash, and all naval stores, such as masts, yards, tar, pitch, pig and bar iron, copper ore, and turpentine. Colonial merchants thus were prohibited from directly exporting these commodities to a foreign port. The Staple Act of 1663 led to further control over colonial markets by requiring all European goods, with minor exceptions, to be imported into the British colonies by way of a port in the British Isles. European goods thereafter had to be unloaded in England or Scotland, duties paid, and goods reloaded and shipped to the colonies.

These regulations gave British shipowners and merchants almost exclusive dominance in the carrying trade within the British Empire. Robert Paul

Thomas estimates that the "freight factor," the increase in price of goods due to transportation, averaged 20% in the eighteenth century, meaning goods were sold in colonial ports at 20% higher prices than in the ports of Britain.[57] Monopolizing the carrying trade improved England's balance of trade by reserving the revenue generated by the carrying trade to British merchants, at the expense of the colonists who would have benefited from greater competition.

The near-monopoly on shipping within the British Empire imposed by Parliament was initially met with colonial resistance because the Dutch offered shipping at lower rates and on better credit terms. Southern colonies suffered from the loss of competition in the tobacco export business. At the same time, the stimulus to shipbuilding generated by the monopoly helped boost the New England economy. The lower relative cost of materials in New England led it to become the center of shipbuilding within the British Empire. Over time, rapid expansion of the British mercantile fleet and increased competition meant British shipping rates and credit terms fell to levels equal to the rates formerly charged by the Dutch. The British shipping monopoly also made it easier to combat piracy: limiting all colonial ports to English-owned ships reduced the bases from which pirates and privateers in foreign-owned ships could operate. Insurance costs for shipments declined.[58]

The monopoly on shipping required under Navigation Acts led to an English and Scottish monopoly over the supply of credit to the colonies. Colonists were not prohibited by law from obtaining credit outside Britain. But by monopolizing shipping, by prohibiting non-British subjects from acting as factors or merchants in the colonies, and by requiring that European goods be imported into an English or Scottish port before reexport to the colonies, the Navigation Acts made it extremely difficult for colonists to obtain credit from European sources, either directly or through a middleman. Colonists from all regions were steady consumers of imported manufactured goods and were therefore perpetually in debt to their creditors in Britain.

REGULATING COLONIAL EXPORTS

From the perspective of the colonies, the most onerous regulations were those that impaired trade with Europe. Restrictions on trading with Europe were the central reason that the British Isles became the exclusive source of financing of external colonial credit. As mentioned, the Navigation Acts required that certain enumerated items, including tobacco, rice, indigo, and other goods, be exported directly to the British Isles to enable merchants from the mother country to dominate the international marketing of the goods and to improve the balance of trade. The goods subjected to this requirement were typically the most profitable items produced in the colonies, the importation of which would not lead to competition with goods produced in the British Isles.[59] London and Glasgow, for example, became global centers for the marketing of tobacco and rice. This requirement also effectively excluded colonial merchants from exporting these goods directly to Europe, which drastically reduced their profits in comparison to what might have been earned had the colonists been able to trade in European markets directly. Robert Paul Thomas found that 85.4% of the goods enumerated by the Navigation Acts were reexported to Europe after being imported to Great Britain.[60]

Not every commercial regulation discriminated against the colonies. The Navigation Acts allowed an entirely free trade between colonial merchants and merchants of foreign countries in all commodities that had not been enumerated for exclusive export to England, as long as the goods were carried in British ships. Free trade was permitted in many important colonial goods, including grain of all varieties, lumber, salt, fish, sugar, and rum. These commodities could be transported directly to cities in Holland, France, Portugal, Spain, and Africa, and to any of the European colonies in the Caribbean.

OPPOSING VIEWS OF THE NAVIGATION ACTS

One of the principal contributions of Adam Smith's *The Wealth of Nations* (1776) was to describe the seemingly ad hoc regulations governing trade within the British Empire as the embodiment of a system of political economy that, while coherent in itself, rested on flawed assumptions and empirical beliefs. Smith's critique related, in part, to the credit flowing to the colonies. Smith explained that European governments' bullionist emphasis on specie flows misunderstood the deeper basis of wealth. The wealth of a nation derived from the value of the goods and services that the nation produced, not from the amount of specie circulating within its borders. The effort by a government to micromanage commerce in order to improve its balance of trade did not enhance basic productivity and often diminished it. Government trade regulations distorted incentives by inflating profits in particular areas, thereby diverting investment from products that could provide greater economic return.

Smith's criticism of what he referred to as Britain's "mercantile system" focused on its negative effects on the British, not the colonial, economy. In Smith's account, the primary beneficiaries of the Navigation Acts were British merchants, whom he believed controlled British trade policy, and colonial subjects. The enumeration of goods—which constrained their export to England or Scotland—increased profits for merchants in Britain dealing in those goods and led to excessive investment in their production.[61] Moreover, merchants pressured the government for continued military expenses for colonial defense. According to Smith, the colonists were free riders benefiting from British military protection and not contributing their share. Writing in 1776, Smith opposed fighting to retain the American colonies. He believed that a better course would be to negotiate a trade treaty with America so that trade relations would be maintained without the costs of military defense.

The British colonial regime of the eighteenth century consisted of dispersed constituencies, integrated loosely by a shared cultural and legal tradition, by market relationships, and by the relatively weak superstructure of parliamentary and Crown rule. Until the 1760s, colonists were generally content with their status as subjects to the British Crown. The two principal counterfactual alternatives—independence during the eighteenth century or colonial dependency on another European government—might each have been inferior in terms of colonial livelihood when compared to remaining a colony of Britain. Seventeenth- and eighteenth-century British commercial regulation had dual effects: the laws were designed to ensure that the English would receive the principal financial benefits of trade within the empire, but the colonial regime worked to the advantage of the colonies as well. The vice-admiralty courts, which were established for the purpose of enforcing the Navigation Laws to the detriment of individual colonists, greatly benefited colonial economies by applying a consistent body of law to resolve disputes emerging on the seas. The existence of a uniform law of bills and notes allowed payments by bills of exchange anywhere in Britain and the colonies. Finally, in very crude terms, British bankers and merchants financed operations in the colonies because the colonies shared a legal tradition of formalistic enforcement of contractual obligations.

By the 1760s, however, the colonists began to emphasize the direct, tangible costs that the Navigation Acts imposed on their economic activity. The colonists viewed themselves as supporting the mother country in four ways: by stimulating English industry through the purchase of imports; by paying the interest costs of the goods they bought on credit; by paying import duties; and, particularly in the South, by suffering the British monopoly on goods they exported like tobacco and rice.

The following chapters turn to the legal institutions and laws that formed the basis of the colonial credit economy. They offer a history of title and mortgage recording, and the laws defining the assets available to be taken to satisfy debts. Issues of federalism within the British colonial framework were at play: initially colonial governments had the authority to set their own policies pertaining to the remedies available to creditors. Prior to 1732, each colony established laws and procedures governing property, inheritance, and the satisfaction of debts. The colonial property law and legal institutions reflected the tensions between local control and imperial regulation.

2

The Backbone of Credit: The Institutional Foundations of Colonial America's Economy of Credit and Collateral

In the winter of 1710–1711, the New Jersey Assembly enacted a law to allow residents to record deeds to property locally in each county. One might think that offering local title recording would have been an innocuous, positive development in the colony. In this case, the governor-appointed council rejected the act. Why? A member of the council explained in a letter that local deed recording would deprive the colony's secretary of the recording fees to which he was entitled. The council member's letter emphasized that the act "took away the Only Valuable Perquisite belonging to the Secretaries Office, & was directly contrary to his Patent."[1] For complicated reasons, the colony of New Jersey had recently come under the authority of New York's governor, and New York's recording law of 1683 required local officials to send fees to the secretary's office every year.[2] The letter went on to criticize the county clerks, stating that the "the Clerks of many Counties being Scarce able to write, & having no particular Offices, and on Other Acco'ts most Incapable of Such a Trust." He continued that "It was moreover proved, that the Records of Severall Counties have been lost or embezzled by the Negligence or Roguery of the Clerks."[3] On these grounds, the council prohibited the act from taking effect.

Yet, in 1713–1714, the assembly enacted the same law another time. The act described the problem it addressed as the fact that the "Inhabitants of this Province are under great Inconveniences, and put to much trouble and Charges by reason there is no Records of Deeds and Evidences of Lands kept within the respective Counties."[4] The new act allowed deeds to be proved and recorded at the common pleas courts in the counties and required that the clerk of the common pleas "keep a Book or Books, wherein all Deeds, Conveyances and Evidences of Lands, lying within the same County, . . . shall, or may be Recorded by him." The law stated that the records would be publicly searchable: "all Persons concerned may have recourse to the said Records, as they shall have occasion."[5] Yet again, the New Jersey Assembly's efforts were thwarted. The act was disallowed by Parliament's Privy Council in January 1722. William Burnet, who served as governor of New York and New Jersey from 1720 to1728 wrote the Board of Trade in May 1722, explaining that the act "hurt the Prerogative" of the secretary's office.[6]

The New Jersey Assembly reenacted the law a third time, in 1727.[7] This time the assembly offered the secretary a stipend of twenty-five pounds a year to reduce his losses. Estimating the loss of his fees as totaling more than sixty pounds a year, the secretary of New Jersey, James Smith, wrote desperately to the Board of Trade in November 1728, explaining that the assembly had paid 600 pounds to Governor Burnet to get his approval of the new act. According to Smith:

> Notwithstanding which Disallowance; the late Governour William Burnet, Esq. did, in the Year 1727: for the Sum of Six hundred pounds given to him by the Assembly, under the name of Incidental charges, Reenact the Aforesaid Laws, and caused a New Ordinance to be Made in which the fees only of the Secretary are Reduced very near to what they were when first complained of.[8]

Smith goes on to state that some objections were made by the New Jersey Council about reenacting the laws "[t]o remove which; the Assembly voted to the Secretary twenty five pounds a year . . . in consideration of the loss his Office would Sustain thereby, which he is Sure will be more than Sixty Pounds a Year." Yet, Smith explained that when he raised his loss of fees in the Council, he "found it was to no purpose, and if he did not accept of the said twenty five pounds a year, he would have nothing."[9] Although it appears the 1727 act was allowed to stand, the assembly enacted a similar law (for the fourth time) in 1743, stating that many of the inhabitants of the colony "live at a great Distance" from any of the officials permitted to record deeds, and in those areas "People labour under considerable Inconveniencies for want of a Law for acknowledging Deeds and Conveyances of Land."[10]

The New Jersey Assembly's efforts to create locally run institutions for publicly searchable title recording is merely one example of how, in all regions of British America, the colonial assemblies enacted laws that shaped the local institutions, securing property rights and enforcing credit agreements. The creation throughout the colonies of an institutional infrastructure surrounding dispute resolution and land conveyancing was profoundly important. Colonists typically wanted institutions that secured property rights and that resolved disputes and wanted them run by representatives in local communities. In a foreshadowing of the explosive 1765 Stamp Act conflict, colonists at times opposed the imposition of fees benefiting crown-appointed officials. The colonial governors and their appointees expressed competing claims to authority in their struggle to regulate land distribution, to collect fees and taxes, and to control the expanding institutional infrastructure. This chapter takes a broad look by compiling and presenting colonial laws, which have not previously been published together, along with evidence from the existing secondary literature, to offer a historical overview of the colonial courts and land title registries, the institutional underpinnings of the American property system that persists today.

The chapter begins by discussing the role of the common pleas courts in colonial credit relations, followed by an examination of the early history of title recording. Historical sources reveal that in most colonies, the adoption of local public title recording was driven both by concerns over convenience and by concerns about fraudulent conveyances, that is, problems arising from a lack of transparency in the purchase and mortgage markets. Most colonies offered a simple solution: mortgages and deeds could be recorded at the sessions of the common pleas courts. As we shall see, public authentication of deeds and title recording streamlined the existing English conveyancing practices and allowed for the recording of all forms of property serving as collateral, including, most consequentially, slaves. The account also demonstrates how the process of securing property rights made some of the colonial legislatures stronger and more deeply intertwined with local institutions than they were before. Creating and empowering local administrations required the colonial legislatures to assert their authority, at times in the face of countervailing assertions of power by crown-appointed officials.

Courts and Credit: Debt Litigation and Property Titles

Title recording in most British colonies of the seventeenth and eighteenth centuries started in the colonial common pleas courts, which were the courts for civil (noncriminal) disputes in the colonies. By the early eighteenth century, each colony hosted courts of common pleas, typically in local counties four times a year on a rotating basis.[11] At the common pleas sessions, for a fee, clerks of the court recorded debt litigation based on various forms of debts or mortgage bonds.[12] The common pleas courts also confirmed property titles in legal actions brought by property owners. These institutional services secured property rights and conveyed important market information to interested members of the community.The official production of court records at the quarterly court sessions provided a venue for the broader transmission of information throughout a community by word of mouth. Court days were highly popular events. Entire communities would converge at the location of the court sessions to hear about the court business of the day.[13] On court days, individuals could personally observe or hear about land conveyances, mortgages, the probate of wills, and lawsuits based on debts. As A. G. Roeber describes, court days were an essential time to discover "who was recovering against whom and what their own roles might be at any given moment."[14] The role of institutions was therefore twofold: to create a formal record of the legal actions related to property, and to provide a forum where the entire community became informed of property-related status changes.

In the colonial era, like today, people would go to great lengths to avoid litigation in the course of ordinary commercial transactions. Family relationships, personal acquaintances, and the spread of information about an individual's reputation and honor were centerpieces of colonial society. Maintaining your credit meant gaining a reputation for paying back debts. In the small transactions taking place within local communities, litigation was an unfortunate event. Being sued on court day informed the whole community that a debtor failed to pay his debts, undermining the debtor's reputation and credit. Moreover, court fees were imposed to compensate officials for every aspect of the paperwork involved. In litigation, court fees were charged to the losing party, who were usually debtors already lacking the means to pay their creditors.

Although those entering commercial dealings naturally tried to avoid litigation in settling disputes, private behavior operated in the shadow of the legal system. Where today, routine market transactions take place by means of cash, credit cards, and electronic payments, in the colonial era, individual community members were bound together by webs of debt. Colonial market transactions often involved unsecured debts on book accounts and promissory notes (analogous to a check).[15] Throughout New England and in rural areas, there was often little cash on hand, and members of the community extended credit and were repaid in goods and services over time. Individuals also frequently took out lines of credit with merchants and shopkeepers, satisfying the debts later through crop harvests or other goods.[16] Cases from the Inferior Court of Common Pleas in Plymouth, Massachusetts, for example, demonstrate that creditors sued on book accounts for transactions ranging from " sundry goods," to the balance due for " boots and shoes," for that " remaining due for a yoke of a young oxen," to a sum of money " to Ballance for English Hay," to " time, travel and assistance," or for " Shoes, Drink, Entertainment, and Wares," to " work done at the furnace in Pembroke and a canoe sold," to "one freight of Lumber from Rochester to Chilmark, in the Sloop *Adventure*."[17]

In addition to unsecured debts, colonists also borrowed money against specific collateral using sealed bonds and mortgages. Like today, land was a central form of collateral. In many areas, land was a principal store of colonial wealth. Alice Hanson Jones studied probate records at the time of the American Revolution, which revealed that land reflected 81.1% of wealth in New England, 68.5% in the mid-Atlantic region, and 48.6% of wealth in the South, with slaves constituting 35.6%.[18] Mortgages extended on the basis of land and slave property were an essential source of credit.[19] G. B. Warden's study emphasized the use of land as a means of exchange in colonial Boston, finding that 3,617 mortgages were recorded in Boston between 1692 and 1775 with a total value of £94,380.[20]

In areas relying on slave labor, slaves were a primary form of collateral and were often used to pay off debts when their owners failed to meet their obligations. The historian Bonnie Martin examined mortgages in three colonies and found that, although only 39% of the total number mortgages used slaves for some or all collateral, the mortgages that used slaves as collateral account for two-thirds of the funds extended.[21] What Martin describes as "slavery's invisible engine" refers to the evidence she collected, suggesting that the majority of total credit extended in the Southern colonies was secured by agreements that used human beings as collateral. Russell Menard's study of mortgages of land and slaves in eighteenth-century South Carolina found that by means of mortgages, capital flowed "from the city and mercantile fortunes toward the country and plantation development."[22]

Debt litigation on unsecured debt and mortgages dominated the business of the courts. Bringing a lawsuit on a debt established a creditor's priority to the debtor's assets. A creditor first sued on the debt to obtain a judgment by the court that the debtor owed a sum of money. At the creditor's discretion, the judgment could remain on the record with no further action. In a second step, the creditor requested that the court issue a writ of execution empowering the sheriff to physically seize the debtors' assets.[23] (The various writs of execution will be discussed in chapter 3.) Debt records served as a priority list of creditors' claims against defaulting members of the community: Debts were satisfied in the order in which creditors requested writs of execution.[24] Word that one creditor was bringing a debt action against a debtor would, of course, be highly relevant to all of that debtor's other creditors. In times of general economic recession or uncertainty, litigation volume skyrocketed as creditors scrambled for a place in line.

In a striking example from colonial Massachusetts, a pamphlet literature emerged advocating the issuance of paper currencies to boost the economy and to provide liquidity as a means of stemming the tide of debt litigation. John Colman gained notoriety advocating a land bank proposal, which would have printed private money secured by mortgaged land. In 1720, Colman wrote a pamphlet criticizing the government's failure to print money or to allow private banking.[25] Colman's pamphlet emphasized the prevalence of lawsuits that operated unfairly on debtors in an environment of currency shortage. Colman also protested the fees set by the Massachusetts assembly and collected by clerks and lawyers. According to Colman:

> We find already the miserable Effects of the want of a Medium in these Instances; besides a Torrent of other mischiefs breaking in upon us, *viz.*
>
> The vast Number of Law Suits occasioned thereby, the Courts are open, and every Term, four or five hundred Writs (and perhaps more) given out against good honest Housekeepers, who are as willing to pay their Debts as their Creditors would be, and have wherewith to Pay, but can't Raise Money, unless they will Sell their Houses at half Value, which they have been Working hard for, it may be these Twenty years, and so turn their Families into the Streets; and this because they are obliged to Work for half, nay, some for two thirds Goods, and their Creditors will take nothing but Money; and so they are Squeezed and Oppress'd, to Maintain a few Lawyers, and other Officers of the Courts, who grow Rich on the Ruins of their Neighbours, while great part of the Town can hardly get Bread to satisfie Nature.[26]

Like the New Jersey Assembly's conflict over the secretary's fees, also occurring in the 1720s, the fees imposed by the courts were seen as oppressing to the colonists. The pamphlet led to Colman's arrest and trial for disturbing the peace.

In a similar instance during a recession in 1738, Massachusetts residents developed plans for a Land Bank, which would issue notes backed by mortgages of close to 400 private individuals. The bank was put into operation in 1740. On March 27, 1741, Parliament suppressed the Land Bank by applying to the colonies the Bubble Act—enacted in the wake of the South Sea bubble—which banned joint-stock companies. John Adams later claimed that the "act to destroy the Land Bank scheme *raised a greater ferment in this province than the Stamp Act did*."[27] According to Governor Thomas Hutchinson's history of Massachusetts, Sam Adams, the famous revolutionary, "first made himself conspicuous" during the resolution of Land Bank affairs. Officers of the court, under writ of execution, attempted to seize and to put up for public auction several buildings on his father's estate in order to repay alleged debts still outstanding from the Land Bank. Adams harassed both the auctioneers and the potential buyers of the estate with such vehemence that the auction was called off, which increased his notoriety as a staunch advocate of colonial liberties.[28]

The Massachusetts Land Bank events are a dramatic example of the political nature of courts, fees, and officials occurring throughout the colonies. Debt was pervasive in the colonial economy. The colonial courts offered valuable remedies to creditors (the specifics of which are outlined in the next chapter). Although litigation was a last resort, colonial court records reveal that suits on unsecured debts and mortgages were routine, particularly during times of economic downswings. The courts provided a backdrop to the large volume of transactions taking place on the basis of credit.

The Novelty of the Colonial Land Title Registries

Initially, colonial governors and proprietors maintained records of the land they granted in the course of exercising their royal prerogative to control the distribution of crown lands. Eventually, most colonies introduced a means of recording conveyances and mortgages in closer proximity to the relevant property.[29] The historical evidence suggests that it was the desire for better functioning property and credit markets that led to the widespread innovation of county-level public records of property conveyances.

English law required the Crown to maintain public records of its grants of land, an early and important precedent for government transparency. As Blackstone's treatise on the common law describes, "[N]o freehold may be given to the king, nor derived from him, but by matter of record." The records of such grants were to be publicly known. The "patent" granted by the King meant "open," according to Blackstone, "so called because they are not sealed up, but exposed to open view, with the great seal pendant at the bottom; and are usually directed or addressed by the king to all his subjects at large."[30] By extension of the King's authority in the colonies, the proprietors and governors of the British colonies kept open records of their own land grants. Imposing fees for placing royal seals on land grants was often treated as an important crown prerogative and a source of revenue.[31]

Acting independently, starting in the 1620s and continuing through the colonial era, each of the British colonies in America and the West Indies instituted courts and land title recording. Records of colonial grants of land were initially kept and maintained by high-level officials of the founding corporations, proprietors, and governors' offices. The recording of subsequent land conveyances became a matter over which the colonial assemblies asserted control.

What was innovative about title recording in the colonial courts? Title recording existed in England of course, but in the colonies, publicizing conveyances in open records became widespread practice and was normalized in a manner not achieved in England until the late nineteenth and early twentieth centuries.[32] The first innovative aspect was that, procedurally, authenticating conveyances and mortgages in public institutions allowed for vastly simpler and less expensive methods of conveying title in comparison to the typical combination of procedures and formalities relied upon in England. Second, the court records and title registries publicized conveyances and mortgages to the broader audience of purchasers and creditors. Public records lowered the cost for creditors to gain relevant information about the status of property. The third innovative characteristic was that recording of conveyances and mortgages could be used for any kind of property. English procedures and formalities, in contrast, distinguished between land and chattel goods. From the start, particularly in the Southern colonies and in the West Indies, mortgages in slaves and other chattel goods were a major source of credit. Moreover, by means of successive statutory enactments, the colonial legislatures could modify and improve the design of the institutions, make changes to the methods of selecting clerks and registers (election? appointment?), and could control the fees and costs associated with their use.

THE SIMPLICITY OF COLONIAL TITLE RECORDING

As described above, to provide reliable information to potential purchasers and creditors at a low cost, most colonial laws simply held that the first conveyances (land transfers or mortgages) to be recorded had presumptive validity over other claims. Creditors were therefore notified, through publication, of prior claims against an asset. Colonial land conveyancing began with a written deed or mortgage bond executed by two parties. The form and content of the deeds themselves closely replicated the forms used in England.[33] In colonial law, however, the deed itself fully conveyed the property. This was possible because having the deed authenticated or "proved" in court and recorded in the court records or registry provided the required element of "notoriety" of the transaction.

Simple conveyancing and local recording existed in England since the Statute of Enrolments of 1536, under which a "bargain and sale" contract for land would convey legal title when it was registered in "one of the King's courts of record at *Westminster*" or "within the same county or counties where the same manors, lands or tenements, so bargained and sold, lie or be" before at least two officials.[34] The letter of the statute required the recording of land conveyances. Nevertheless, landowners found a loophole, which is that the statute requiring recordation did not apply when a tenant under a lease purchased the land. According to the English historian J. H. Baker, by the 1620s, the legal practice of leasing for one year prior to the full conveyance, known as "lease and release," was in "general use."[35] Although practices varied by county, English landowners generally maintained a private system of land conveyancing well into the nineteenth century.

English landowners relied on private methods of conveying land and confirming title. Lawyers pored over documents relating to the property to verify ownership. The deed was (and is) a writing executing the conveyance.[36] In England, however, the conveyance was required to be perfected in a public ceremony called "livery of seisin."[37] The purpose of the ceremony was to publicize the conveyance to the community. As described by William Blackstone, the ceremony's function was to be a "public and notorious act, that the country might take notice of, and testify the transfer of the estate: and that such, as claimed title by other means, might know against whom to bring their actions."[38] The ceremony involved the parties and their attorneys coming to the land itself, and in the presence of witnesses, declaring the property to be conveyed. The prior owner would deliver to the new owner "a clod or turf, or a twig or bough there growing" and state that "I deliver these to you in the name of seisin of all the lands and tenements contained in this deed."[39] Done properly, the livery of seisin would be documented in writing on the back of the deed with a list of witnesses and details about the manner, place, and time of the ceremony. According to Blackstone, because the ceremony was relied upon for notoriety of the conveyance, if a deed conveyed land in different counties, "there must be as many liveries as there are counties."[40]

In contrast, a principal benefit of having land conveyances authenticated and recorded in the colonial courts and land title records was that it eliminated the need for the livery of seisin ceremony, and the attendant time and expense. As stated in a conveyance law enacted in 1715 in North Carolina, deeds proven in court and registered in the precinct shall be valid "without livery of seizin, attournment, or other ceremony in the law."[41] In fact, publicly searchable records were later celebrated for improving upon the livery of seisin ceremony in providing notoriety regarding land conveyances. Zephaniah Swift's 1795 treatise on Connecticut law emphasizes that Connecticut's recording act was

> founded in the highest wisdom and policy, and has a most effectual operation to reduce the titles to things real to certainty, and lessen the sources of litigation. The records and files of the towns, *will shew to every person, that is pleased to enquire, in whom is vested the legal title to lands, and inform him whether he can purchase with safety. This renders all conveyances of lands a matter of much more public notoriety, than the ancient method of livery of seisin.*[42]

By having the records give "notoriety" to the transaction, once the deed was "proven" in court, the transfer of title was complete.

CREATING A NORM OF PUBLICLY SEARCHABLE TITLE RECORDS

As Swift's treatise emphasizes, the public's access to court records and land title records was a central feature of colonial institutions. The Massachusetts recording law of 1658, for example, stated that "every Inhabitant of the Country shall have free liberty to search and view any *Rolls, Records, or Registers,* of any Court or Office, except of the Council and to have a transcript or Exemplification thereof written, examined and signed by the hand of the Officer, paying the accustomed fees." A 1720 Massachusetts law, which confirmed a process of electing county registers every five years, provided that each person chosen as register "shall reside and keep his office daily open in the respective shire town of each county, and therein keep the books, records, files and papers to the said office belonging."[43] A 1698 law enacted for the Carolinas held that if the Register or Secretary falsely certified that no sale, conveyance, or mortgage had been recorded on a parcel of land or "Negroes and other Goods and Chattels," the official would be liable for costs and damages to "such Person who made Enquiry and is damaged by Reason of such false Certificate."[44] New Jersey's recording acts of 1714 and 1727, described at the outset, stated "all Persons concerned may have Recourse to the said Records, as they shall have occasion."[45] A later New Jersey statute detailing the information that needed to be recorded stated that "all Persons whatsoever, at proper Seasons may have Recourse and Search" the mortgage book for the legislatively approved fee.[46] The 1753 New York "Act for preventing frauds by Mortgages" stated that "all persons whatsoever at proper Seasons may have Recourse and Search" the register of mortgages."[47]

The *public* nature of the court records and land title records was strikingly different than English conveyancing practice. As mentioned above, there were various movements to introduce public registries in England in the seventeenth and eighteenth centuries, but large landowners opposed the proposals.[48] In England, the public debate over court authentication and registries resulted in a vastly different outcome than the simultaneous institutional development in the colonies. Rather than relying on recording, Parliament enacted the Statute of Frauds in 1677, which simply required land conveyances to be put in writing (rather than be made orally). The English Statute of Frauds was enacted "[f]or prevention of many fraudulent practices" involving land conveyances. It held that conveyances executed without a writing, that is, orally or by the livery of seisin ceremony, would be treated as leases or held at the will of the owner.[49] The act failed to establish local public records or to disrupt the private system of conveyancing. Open records would have reflected a cultural and political shift: The English landed elite favored privacy in matters relating to their finances, including the existence of mortgages on their land, and were more comfortable relying on reputation as a driving force in credit markets.

York County and Middlesex County, England were two exceptions. Although widespread registration was not instituted in England until 1869, registries were adopted in the county of York (West Riding in 1703, East Riding in 1707, and North Riding in 1735) and Middlesex in 1708.[50] The law for West Riding explains that the residents of the county were interested in using their land as collateral for debts but were unable to because of the lack of a registry. The West Riding statute states:

> West Riding of the County of York is the principal Place in the North for the Cloth Manufacture and most of the Traders therein are Freeholders and have frequent Occasions to borrow Money upon their Estates for managing their said Trade but for want of a Register find it difficult to give Security to the Satisfaction of the Money-Lenders (although the Security they offer be really good), by Means whereof the said Trade is very much obstructed and many Families ruined. [51]

It is notable that the statute emphasizes the desire of "Traders" to mortgage land for funds to use in commerce. Moreover, the traders are "Freeholders," meaning they own land in a form that allows them to mortgage it. They have "really good" credit and security, but without a public record of mortgages, they are unable to convince "Money-Lenders" to extend funds on the basis of their land. In other words, the traders of York desired to use the wealth held in land as collateral to obtain funds to expand their trading operations. They thereby distinguished themselves from the landed elite, who often held some portion of their estates in illiquid form for the benefit of heirs, and for whom the property law offered political, economic, and social stability. The English county-level statutes reveal that contemporaries believed public mortgage recording to have great benefits for credit markets.

SLAVERY AND THE INTRODUCTION OF CHATTEL MORTGAGES

Another dramatic departure from the English common law involved the recording of slave mortgages. The simple colonial court procedures adopted to record conveyances and mortgages of land were adapted for chattel property. Virginia law recognized chattel mortgages in 1656.[52] Carolina's recording statute of 1698 stated that, in addition to recording land transactions, "the Sale or Mortgage of Negroes, Goods or Chattels which shall be first recorded in the Secretary's office in Charles-Town, shall be . . . held to be the first Mortgage" in all the courts of the state, any "Sale or Mortgage for the same Negroes, Goods and Chattels not recorded" notwithstanding.[53] Slavery is therefore an important driver of an institutional legacy that persists in the modern United States, which is an openness to the types of goods that can serve as commodified collateral. The unique legal path of the British American colonies originated in chattel mortgages for slaves.

County-Level Recording as an Institutional Response to Fraudulent Conveyances

In the late seventeenth and early eighteenth centuries, colonial assemblies passed laws to move recordkeeping of conveyances and mortgages to the counties. The decentralization of recordkeeping followed a different time line in each colony. In Virginia, for example, the Virginia Company maintained land records beginning in 1619. When Virginia became a royal colony in 1624, grants of land were first confirmed in England. The grants were then reported to Virginia for recording in a colony patent book.[54] In 1629, an act reflecting the executive's desire for full information on subsequent conveyances required the recordation of all land conveyances in one central location near the governor and council in Virginia's capital. The act states that "all sales of lands & deeds of gift of land made & agreed on between partye" must be "brought in to ye Court at James Citty & there recorded & enrolled w'thin one year and a day."[55] Even boundary disputes were required to be resolved in the capital. Statutes of 1624 and 1632 require that the governor and council resolve all disputes of "mayne importance" about the "bounds recorded."[56] Only "petty differences" could be resolved by local surveyors.[57]

A broad survey of colonial laws reveals that, across the colonies, county-level, public title recording typically was adopted for the stated reason of bringing greater transparency to ownership interests in land and slaves by addressing the problem of fraudulent conveyances. There is often a presumption of ownership in the person who is in possession of property. Mortgages are structured to encumber property with a debt with no visible change in possession, and therefore create a potential transparency problem. How is a creditor to know when property has been previously encumbered by a mortgage? Under the new colonial laws, recording a mortgage gave the creditor legal priority to the property over others who might claim an interest in it. Making mortgage records public gave transparency to any prior claims. Creditors who searched the body of records would know that, if there were no prior mortgages, once they recorded a mortgage interest their claim would have priority.

In Virginia, for example, in 1639, the problem of transparency in mortgage markets was addressed by introducing county-level recording. A 1639 statute states that "Whereas divers persons (as daily experience informeth) do closely and privately convey over their estates by way of mortgage not delivering possession whereby their creditors are defrauded and defeated of their just debts." The law moved recordkeeping of conveyances to the court sessions held in the newly created counties. The act required that deeds or mortgages "made without delivery of possession" be acknowledged and entered into the records of the "Quarter or Monthly court."[58] In 1656, the legislature, again addressing the problem of conveyances "whereby [a landowner's] creditors not haveing knowledge thereof, might be defrauded of their just debts unless such conveyance were first acknowledged," gave the parties the choice of either recording their conveyance "before the Governour and Council or at the monthly courts . . . in a book for that purpose within six months after such alienation."[59] Importantly, the 1656 act extended its scope to the recording of chattel mortgages. It states that "no part of any estate, whether in lands, goods or chattels shall be made over" without being recorded within six months.[60] A similar statute was enacted in 1662 that stated its goal was to prevent creditors from being defrauded and to allow recording of transactions in all "lands, goods or cattle," either before the "governor and councell at the general court, or before the justices at the county courts."[61]

As corporate colonies throughout the colonial era, Massachusetts and Connecticut had a different system in that towns were delegated control over granting land as early as 1629. In 1640, the first recording act appears to apply specifically to mortgages because it refers only to conveyances "without transfers of possession." The act states that its purpose was "avoiding all fraudulent conveyances and that every man may know what estate or interest other men may have in any houses, lands or other hereditaments they are to deal in . . . no mortgage, bargaine, sale or graunt . . . where the Graunter remains in possession shall be of force against other persons except the Graunter and his Heirs" unless it is recorded.[62] Similarly, by 1678 in Maryland, land sales were recorded by clerks of the county courts.[63] In New York, an act was passed in 1683 which stated that "No grants deeds Mortgages or other conveyances whattsoever of any Lands or Tenements . . . shall bee of force, power or validity in Law" unless the conveyances are "entered & recorded in the Register of the County wherein such lands or Tenements do lye" within six months.[64]

In 1715, North Carolina law recognized that the founders, the Lords Proprietors, granted as one of the colony's "privileges and immunities" the power of the free men to "choose public registers." The colonists were concerned about the politicization of the office of the register. With the end of "the more effectual prevention of fraudulent deeds, alienations, and mortgages," the freemen of each precinct were to elect three candidates for public register, of which one would be chosen by the colony's governor.

The law required that all conveyances except mortgages were required to be authenticated "by one or more evidences, upon oath" either before the chief justice or in the court of the precinct, and then registered by "the public register of the precinct where the land lieth."[65] Recording a mortgage was not required, but gave priority over subsequently executed debts. The power to select the public register was given fully to North Carolina's counties after the Declaration of Independence, in 1777.[66]

Pennsylvania similarly allowed local recording by 1706. In contrast to North Carolina, the mandatory recording in the "office of deeds of every county" applied only to mortgages, with voluntary recording available for titles.[67] What were the tradeoffs relating to mandatory or voluntary recording? Mandatory recording acts stated that all conveyances (sales, mortgages, gifts, etc.) were required to be recorded in order to effectively execute the transaction. The benefits of mandatory recording were that the public records became far more complete, which created greater transparency. The problem with mandatory recording, however, was that colonists often executed agreements without recording them. These statutes held unrecorded sales or security agreements to be defective after a time. Innocent parties who had executed land sales or mortgages but had failed to record were therefore unfairly penalized. In contrast, voluntary recording systems had the advantage that they did not invalidate unrecorded agreements. When recording was voluntary, the first recorded sale or mortgage was privileged over other agreements. If one did not record a mortgage, it would not get priority over another recorded claim. Unrecorded agreements were still legally effective, however, and could be proved in court at a later time. (Like contracts today, for example, where debt to a credit card company is not invalid simply because it is not publicly recorded.) And in the absence of competing claims, why hold invalid an agreement the parties intended to make enforceable, simply because it was not recorded? In a frontier society, in a culture where public recording was largely a novelty, voluntary recording proved to be the dominant approach.

Developing Institutions and Political Struggle

It is beyond the scope of this work to describe all of the political tensions over land, its distribution, and the institutional structure in the British colonies in America. Closer examination, however, reveals an atmosphere fraught with confusion, disagreements, and at times disruptive tensions over land ownership and officals' desire to collect fees they viewed as a prerogative of the

Crown. In the Massachusetts Bay colony, for example, under the 1629 charter, the colonial leadership clearly had land-granting authority. Nonetheless,
the historian David Thomas Konig's close study of Massachusetts land policy
in the seventeenth century concludes that "early land use was characterized
by inexactness in distribution, inattention to recording, and neglect of the
most basic statutory requirements of occupancy and fencing."[68] Lack of a
uniform surveying system and laxness on the part of those allocating land led
to uncertain boundaries and confusion over ownership. Konig notes that by
the 1660s and 1670s, greater pressure for land led town authorities to focus
more attention on the recording of deeds and the firming up of boundary
lines. A wave of land titling took place both in the individual towns and at
the level of the largest landholders, some of whom had acquired vast parcels
after King Philip's War of 1675–76.[69]

In 1686, however, King James II created the Dominion of New England,
with the intent to subject all of the New England colonies to firmer royal
control, and placed Massachusetts within it. When Sir Edmund Andros was
appointed governor in 1686, his commission and royal instructions specified
that he was to review the land titles that colonists had formalized outside of
the official processes for granting royal land. Andros was highly suspicious
of the actions of the previous administrations and ruled that all land titles in
Massachusetts were effectively invalid.[70] He announced a program whereby
residents would apply for new land patents, with the land surveyed by his
office and with titles formalized with the royal seal. In addition to surveying
costs, he imposed fees for obtaining the new land patents. Andros's decision
to invalidate land titles undermined the legitimacy of the primary asset held
by most Massachusetts residents.[71] Thus it is not surprising that he created
an uproar throughout the colony. With regard to the fees imposed, a 1691
account of the events written by members of Andros's Council emphasized
that *"[I]t hath by some been computed that all the money in the Country would
not suffice to patent the lands therein contained."*[72] The land patent issue was
central to Andros being violently overthrown in what was referred to as a
"Revolution."[73]

A central issue in the colonies was whether the records would be maintained centrally or in local communities. The crown-appointed governors
perceived the need to maintain records of subsequent conveyances to retain
control over land distribution and, in many colonies, to promote the collection of quit rents, a form of land tax. As was described in the case of the
New Jersey Assembly's laws, when institutions moved to the county level,
more of the fees went to county officials, not the crown-appointed officials in

the colonial capitals. But the inconveniences of keeping all records with the governors and councils in colonial capitals meant that subsequent transfers and conveyances often went unrecorded.

In contrast, a New York law of 1683 which established recording in the counties also required that the local county officials send the records and, importantly, the secretary's fees to the secretary's office every year. According to the act, the records must be "Transmitted once every yeare to the Secretarys office att New Yorke with the fees ordained for the same, there to be registered and Entered." If the clerk or register failed to transmit the records and fees to the secretary's office, the "Clerk shall loose his place & be made for ever incapable to Execute any place or office of trust within this Province." [74] In 1693, a *Catologue of Fees Established by the Governour and Council* at the New York Assembly's request noted various fees owed the governor, for example, "For the great Seal to every Patent for and under 100 Acres, 12 shillings."[75] The "Secretary's Fees" included "For a Patent for a House, Lot or Confirmation of Land, formerly possessed, 12 shillings"; "For a License to purchase Land of the *Indians*," 6 shillings.[76] Under the section "Fees for the Justices in or out of Sessions" is listed "Acknowledging a Deed of Sale, 2 shillings, 3 pence."[77] The section on "Fees to the Clerk of the Sessions and Common Pleas" includes "Searching the Records within one Year 6 d" and "Every Year backwards, 3d more."[78]

Then in 1753, New York law incorporated a special provision for mortgages that made no mention of sending records and fees to the secretary's office. The act recognized that "many frauds and Aubuses have been Committed as well by Persons Mortgaging their lands Tenements and Real Estate and afterwards Selling the Same Lands to other Persons who were Ignorant of Such Mortgages."[79] It noted that "many Persons have been defrauded of great Sums of Money Wherefore for preventing those Evils for the future." The 1753 law required that "Each and every of the Clerks of the Several and Respective City's and County's within this Province Shall provide a fit and proper Blank Book for the Registering of all Mortgages of Lands Tenements and Real Estate lying within their Respective City's & County's."[80] Subsequent laws in the colony repeatedly tried to improve upon the recordkeeping in the local mortgage books required in the 1753 law.

The struggle between colonial legislatures and the King's Privy Council is well illustrated by Pennsylvania, which in January 1706 passed a law providing for recording of conveyances in the city or county where the land existed. The law was repealed by the Privy Council in 1709.[81] In February 1711, the legislature enacted a similar law setting up an "office of record, which shall be called and styled the enrolment office" in the towns and counties. Under the law, the recorder was required to keep books of conveyances and mortgages, which could be searched. The Privy Council repealed the law in February 1714.[82] In May 1715, the legislature reenacted the law. This time, the Privy Council failed to respond and the act remained effective "by lapse of time."[83]

With regard to South Carolina, it appears that county-level recording did not become the law until 1785. South Carolina retained a centralized system throughout the colonial era. In the Carolinas, recording first took place in two centralized offices in Charlestown. A 1698 "Act to prevent Deceits by Double Mortgages and Conveyances of Lands, Negroes and Chattels" stated that it was intended to prevent "knavish and necessitous" persons from making two or more sales of "the same plantation, negroes, and other goods and chattels" which led "buyers of plantations, and lenders of money" to lose their money.[84] It established a system of voluntary recording, which held that, with regard to the sale, conveyance or mortgage of *lands*, those first registered in the Register's Office in Charlestown would be deemed the earliest and given priority. That statute provided that recording the sale or mortgage of "negroes, goods or chattels" was available in the Secretary's Office in Charleston. The recording fees would be collected by the Register and the Secretary, respectively.

In 1729, the Carolinas came under direct rule of the Royal Government (became British Crown colonies) as two separate colonies. An Act of 1731 stated that the colony of South Carolina was now ruled directly by "his Majesty." It recognized that "it having been found by experience" that the office recording titles "has had the good effects expected by the same, and has been of great use and service to this Province, as it has been distinct and separate from any other office."[85] Under the act, the "recorder or register of deeds and conveyances of land and mortgages, shall be and continue separated and distinct from any other office."

It is clear that local, county-level recording in South Carolina was established by 1785 when the South Carolina legislature enacted "An Act for establishing county courts," which required the recording of conveyances of land "in the Clerk's office of the county where the land mentioned to be passed or granted shall lie."[86] The 1785 law, however, still provided for an additional central secretary's office where records of all conveyances would be kept. The act states that "to the end that persons who are inclined to lend money upon the security of lands or Negroes or to become purchasers thereof, may more easily discover whether the lands or slaves offered to be sold or mortgaged, be free from incumbrances," the state of South Carolina would maintain one registry in the secretary's office. Under the 1785 Act, the clerks of the county courts were required to "transmit memorials" of all recorded conveyances to the central office every January and June.[87]

In sum, colonial era society became more heavily reliant on legal institutions than was true in England. British policy led to massive land distribution in the colonies to individuals willing to cultivate it. Far more than in traditional English society, however, land was often viewed as a source of wealth that could be bought and sold, and used for collateral for debts. Slaves too were treated as assets and were a primary form of collateral driving the economy in many areas. Colonists relied on local institutions to publicize records of transfers and mortgages of land and slaves.

Colonial title recording involved no massive government surveying effort and was not linked to taxation. Although some colonies experimented with requiring recordation, most established a voluntary process. Under the voluntary recording system, whoever recorded a title or a mortgage gained priority over subsequent parties claiming an interest in the same property. The records did not confirm the validity of the title—what is referred to as registration—instead, they established a priority rule in the case of a title conflict. The statutes enacting the recording regime were rooted substantively in older English fraudulent conveyance law, but publicly searchable records were a new institutional solution to fraudulent conveyances that had not gained widespread acceptance in England. Colonists adopted a low-cost way to secure property rights and to promote credit markets. In addition, representative assemblies were very active in creating the institutions and in setting fees. In the process, they empowered themselves vis-à-vis the Crown. As chapter 6 will describe, this made the issue of the fees imposed for institutional services highly political.

The Stamp Act of 1765 was a parliamentary tax on institutional services such as court processes and title recording. As we shall see, Parliament's decision to tax basic institutional services was viewed as a betrayal of the understood delegation of authority over fees and taxes to colonial legislatures. Moreover, by using these institutions to generate revenue for the Crown, the Stamp Act would have suppressed economic activity, making it more costly for colonists to avail themselves of legal services they had come to rely upon. That the Stamp Act served as a breaking point, propelling the movement for Independence, reveals just how important these institutions were to the colonial economy and to the colonists' sense of the proper realm of authority of their colonial legislatures.

PART II

Property Exemptions

COMMODIFYING LAND AND SLAVES IN COLONIAL AMERICA

3

English Property Law, the Claims of Creditors, and the Colonial Legal Transformation

In the seventeenth and eighteenth centuries, England was a vibrant commercial society with active land and credit markets. And yet, those credit markets were constrained by laws that followed long-standing social norms which privileged maintaining the integrity of landed estates and limited the extent to which families' ownership interests would be subject to commercial and other financial risks. By social convention, owners of the larger estates were expected to pass them from one generation to the next in at least a similar, or perhaps even an augmented, condition. As described by Sir Lewis Namier:

> The English political family is a compound of "blood," name, and estate, this last . . . being the most important of the three. . . . The name is a weighty symbol, but liable to variations; . . . the estate . . . is, in the long run, the most potent factor in securing continuity through identification.[1]

The landed elite maintained by these estates had incentives to protect the status quo. The law of inheritance was crucial to the English social and economic framework. John Locke, best known today for his emphasis on an individual's natural right to property acquired through labor, defended the English inheritance system on the ground that all children—irrespective of whether they labored on behalf of the family—naturally enjoyed a shared title with their parents to the family property. Locke viewed England's inheritance system as a natural consequence of the powerful instinct of humans to procreate, which led to a sense of obligation of parents to provide for their children. According to Locke, this principle "gives Children a Title, to share in the *Property* of their Parents, and a Right to Inherit their Possessions. Men are not Proprietors of what they have meerly for themselves, their Children have a Title to part of it, and have their Kind of Right joyn'd with their Parents."[2]

Of course, there were tradeoffs between protecting ownership of property through the generations and the economic benefits of using land like a liquid asset. The desire to pledge land as collateral to borrow money to make improvements, to invest in new equipment, or to acquire more land was powerful, even in a traditional society like Great Britain. Throughout history, societies have always experienced economic cycles, however, and widespread voluntary borrowing in an upswing will often cause widespread financial stress in a downswing. In societies with active credit markets, the downside risks of foreclosure, seizure of property, homelessness, and social instability can be reduced by laws that protect assets from creditors' claims. The tradeoff is that protections against creditors' claims raise interest rates and decrease investment.

Through the early nineteenth century, English law balanced these tradeoffs by distinguishing between involuntary and voluntary conveyances. Unsecured credit is borrowing where no property is specifically pledged as collateral. As will be described, in the early modern period, the common law offered extensive remedies that allowed unsecured creditors to take property involuntarily, but notably protected ownership interests in land from their claims. In contrast, mortgages and other forms of secured credit involve a debtor voluntarily pledging particular property as collateral for the debt. Under English law, mortgage creditors could foreclose upon land in the Court of Chancery (a court of equity with jurisdiction over land law issues and other matters). As we shall see, however, judges' discretionary decisions in the Court of Chancery displayed a bias in favor of inheritance, and the courts offered procedural hurdles to foreclosure on land. Moreover, in early modern England, individual families used legal means like trusts and fee tails to segregate the assets that would be protected for future generations (which could not be sold or mortgaged) from the assets held in liquid forms (which could be sold or mortgaged). The social norms of early modern society dictated that the primary land of the larger estates was often held in a form protected from creditors and sale, while outlying land might be held in a form that was more liquid.

As the second part of this chapter describes, the colonial context was completely different and led to radical change. Initially, many colonies adopted the English framework, including legal protections on land from unsecured creditors. Some colonies recruited immigrants by announcing that landowners would hold "estates of inheritance" like in England. Starting in Barbados in 1656, Massachusetts in 1675, and West New Jersey in 1682, some colonial legislatures began adopting a much more credit-friendly approach, which commodified land and slaves by treating them not as "land" in England, but as "chattel." This meant that when unsecured creditors obtained judgments against debtors, land and slaves could be used to satisfy the debts in streamlined court processes, without foreclosure. Other colonies, like Virginia, consciously attempted to replicate the English system.

This chapter and the next describe the complicated history as the colonies, under British oversight and imperial regulation, diverged from English property and inheritance law while laying the foundations for colonial economy and society. Until 1732, under the federal system of the British colonial regime, each colonial legislature had the authority to determine which protections from creditors, court processes, and currency policies to adopt. The next chapter describes how Parliament assumed control over creditor protections and court processes in 1732.

The Protection of Family Ownership of Land in English Law

In England, the doctrine of primogeniture was the most obvious example of the preference for maintaining estates through the generations. Under primogeniture, the eldest male heir inherited the family's primary estate in land, thereby ensuring that it would remain concentrated in one undivided parcel.[3] Primogeniture was a default rule, that is, it operated by law when there was no will, that persisted until 1925. The members of most elite families wrote wills, however, and formalized primogeniture in "settlement" agreements entered into at the time of the eldest son's marriage. The settlement agreements often gave the primary estate in land to the eldest son and required him to make payments from the land's income for the benefit of his mother (her dower or jointure interests as a widow), his wife (specified pin money), and his younger siblings (called "portions") either in lump sums or in annuities.[4] Settlement agreements often specified the terms of a trust describing the land that could not be sold or mortgaged, while also designating some land to be held in fee simple (the form most commonly used in the United States today, which can be sold or mortgaged[5]). The landowner's interest could also be circumscribed by a will "entailing" the land, which meant that the land would descend through the family line in perpetuity, unless the owner went through a legal proceeding to remove the entail. Settlements and entails provided for wealth distribution within the family while appointing one person (typically the eldest son) as manager of the entire estate.

Historically, the English law of property was defined by stark distinctions in the treatment afforded land (real property) and personal property (chattel).[6] With regard to the claims of creditors, the law maintained the cohesion of English estates and protected land from involuntary seizure in two ways. First, English law protected title ownership in land from the claims of all unsecured creditors. Second, the Court of Chancery protected land by creating procedural hurdles to foreclosure on land to satisfy secured debts and by privileging the long-term family interests in inheritance proceedings. These laws and practices are discussed below.

THE PROTECTION OF FAMILY ESTATES IN ENGLISH COURTS OF LAW

From the late thirteenth century onward in England, an unsecured creditor obtaining a judgment against a debtor in a common law court could request one of four writs of execution to enforce the judgment. First, the writ of *fieri facias* directed the sheriff to seize the goods and chattels of the defendant, to sell the items, and to deliver the proceeds to the plaintiff.[7] Second, the writ of *levari facias* directed the sheriff to seize and sell the debtor's goods and chattels, like the writ of fieri facias, but additionally imposed a lien on behalf of the creditor on the future earnings of the debtor's land until the debt was satisfied.[8]

Third, in contrast to the writ of levari facias, the writ of *elegit* allowed for a limited tenancy in the debtor's land.[9] Blackstone described the elegit as a "speedier way for the recovery of debts" and a "benefit to a trading people."[10] Under the writ of elegit, the sheriff obtained an appraisal of the debtor's goods and chattels, which the creditor accepted at the appraised value. If the debtor's goods and chattels failed to satisfy the debt, the creditor acquired a tenancy of one-half of the debtor's land for the number of years necessary to satisfy the remainder of the debt, based on a court-ordered appraisal (like a lease, with no rent).[11] The debtor retained possession of half of his property, as well as "his Oxen and Beasts of his Plough,"[12] presumably to ensure that he was able to fulfill his obligations to his landlord and to the King, as well as to provide for his family. A closely related but more valuable remedy could be obtained if a debtor appeared in the Merchant Court or the Staple Court to formally acknowledge his debt. These courts offered creditors the remedy of a temporary tenancy of all of the debtor's land until the debt was satisfied (a "tenancy by *extent*").[13] Creditors who took possession of their debtors' property as tenants by elegit or extent could maximize the productivity of the land during the years of their tenancy.[14]

Fourth, under the writ of *capias ad satisfaciendum*, the sheriff seized the body of the debtor for imprisonment.[15] While the debtor was in prison, the creditor could not touch the debtor's land.[16] The principal use of the writ of capias ad satisfaciendum was to threaten the debtor and his family in order to encourage them to pay the debt or to provide security for the debt.[17] Less frequently, a debtor would use debtors' prison to his advantage by having a "friendly" creditor imprison him to allow his family to remain in possession of all of his land.[18]

Notably, none of these remedies jeopardized a landowner's title interest (ownership) in his land and the heir's ability to inherit it. The writ of fieri facias was limited to the debtor's goods and chattels. The writ of levari facias allowed the creditor to take the income from land for a temporary period. The writ of elegit offered a creditor temporary possession (not ownership) in one-half (not all) of a debtor's land. The writ of capias ad satisfaciendum put the debtor in jail, but preserved his land.

Moreover, each of these remedies was limited to the life of the debtor. The inheritance of unencumbered land was considered a birthright of the eldest son. According to the prevailing custom, when a property owner died, the unsecured creditors of the deceased instituted debt actions against the executors of the deceased's estate.[19] The executors of the estate assumed control over the deceased's *personal* property, but not the land.[20] The executors satisfied the debts out of the deceased's personal property. In the absence of a will, the land immediately descended to the eldest male heir. Inherited land never came under an executor's control.[21] According to the historians Pollock and Maitland, "[T]he executor had nothing to do with the dead man's land, the heir had nothing to do with the chattels."[22] The landed inheritance remained legally protected from all unsecured creditors, unless the deceased explicitly stated in his will that the land should be sold to pay his debts.[23]

If the personal property was insufficient to satisfy the debts, the unsecured creditors would simply lose the value of the remaining debts, unless the heirs and devisees felt obliged to pay the debts out of a sense of honor, or wanted to extend the ancestor's credit line for their own purposes.[24] Of course, to maintain the family credit, most landowners would want to repay their father's debts voluntarily, but they were under no legal obligation to do so.

THE PROTECTION OF FAMILY ESTATES IN THE CHANCERY COURT

Mortgages were treated entirely differently under the law. Mortgage creditors and other secured creditors—those who extended credit on the basis of specific pledges of land as collateral, formalized by signatures and the debtors' seals—could foreclose upon the land that was pledged.[25] When landowners pledged land under a mortgage or sealed bond, they could bind themselves as well as their heirs. Before 1691, the way to bind future heirs was to explicitly state in the credit agreement that all "heirs, executors, and administrators" were responsible for the debt.[26] When the generic "heirs" were made parties to the secured credit agreement, the creditor could pursue a cause of action against the heir after the debtor's death, and the heir might be compelled to discharge the debt out of the land that he inherited. The requirement that heirs were only bound by mortgage agreements that explicitly included the heir as a party was expanded by the English courts into a broader "privilege" allowing the heir a procedural right to contest any action in which he might lose the landed inheritance. Blackstone, in describing the features of what he referred to as the "absolute" right of property, emphasized the English laws, stating that "no man shall be disinherited, nor put out of his franchises or freehold, unless he be unduly brought to answer, and be forejudged by course of law."[27]

Parliament strengthened the remedies of secured creditors in a 1691 law, the Statute of Fraudulent Devises, which stated that secured creditors could pursue causes of action against heirs of deceased debtors as well as devisees, even if they were not mentioned in the secured credit agreement.[28] An owner of land might write a will that devised land to a family member or non–family member.[29] Under the Statute of Fraudulent Devises, attempts by the deceased to devise land that had been previously pledged as security, or attempts by the heirs or devisees to transfer that land to another party, were deemed fraudulent.[30] (Interestingly, there was debate in the colonies as to whether this statute, a parliamentary law that did not reference the colonies, automatically applied.)

Secured creditors seeking to satisfy a debt with land the debtor had pledged, however, could not do so simply by bringing an action in the common law courts.[31] In the early seventeenth century, the Court of Chancery determined that a mortgagor held a right to redeem the land within a reasonable period, irrespective of the actual terms of the mortgage agreement.[32] The right to redeem the land was called the "equity of redemption." (This term resembles the modern description of someone's ownership interest as the "equity" they have in property.) Recognition of the equity of redemption meant that, in order to gain secure title in the land, the mortgagee (the lender) was required to obtain both a legal judgment in the common law courts on the debt and a separate decree of foreclosure in the Court of Chancery.[33]

What was the Court of Chancery? The Chancery began as an office of the Crown, charged with "keeping the great seal," which was used to authenticate "royal grants of property, privilege, dignity or office, charters, writs and commissions."[34] It became an independent judicial institution in the fourteenth and fifteenth centuries. The common law courts were viewed as merciless and heavily formalistic. Parties began passing on to the Court of Chancery "bills addressed to the king in council, complaining of interference with the common law."[35] The Court of Chancery was able to overrule decisions of the common law courts, which it did on the basis of fairness issues (including fraud, opportunism, and conflicts of interest). Over time, the court's jurisdiction expanded and it came to be the primary court for land law issues, trusts, and guardianship, among other things.

Chancery was known for its high costs and procedural delays. According to the historian J. H. Baker, "[f]or two centuries before Dickens wrote *Bleak House*, the word 'Chancery' had become synonymous with expense, delay and despair."[36] Actions in Chancery inevitably took a long time because the docket was large, the court did not meet continuously, and all relevant parties were given the opportunity to be heard and to appeal the court's decisions.[37] Secured creditors seeking to foreclose upon land that had been pledged as security had to contend with the claims of family members in all preexisting family settlement agreements. Settlement agreements were treated like secured credit agreements in the sense that they established prior claims against the land over subsequent creditors.[38] Contending with family members who claimed under family settlement agreements was an immensely costly component of foreclosing in Chancery. Moreover, prior to obtaining a formal foreclosure in the Chancery court, and at times *after* the creditor obtained a foreclosure, the mortgagor was permitted to redeem the property from the mortgagee by paying the remaining amount due on the mortgage, plus interest and costs.[39] These complicated procedures for foreclosure of course added costs to the process of acquiring title to land under a mortgage.

As described by the legal historian Robert W. Gordon, "while the common law promoted alienability, equity promoted dynastic preservation."[40] Chancery court judges at times exercised discretion on behalf of family members at the expense of creditors in order to pursue a policy of privileging the preservation of families' long-term interests in land. In his study of Chancery court decisions that favored family members over creditors, Adam Hofri-Winogradow describes an example of Chancery interpreting a will as entailing land on behalf of the possible future children of a then-childless, estranged couple in their fifties (a couple not likely to have children) in order to prevent a sale of the land to pay debts.[41] Chancery judges chose to preserve the family's ownership of land when faced with language in a will that was ambiguous as to whether the land should be sold to pay debts. Moreover, Chancery judges upheld family settlement agreements that protected land when faced with creditors' challenges to the validity of those agreements.[42]

Chancery's general policy was to protect the integrity of the family estate in land whenever possible. The most prominent example of this policy was that mortgage debts, in which parcels of land were specifically pledged as collateral, were charged to the landowner's personal property first, rather than to the land that had been pledged as security. The mortgaged land would be sold only if the personal property was insufficient to pay the debt.[43] By paying mortgage debts with chattel property, Chancery reduced the encumbrances on the family land. In doing so, it privileged the heir at the expense of the deceased's other children, who typically inherited equal portions of the deceased's personal property after the unsecured debts were paid.[44]

CREDITORS' REMEDIES AGAINST LAND IN ENGLAND

In sum, the English legal regime of the early modern era allowed land markets and mortgages but, with regard to unsecured creditors, the common law courts offered no remedy that directly threatened a family's freehold interest in land. The integrity of estates and the inheritance of land were further protected in the Court of Chancery by its practices of recognizing the equity of redemption and of privileging landed inheritance over the interests of creditors in its proceedings.

The presence of these protections on land ownership, however, did not mean that English landowners never sold their land to satisfy unsecured debts. The most common circumstance in which family property was sold was when a landowning family's debt became so large (possibly after accumulating over the generations) that, without a sale of land, family members were unable to access credit for resources needed to manage the remaining property.[45] In addition, the threat of debtors' prison or of the sheriff stripping away all of the family's goods and chattels and selling them at auction also induced landowners to sell their land to pay unsecured creditors.[46] Landowners whose powers to convey property were circumscribed in family settlements could petition for a private Act of Parliament to allow a sale of settled land.[47] An entail could be removed through a conveyance referred to as a "common recovery."[48]

In each of these circumstances, however, the law gave landowners the privilege of voluntarily choosing to sell the land, and the land was sold only on terms to which they consented. The inability of an individual unsecured creditor to force a seizure and sale of the land gave landowners important opportunities to delay the repayment of their debts. English law therefore limited the extent to which a family's ownership interests would be subject to commercial and other financial risks. This was the legal regime that formed the foundation of the property law of the British colonies in America.

The Transformation of Property Law in Colonial America

How would this English body of law be instituted in the colonies? The charters and patents that conveyed legislative power to the colonial governments generally prohibited colonial legislatures from making laws "repugnant to" the laws of England or requiring that the enacted laws be "not contrary to but as near as conveniently may be made agreeable to the Laws, Statutes & Government of this Our Realm of England."[49] Yet, land was inevitably a different kind of asset in a colonial context where the settlers, after usurping or purchasing the land from native Americans, acquired land in a more rudimentary state. The British policy of distributing land in small headrights was merely one formal recognition of how different land was as an asset in colonial society. The English legal tradition, however, carried great weight among the colonial settlers and shaped the underlying legal regime. Moreover, many immigrants (not slaves) came to the colonies with the aspiration of owning a landed estate, which often would have been out of their reach in England.

COLONIAL CREDITORS' REMEDIES AGAINST THE LAND PRIOR TO PARLIAMENTARY REGULATION

Not surprisingly, the originating documents and early statutes of many colonies promised adherence to the English protections to land from creditors' claims. New York's 1683 Charter of Liberties, for example, promised its residents that land would not be characterized as chattel property, but as "an estate of inheritance" according to the laws of England.[50] The Charter explicitly stated that courts in New York had no authority to "grant out any Execucon or other writt whereby any mans Land may be sold . . . without the owners Consent."[51] A 1647 Connecticut statute adopted the English body of remedies, clarifying that creditors could take possession of debtors' land only until their debts were satisfied, as under the writ of elegit.[52]

Indeed, several colonies adopted remedial regimes that were even more protective of land than English law in that they did not offer the writ of elegit. The absence of the writ of elegit likely reflected the fact that a temporary possessory interest in land was not a valuable remedy in the early stages of agricultural development when profits from land were low. A Virginia statute of 1705 outlined the procedures according to which sheriffs could seize either the "goods and chattels" or the body of a debtor to satisfy debts.[53] Maryland statutes enacted in 1705 and 1715 limited execution to the seizure of "goods chattels and credits" to satisfy debts.[54] The Maryland acts exempted from creditors' claims property that would "deprive [debtors] of all Livelihood for the Future[, such as] Corn for necessary Maintenance, Bedding, Gun, Axe, Pot and Labourers necessary Tools, and such like Houshold-Implements and Ammunition for Subsistence." A Jamaican statute of 1681 allowed the sheriff to seize "goods and chattels," and if the goods and chattels were insufficient, then "negroes, working cattle, or necessary utensils," but did not mention the writ of elegit or other claims against the land.[55] In St. Kitts, the writ of elegit was not available, freehold property interests were entirely immune from the claims of unsecured creditors, and freehold property owners were exempt from arrest and placement in debtors' prison.[56]

Merchants lending to residents of these colonies, however, often complained about the fact that unsecured creditors were prohibited from seizing their debtors' land. In 1715, the Board of Trade issued a formal instruction to the governor of Jamaica directing him to persuade the legislature to introduce a remedy against the land by elegit or extent. The instruction described the lack of such a remedy as "a great prejudice to creditors and discredit to trade."[57]

Others emphasized that the English legal regime threatened credit because English inheritance laws protected land from unsecured creditors when a debtor died. As an example, Robert Carter, one of the most prominent planters in Virginia, complained that he suffered the negative impact of these laws personally after lending money or goods to a Mr. Lee.[58] After Lee died, Carter found that Lee's personal property was insufficient to satisfy his debts, but that his estate included recently acquired land. Carter suspected that Lee had purchased the land to avoid paying his debts "just as Lee found himself tottering, to defraud his creditors, and to do something for his wife and children at other men's cost."[59] In a 1720 letter to his son John, Carter described his concern about the impact on credit of applying English protections to land from unsecured creditors:

> If this be law, we in the Plantations are in a very dangerous condition, for we have nothing but the merchants' accounts for our security, and any merchant for the advancement of his family may throw all the money he has of others to purchase a real estate with; and when he's dead his family goes into the possession of it and his claimers are without remedy.[60]

A 1723 letter from a Virginia factor to the Bristol merchant Isaac Hobhouse described a similar problem.[61] The factor explained that the merchant would not likely be paid because the debtor's land was devised to the debtor's son:

> Its my Opinion yt Mr Lyd's nor yr Selves wont be half pd without ye Land could be Sold: wch wont be done by no means what ever: for its Left to ye Son of Mr Robt Baylor after ye Death of Jno Baylor: wch is a very Strong Argument for: Robt not to agree to ye Sale.[62]

In an effort to attract credit on better terms, however, the legislatures of some colonies offered greater protections to creditors than existed under English laws and Chancery practices. As mentioned, the colonial charters and patents typically authorized the colonial legislatures to enact laws that were "not repugnant" to the laws of England. In most cases, the "repugnancy" requirement was understood to mean that English law applied in the colonies. Colonial enactments that reformed English law for the purpose of advancing creditors' interests were not automatically "repugnant" to English law, however, because they were consistent with another overarching and widely accepted English policy: that the role of the colonies was to advance

British mercantilist economic interests.[63] Moreover, colonial authorities in Britain came to accept that not all English laws and practices were appropriate to unique local conditions.[64] The colonial authorities were amenable to legal reforms that responded to local needs *and* that advanced the interests of the colonial regime by providing greater security to English and Scottish creditors.

Some colonial legislatures made modest modifications to the English remedial regime. The legislature of New Plymouth (later part of Massachusetts), for example, enacted a law in 1633 that departed from English law by stating that if a creditor could demonstrate that a debtor had purchased land for the purpose of avoiding the payment of his unsecured debts, then the land would be available to satisfy those debts.[65] The law provided, however, that notwithstanding any improper motives of the debtor in purchasing the land, if the land was found to be necessary for the subsistence of the deceased's family, "such lands remaine to the survivors his or her heires no seizure being allowed the creditors in that case."[66] William Penn's Charter of Liberties of 1682 included a section that departed from English law by providing generally for the liability of lands for debts. The provision protected the inheritance rights of eldest sons by stating that once a debtor had a child, the amount of land available to satisfy his debts would be limited to one-third of his holdings.[67]

In 1700, however, the Pennsylvania legislature radically revised its remedial regime and adopted a statute making all of a debtor's land available to satisfy unsecured debts, even if the debtor had a child.[68] Five years later, the Pennsylvania legislature apparently decided that its law subjected landowners to excessive financial risk. It enacted a new law (which, notably, became the law of the Northwest Territory in 1795) according to which, if the debt could be satisfied out of the *earnings* from land within seven years, then the creditor would be limited to a tenancy by elegit, that is, possession of the land for a term.[69] But if an unsecured debt was so large that it could not be satisfied with seven years' worth of earnings from the debtor's land, the land would be sold at auction.[70] The 1705 Pennsylvania statute also tried to improve the terms of secured credit within the colony by replacing mortgagors' *equitable* redemption rights, recognized in equity, with a *statutory* redemption right, enforced in the law courts. According to the statute, the use of mortgages for the "payment of monies" was widespread, but mortgages were "no effectual security, considering how low the annual profits of tenements and improved lands are here, and the discouragements which the mortgagees meet with, by reason of the equity of redemption remaining in the mortgagers."[71] The statute allowed mortgagees to force the sale of mortgaged land no sooner than one year from the day on which a debt was owed. At the end of the year, the mortgagor or his or her "heirs, executors or administrators" were given the procedural privilege of an opportunity to contest the sale in court.[72] If they could not provide an acceptable defense to the court action, the property was to be sold at auction, with a fee simple title going to the purchaser.[73]

What about Chancery in the colonies? In the eighteenth century, Chancery courts were established in the royal colonies (New Hampshire, New Jersey, New York, Virginia, North Carolina, South Carolina, and Georgia, as well as Massachusetts, eventually), and also in Maryland and briefly, Pennsylvania, often with the governor acting as chancellor. As the historian Stanley Katz has described, "[t]he inescapable problem of such chancery courts was that few colonial governors had either the legal training, the time, or interest to exercise judicial office adequately."[74]

THE EARLY RADICAL COLONIAL TRANSFORMATION IN CREDITORS' REMEDIES

Some colonial legislatures experimented with more fundamental changes to the English property and inheritance laws in the late seventeenth and early eighteenth centuries. In Barbados as early as 1656, land and slaves were treated as legally equivalent to chattel property in all debt collection proceedings.[75] The Barbados legislature, however, appears to have changed course several times soon thereafter. In 1668, the legislature enacted a law declaring slaves to be real estate and making both slaves and land exempt from the claims of unsecured creditors.[76] Then, in a reversal, a 1672 law declared that slaves would be treated as chattel and subject to the claims of unsecured creditors. Creditors of the Barbadian planters, however, complained about the exemption of land from the claims of unsecured creditors. A royal instruction of 1673 directed the Barbadian governor to "get the assembly of Barbados to reenact that law whereby all lands seized by process of law for the satisfaction of debts should be sold as formerly by outcry [auction]."[77] According to the instruction, merchants extending credit suffered "great inconveniences and prejudice" in trying to recover their debts, and failing to strengthen creditors' legal remedies would "draw certain ruin upon the place."[78] Although no statute has survived, by 1677 Barbados appears to have returned to the policy of treating both land and slaves as legally equivalent to chattel for the purpose of satisfying debts.[79]

Some colonial legislatures—in New England and New Jersey—also made fundamental changes to the body of English law on remedies. The legislature of West New Jersey, in 1682, enacted a law making land liable for unsecured debts if the debtor's personal estate was found to be insufficient to satisfy the debts.[80] A Massachusetts law from 1675, like the practice in Barbados and New Jersey, was revolutionary in that it explicitly permitted a creditor to take an individual's freehold interest in land to satisfy an unsecured debt.[81] The act was reenacted in 1692 with more explicit language, stating that "all lands or tenements belonging to any person . . . in fee simple shall stand charged with the payment of all just debts owing by such person, as well as his personal estate, and shall be liable to be taken in execution for satisfaction of the same."[82] Unlike the 1705 Pennsylvania statute, the Massachusetts law did not establish a minimum debt amount below which creditors would be unable to take debtors' land. Other New England colonies enacted similar laws in the same period. Connecticut enacted a statute in 1702 making lands liable for debts.[83] In 1718, New Hampshire adopted a statute making lands, but not houses, liable for the debts of a debtor who was alive.[84] Upon the debtor's death, however, the executor could distribute the lands and the house of the deceased debtor to his creditors.[85]

The New England and post-1677 Barbados practices modified English law in two important respects. First, they enabled creditors to seize a debtor's freehold interest in land in addition to his personal property to satisfy unsecured debts. In Massachusetts after 1701, for example, the legislatively prescribed form for the writ of fieri facias directed the sheriff to seize the debtor's "goods, chattels or lands," instead of simply "goods and chattels."[86] The writ of elegit fell out of use entirely because title to a debtor's land was more valuable than possession of the land. As Governor Thomas Hutchinson described in his history of Massachusettts, "[The county courts] consider[ed] real estates as mere *bona*, and they did not confine themselves to any rules of distribution then in use in England. . . . [These legal modifications were excusable] in a new plantation, where most people soon spent what little personal estate they had, in improvement upon their lands."[87]

Still, the New England colonies and Barbados, unlike Pennsylvania and Delaware, imposed a unique limitation on creditors' remedies. Lands seized in execution were not sold at public auction as chattel property ordinarily would have been; the laws in these colonies instead provided that land would be appraised and then transferred to creditors in satisfaction of their judgments. The creditors thus had to accept an in-kind remedy, not cash after an auction. *Phillips v. Dean*, a 1720 court case in the Plymouth County,

Massachusetts Court of Common Pleas, illustrates how the Massachusetts law functioned. Joseph Phillips successfully sued Thomas Dean on a book account debt for "Sadlary Ware" and received a judgment of eight pounds, ten shillings, and nine pence, plus court costs. The court issued a writ of execution for the sheriff to satisfy the debt. Three people were appointed to appraise Dean's land. The sheriff then put Phillips in possession of just over six acres of Dean's land.[88] Under the law, once Phillips recorded his interest in the county registry, he would have full legal title—a fee simple interest— to the land. To convey by piecemeal a six-acre parcel of an estate to satisfy a simple book account debt is a stunning contrast to English law, which privileged the integrity of estates and inheritance and created innumerable legal hurdles and fees to buffer against creditors' claims.

The second effect of enormous significance of the New England and Barbados practices was to allow unsecured creditors priority over the heirs in the distribution of the deceased's land in inheritance proceedings. The 1692 Massachusetts statute explicitly stated that it intended to remedy the problem that, although debtors' houses and lands "give them credit," some debtors are "remiss in paying of their just debts" and "others happen[] to dye before they have discharged the same."[89] The broader consequence of the 1692 law was that the inheritance of real property could no longer be viewed as an inevitable occurrence or a birthright: heirs took real property subject to the claims of all of their fathers' unsecured creditors. Land—the inheritance—could be taken involuntarily based on highly informal obligations such as book accounts without the participation of the heir and without the landowner expressly signing a mortgage or other security agreement, a grant, or a will.

The colonial laws described thus far implicitly reveal an important feature of regulation within the British colonial regime prior to the 1732 Debt Recovery Act, described in the next chapter. Lawmaking authority relating to debt collection and creditors' remedies was initially firmly vested in local colonial legislatures and courts. The Board of Trade and the Privy Council reviewed and modified colonial law to advance British economic interests.[90] Parliament, however, initially chose not to legislate directly in the realm of legal remedies and colonial court procedures. In resolving intercolonial disputes, the Privy Council and House of Lords, which had appellate jurisdiction over litigation initiated in the colonies, applied not English law, but the relevant local colonial law. Colonial laws were overturned if they were found to be repugnant to the laws of England, but in the absence of such a ruling, colonial law prevailed.[91]

4

Parliamentary Authority over Creditors' Claims

THE DEBT RECOVERY ACT

Under the decentralized British colonial rule of the early eighteenth century, local colonial governments defined the treatment of property in their courts, established the remedies available to creditors, and issued their own currencies.[1] In the late 1720s and 1730s, a sharp decline in the prices of both sugar and tobacco, as well as general conditions of recession throughout the Atlantic economy, transformed the relationship between the colonial legislatures and the authorities in Great Britain.[2] Large numbers of colonial planters were unable to pay off debts to their factors and merchants. Such depressed economic conditions made creditors' remedies a central issue in colonial politics. This chapter describes the history and impact of Parliament's Debt Recovery Act of 1732, which created a legal regime strengthening creditors' remedies against land and slaves throughout the British colonies in America and the West Indies.

Credit and the Legal Status of Slaves

Parliament enacted the Debt Recovery Act in response to concerns among English creditors that the colonists were defeating their efforts to collect on debts by invoking traditional English legal protections to land. The merchants were centrally interested in the laws of Virginia and Jamaica, where planters relied on credit to purchase an increasing supply of slave labor. With some exceptions, colonies relying heavily on slave labor to produce staple crops were more likely than other colonies to uphold the English protections to land and inheritance from unsecured creditors. In Virginia, for example, the owners of the most profitable colonial estates were seemingly replicating the social and political environment of England through their treatment of land, including protections for landownership and inheritance, and use of the fee tail. There were also economic reasons for protecting estates. According to the historian Richard Pares, "[t]he colonial legislatures were . . . anxious to protect plantations from being pulled to pieces for small debts, or by reason of the scarcity of the currency."[3] Landowners likely wanted to prevent the piecemeal dismantling of their estates—through the seizure of some or all of the slaves, or some of the assembled land—in order to prevent the interruption of the estates' operations and to retain the value that could be captured only when the land was assembled in its entirety. In a characteristic eighteenth-century account, a pamphleteer described a Barbados estate as "like a looking glass which when once broke to pieces will not fetch one quarter part of what it would when kept whole and entire."[4] There are exceptions to this generalization: Barbados, for example, was a colony relying on slave labor that made land liable for debts. [5]

As a general matter, however, the persistence of the English property law in many colonies in the South and West Indies may have been a policy preference that their residents could afford because creditors lent to them on the basis of annual staple crop yields. As described in the last chapter, in New England, land was often defined as a "chattel." New England planters similarly may have feared that allowing execution on land for unsecured debts elevated their exposure to financial risk and could threaten the long-term productivity of farms, but the New England colonies had no equivalent staple crops for which they could obtain credit and suffered more severely from liquidity problems than the South.[6] Most wealth in New England was held in the form of land: in 1774, 81.1% of New England wealth (capital goods) was in the form of land.[7] Abolishing the distinctions between real and personal property expanded credit to New England and increased the viability of using mortgages as "currency" in the absence of other valuable chattel property that might serve as commodity money.[8] Liquidity concerns were less serious in the South, where farmers produced staple crops that served as the basis for English and Scottish credit, and where the laborers—slaves—were also a valuable form of chattel property.

A second concern driving Parliament's enactment of the Debt Recovery Act was that colonial legislatures might at any time enact laws characterizing slaves as "land" and thereby make the slaves legally immune from seizure by creditors under English law. From the moment slavery was instituted in the colonies, each colony had to create a law of slavery. An unavoidable question was how to characterize slaves within the traditional English property regime. Were slaves "land" or "chattels" (personal property)? The question was central to the inheritance of property. When the law defined slaves as "land," under the inheritance practice of primogeniture, slaves and land would both descend to the eldest son at the death of a landowner. This kept estates intact. In contrast, if slaves were characterized as "chattel," under primogeniture, the eldest son would inherit the land, but not the slaves.[9] Rather, primogeniture called for the chattel property to be divided equally among all children after the deceased's debts were satisfied. Yet if the eldest son inherited all the land but few slaves, the plantation would sit idle while he gathered enough funds either to purchase his father's slaves from his siblings or to purchase new slaves. Inherited land on its own was of little value if slaves were distributed to other children.

Characterizing slaves as land under English law, however, diminished credit. If slaves were characterized as land, they would be protected from the claims of unsecured creditors both during the life of the debtor and when his estate was distributed upon his death. An additional threat to creditors was the problem described in Robert Carter's letter, cited in the last chapter: money borrowed on an unsecured basis might be used to purchase slaves for the specific purpose of shielding wealth from the claims of creditors. In a slave economy, the effects on credit would be highly detrimental. As described in a 1727 Virginia statute, "to bind the property of slaves, so as they may not be liable to the paiment of debts, must lessen, and in process of time, may destroy the credit of the country."[10] Slaves functioned as the primary collateral for debts among the wealthy in the Southern colonies. They were valued as an investment in part because they could be sold to pay off debts more easily than was true of land.[11]

In order to secure slaves to the land they worked, Southern and Caribbean legislatures adopted a bifurcated approach: they characterized slaves as land for inheritance purposes, but included special provisions making slaves a form of land that could be sold to satisfy debts to unsecured creditors, even in the event of the death of the debtor.[12] As an example, the 1727 Virginia act mentioned above characterized slaves as real property (land) and authorized the practice of entailing slaves to particular parcels of real property.

Entailing property would ordinarily make the property immune to creditor's claims. The 1727 act noted, however, that credit was usually extended on the basis of a debtor's visible property, and that "the greatest part of the visible estates of the inhabitants of this colony, doth generally consist of slaves."[13] The statute therefore provided that even entailed slaves "shall be liable to be taken in execution, and sold for the satisfying and paying the just debts of the tenant in tail," with the exception of those slaves allocated to the widow as dower.[14] A 1731 Virginia opinion, *Tucker v. Sweney*, interpreted the statute in determining whether slaves born after the death of a debtor could be taken in execution to satisfy his debts. The judge determined that "Negroes notwithstanding the Act making them Real Estate remain in the Hands of the Ex'ors by that Act as Chatels and as such do vest in them for the payment of Debts So that in this Case they are considered no otherwise than Horses or Cattle."[15] The Virginia law is typical of the laws in other American and West Indian colonies.[16] Some colonial legislatures, however, characterized slaves as land despite the negative impact that such laws might have had on credit. As described below, Jamaican lower courts were not permitted to authorize the seizure of slaves. In most colonies relying heavily on slave labor, however, unsecured creditors could claim debtors' chattel property and slaves, but not their land.

A Perceived Need for Greater Parliamentary Regulation of Colonial Property

The Debt Recovery Act responded in particular to actions of the Virginian and Jamaican legislatures. Concern about Virginia emerged in 1727 when, in response to an instruction from England, Governor Gooch requested that the Virginia legislature enact a law allowing English creditors to seize the land of debtors who had formally declared bankruptcy in England.[17] The legislature failed to provide the requested remedy but tried to placate the Board of Trade with a law reaffirming that slaves would be available to satisfy debts. English creditors then complained to the Board of Trade about a 1705 Virginia law establishing a three- to five-year statute of limitations (depending on the type of debt) for bringing a suit against a debtor.[18] In 1730, the Crown repealed the Virginia statute of limitations by royal proclamation.[19] The Virginia legislature enacted a new law to replace the 1705 law,[20] but the new law purposefully omitted a provision of the 1705 law that was highly beneficial to creditors in Great Britain: the provision had allowed an English creditor to prove his debts by swearing to them in England, "in the court of that county where he shall reside," or "before the governor or mayor of the place where he is."[21] By failing to reenact this provision, the Virginia legislature implicitly changed the existing policy from one in which debts could be proved in England to one requiring English creditors to produce evidence in the local colonial courts.

The complaints relating to Jamaica concerned what types of property would be available to satisfy creditors' claims. Jamaican law adopted a unique procedural hurdle for creditors: the inferior common law courts were directed not to "intermeddle with or determine any actions whatsoever, where Titles of land or Negroes are concerned."[22] Creditors wanting to force a sale of land or slaves were required to seek relief in the Jamaica Supreme Court.[23] In 1728, both houses of the Jamaican legislature passed a bill proposing a legal tender law to "oblige creditors to accept . . . the produce of the Island in payment of their debts" at a specified rate.[24] Legal tender laws requiring creditors to accept goods at designated rates (often less than the market rate) were a popular form of debt relief legislation in the colonial era. The governor refused to assent to the law and warned the Board of Trade that the legislature had approved the bill.[25]

Then, as mentioned in the introduction, in August 1731, several merchants in London petitioned the Crown to respond more generally to colonial acts and practices that they complained left them either "without any remedy for the recovery of their just debts" or with remedies that were "very partiall and precarious."[26] In a subsequent memorandum detailing their concerns, the merchants complained specifically about the fact that land and houses were not liable for debts in Jamaica.[27] A letter written by John Tymms, a Jamaican merchant, in September 1731, clarified that the need for a law subjecting real property to the claims of creditors derived from the fact that "[a]s it is, the principal parts of [Jamaican] estates are exempted by law from the payment of debts and negroes are frequently driven away into the woods or mountains out of the Marschall's way."[28] Tymms added that "[t]his is an evil which prevents attempts at the better settlement of the island."[29]

In response to the London merchants' petition, the Privy Council asked the Board of Trade to review the merchants' concerns and to advise the Crown on how to proceed. The Board of Trade drafted a report emphasizing the problems confronting creditors collecting on debts because of the laws in some of the colonies, "particularly that of Jamaica, to exempt their Houses, Lands, and Tenements, and in some Places their Negroes also, from being extended for Debt."[30] It advised the Crown of the need for a parliamentary act on remedies.[31]

THE DEBT RECOVERY ACT

In 1732, Parliament asserted new authority over the colonies by laying out rules expanding creditors' abilities to seize colonial land and slaves throughout all of the British colonies in America and the West Indies. The Act for the More Easy Recovery of Debts in his Majesty's Plantations and Colonies in America stated it was enacted to "retriev[e] . . . the Credit formerly given . . . to the Natives and Inhabitants of the . . . Plantations," and to "advanc[e] . . . the Trade of this Kingdom."[32] The statute assured English merchants that colonial legislatures would no longer be able to defeat debt collection efforts through application of English property law. All forms of property were to be available to satisfy any type of debt. Toward this end, beginning on September 29, 1732, all "Houses, Lands, Negroes, and other Hereditaments and real Estates" were to be liable for "all just Debts, Duties and Demands, of what Nature or Kind soever."[33] These property interests—houses, lands, slaves, and others—were to be "Assets for the Satisfaction" of debts "in like Manner as Real Estates are by the Law of England liable to the Satisfaction of Debts due by Bond or other Specialty."[34] Bonds and specialties were secured credit instruments, or debts made under seal. This meant that houses, lands, and slaves would be treated as if they had been pledged as collateral in unsecured credit agreements. This provision of the statute clarified that the 1691 Statute of Fraudulent Devises—which gave secured creditors priority to a deceased's land over the heirs and devisees—applied throughout the American and West Indian colonies both to secured creditors and to unsecured creditors.

The Debt Recovery Act also provided that houses, lands, and slaves would be "subject to the like Remedies . . . and Process" for seizing and selling the same for "the Satisfaction of such Debts . . . as Personal Estates in the colonies were liable to for seizure and sale."[35] In other words, the statute required each colony's courthouses to use the procedures (public auction, transfers) that were already in place for selling personal property to satisfy debts to similarly sell land and slaves, even though land and slaves were of far greater value and consequence. A separate provision of the statute was equally controversial to colonists: it provided that English merchants could prove their debts and obtain judgments against colonial debtors in English courts.[36]

The Debt Recovery Act took from the British colonial legislatures in America and the West Indies the power to define which property would be available to satisfy unsecured debts. All forms of wealth, including slaves, land, and houses, were now available to satisfy unsecured debts. Notably, the statute was not limited to colonial debts to creditors in Britain. The language of the statute required that colonial courts apply the Act to all domestic cases.[37] The Act applied only in the colonies, however; England retained its traditional protections for land until 1833, a century after the enactment of the Debt Recovery Act.[38]

The context of colonial rule allowed merchants in London to represent their interests to the Crown and Parliament with little input from the colonists. The primary participation by colonists in the process of enacting the Debt Recovery Act was by Virginians who fiercely opposed the Act. After learning of the proposed new law, in 1731 Virginia sent Isham Randolph as its agent to Parliament. Randolph submitted a petition to Parliament requesting a hearing on the Act.[39] Randolph's petition stated that "said bill will greatly affect the rights and propertys in the landed interest of his Majestys subjects residing in the said colony."[40] Randolph received a hearing on March 17, 1731, and voiced his opposition to the statute, but his arguments failed to persuade Parliament.

POLITICAL REACTION TO THE DEBT RECOVERY ACT

The Debt Recovery Act radically changed the legal regulation of property in New York, Maryland, North Carolina, South Carolina, Rhode Island, Virginia (for approximately a decade), and, later, Georgia and Kentucky.[41] The statute was recognized as authoritative throughout New England, though the effects of the Act were more subtle in colonies that had already adopted similar laws independently. The Act did, however, have effects in New England. For example, New Hampshire's 1718 law prevented the seizure of debtor's *houses* during the life of the debtor.[42] The Debt Recovery Act explicitly includes houses in its list of property to be treated as legally equivalent to chattel property for the purpose of creditors' claims.[43] In contrast, in Connecticut, for example, the Act was perceived as simply providing more formal authority for the existing practice.[44]

The Virginians—seemingly alone among the colonists—were immediately hostile to the statute. John Custis, Councillor of Virginia and a major planter (and Martha Washington's father-in-law before her first husband, Daniel Custis, died in 1757), referred to the statute as "cruell and unjust" in a letter to an English merchant.[45] Custis explained that he personally owed "no one in England a farthing" and locally "ha[d] many owing" him, so he had no economic motive in attacking the Act; his comments were "purely the result of [his] thoughts."[46] He expressed his astonishment that land could be sold to satisfy unsecured debts:

> Y]our subjecting our Lands for book debts is contrary to ye Laws of our Mother Country; which cannot touch reall estate without a Specialty and as wee are brittish Subjects wee might reasonably expect Brittish liberty wee desire nothing else than to bee subject to ye Laws of our Mother Country but wee have great reason to think you aim at our possessions who have got most of your possessions by us; . . . and how ever you may flatter your selves to bee gainers by that act you will find yt you have so incensed ye Country; that you will force ym as soon as convenient to have nothing to do with you.[47]

Similarly, Robert Carter, who had complained about the impact of the English property exemptions on his own efforts at debt collection in a 1720 letter, expressed concern about the Debt Recovery Act when it was enacted. Now president of the Virginia Council, he stated in a letter to a merchant in England that the "Severe act of Parliament . . . wearing the title, for the better Recovery of Debts . . . has rais'd so general a fury in the Assembly that hath carryed them into measures which I heartily wish from getting out of one extreme, we may not be involv'd in another."[48] Carter stated that the "general crye" was that Virginians would rather "relye on the mercy of our Prince than . . . be subjected to the tyranny of the merchants who are daily encreasing their Oppressions upon us."[49]

Virginia initially complied with the Act. In 1738, the Virginia General Court issued a decision holding that land could be "sold as Goods taken on a [fieri facias]."[50] The court emphasized that this was the first instance of land being sold under the Debt Recovery Act.[51] Nonetheless, in 1748 Virginia appears to have reversed course and opposed parliamentary authority by applying the Act only to debts involving English and Scottish creditors and not to internal debts.[52]

The Impact in the Colonies of the Debt Recovery Act

As mentioned in the introduction, William Knox, a leading English policy maker in the Stamp Act crisis, asserted that Parliament improved economic conditions by enacting the Debt Recovery Act, the effect of which he described as "subjecting lands and negroes in the Colonies to the payment of English book debts."[53] The Act, Knox said, "may truly be called the

Palladium of Colony credit, and the English merchants' grand security."[54] To Knox, Jamaican protections of land and slaves from creditors were perfect examples of colonial legislatures' propensity to damage credit conditions. Similarly, Joseph Story's *Commentaries*, describing American laws making land liable for debts, suggested that "the growth of the respective colonies was in no small degree affected by this circumstance."[55] Were Knox and Story correct to describe the Debt Recovery Act as a source of colonial economic growth?

LEGAL EFFECTS OF THE DEBT RECOVERY
ACT IN THE COLONIES

In practice, the Debt Recovery Act had three principal effects. First, the Act required colonial courts to treat all land, houses, and slaves as legally equivalent to chattel property for the purpose of satisfying the claims of unsecured creditors. Again, according to the language of the Act, "Houses, Lands, Negroes, and other Hereditaments and real Estates" were to be liable for "all just Debts, Duties and Demands, of what Nature or Kind soever."[56] The colonial courts implemented the Act by expanding the writ of fieri facias—which traditionally authorized the sheriff to seize the goods and chattels of a debtor—to authorize the seizure of land.[57]

A debtor's land remained protected from creditors in only one sense: it was typically the last asset that the sheriff was permitted to seize under colonial writs of execution. As an example, the North Carolina writs of execution enacted after the Debt Recovery Act establish a clear ranking of the types of property a sheriff could take to satisfy debts.[58] The debtor's "Personal Estate . . . (Slaves Excepted)" was to be taken first. If that property was insufficient to satisfy the debt, then the debtor's "Personal Estate . . . including Slaves" was to be taken. The sheriff was authorized to seize the debtor's "Lands, Tenements, Hereditaments and other real Estate" only if goods, chattels, and slaves were insufficient to satisfy the debt.[59] This scheme was similar to that adopted in other colonies.

Second, the Act subordinated the interests of heirs to those of unsecured creditors at the death of a debtor.[60] Many colonies interpreted the Debt Recovery Act as requiring a procedural modification whereby executors would be in charge of distributing a deceased's land as well as personal property. Under English law, the executor marshaled only the personal property of the deceased to satisfy his or her debts. The land automatically descended to the heir, unless it was otherwise devised in the deceased's will.[61] The Debt

Recovery Act, however, stated that colonial courts were to subject land to the same "Remedies . . . and Process . . . for seizing . . . [and] selling . . . [for] the Satisfaction of such Debts . . . as Personal Estates."[62] Thus, colonial courts had to address whether, under the Debt Recovery Act, the executor would take control over the real property when a landowner died. If so, the heirs and devisees would be vulnerable to the executor's discretionary choices about how to satisfy the deceased's debts. Equally important, they would be denied the traditional procedural mechanism that afforded heirs and devisees the opportunity to defend their claim to inherited land in court.[63] In an 1804 opinion, Chancellor James Kent stated that, under the Debt Recovery Act, in New York land was "to be treated exactly like personal property; and it became usual to regard lands and real estates as assets in the hands of executors, and to cause them to be sold on execution against executors."[64]

Third, requiring that courts use the same procedures for selling land and slaves as they would for personal property meant that land and slaves would be sold at auction in most colonies. Selling land at auction, however, raised the additional issue of whether traditional debtor redemption rights to land would be recognized after the sale. The statute explicitly stated that "Houses, Lands, Negroes, *and other Hereditaments and real Estates*" were subject to the Act.[65] Redemption rights were interests in real property that most courts interpreted as being covered by the Act, and therefore subject to sale at an execution auction. As described in *Bell v. Hill*,[66] a 1794 North Carolina Superior Court opinion:

> [I]f a [fieri facias] issues upon a subsequent judgment, and comes to the hand of the Sheriff, and he sells the lands, the title of the vendee under such execution cannot ever afterwards be defeated—it is valid to every purpose.[] Were the law not so, it would be the most dangerous thing in the world to purchase lands at an execution sale.[67]

Nonetheless, it was possible for judges to interpret the Debt Recovery Act as applying only to proceedings at law. The Act did not explicitly state that it applied to proceedings in equity. Equity courts, where they existed could have found that the Act did not apply to their proceedings and that, therefore, they were entitled to recognize traditional English redemption rights.[68] But colonial equity courts faced a problem: when law courts, such as the North Carolina court in *Bell v. Hill*, determined that *all* interests in real property were sold during an auction of real property at law, then on what basis could equity courts hold that some real property interest (the equitable redemption right) remained in the mortgagor after such a sale? The issue had never emerged in England because real property could not be sold pursuant to a legal writ of fieri facias. As we shall see, in most colonies (and later, states) the Debt Recovery Act led to the abolition of equitable redemption rights. The Debt Recovery Act therefore made it easier for both secured creditors and unsecured creditors to use legal process to obtain a remedy for their debts.

Slaves had been used as collateral and sold in judicially supervised auctions long before Parliament enacted the Debt Recovery Act. The Act, however, transformed local practice, which could be overturned by legislation, into an imperial mandate. As was described in the introduction, in 1806, in the first known pamphlet on slave auctions, Bryan Edwards, a member of the House of Commons, describes the practice of auctioning slaves to satisfy the slaveholder's secured and unsecured debts as a grievance "so remorseless and tyrannical in its principle, and so dreadful in its effects," which, "though not originally created, is now upheld and confirmed by a British act of parliament."[69] Edwards says of the Debt Recovery Act: "It was an act procured by, and passed for the benefit of British creditors; and I blush to add, that its motive and origin have sanctioned the measure, even in the opinion of men who are among the loudest of the declaimers against slavery and the slave trade."[70] After describing the horrors of the slave auction and the fact that the practice of selling slaves at auction to satisfy debts "unhappily . . . occurs every day," Edwards states: "Let this statute then be totally repealed. It is injurious to the national character; it is disgraceful to humanity. Let the negroes be attached to the land, and sold with it."[71]

Despite this outcry, the reality was that, in America, the provisions of the Act that required courts to treat slaves as chattel property had little additional effect because colonial legislation already required courts to treat slaves as chattel for the purpose of satisfying debts. The Act's principal effect with regard to slaves was to eliminate the possibility that the colonial legislatures might reform their laws and allow slaves to be protected from seizure for debts.

PREDICTED ECONOMIC EFFECTS OF THE DEBT RECOVERY ACT

The legislative history suggests that the Debt Recovery Act was enacted to eliminate three principal risks facing creditors to the colonies. First, the presence of English property exemptions meant that all unsecured creditors assumed the risk that their debtors might purchase land strategically, which reduced the pool of assets from which the creditors could collect. The effect was exacerbated when the inheritance laws prevented unsecured claims against a deceased's land. The Debt Recovery Act abolished all exemptions that allowed for such strategic behavior.

The second risk the Debt Recovery Act sought to eliminate was more specific to colonies, such as Jamaica and Virginia, where planters relied extensively on credit to purchase slaves. This was the risk that debtors might conceal their slave and other chattel assets from the officials who came to collect on behalf of creditors. If the land was protected from creditors and debtors concealed their slaves, creditors would have no effective remedy. The merchant John Tymms, for example, complained that "the principal parts of [Jamaican] estates are exempted by law from the payment of debts and negroes are frequently driven away into the woods or mountains out of the Marshall's way." When creditors could pursue remedies against debtors' land, debtors' hands were tied. It is likely that, faced with losing their land, they handed over their slaves. In colonies heavily reliant on slave labor, the Debt Recovery Act likely led to greater seizure of slaves for debt satisfaction purposes.

The third risk eliminated by the Debt Recovery Act was the possibility that colonial legislatures might enact debt relief legislation that would hurt creditors' interests. The Act created greater security both by overriding specific colonial laws that protected assets or inheritance from creditors and by taking away from the colonial legislatures legal authority over creditors' remedies and debt collection processes. By enacting a broad uniform rule, applicable throughout all of the British colonies in America and the West Indies, the colonial authorities prevented such legislation.[72]

In addition to eliminating these risks, the Act lowered the costs to creditors of obtaining a legal remedy when debtors defaulted on their debts. Under the traditional English remedies, an unsecured creditor who, say, applied for a writ of *levari facias* to impose a lien upon earnings of a debtor's land might have had to wait years for the debt to be paid off. In contrast, under the regime of the Debt Recovery Act, a creditor could use legal process to force a sale of all of a debtor's real and personal property in a short period of time, either during the debtor's life or after the debtor died.[73]

Moreover, as described, English equity court procedures imposed costs on mortgagees seizing real property upon default of a mortgage agreement. Abolishing rights of redemption vastly reduced the costs secured creditors faced in seizing debtors' land.[74] On the margin, a creditor is likely to pass the costs of collection to the debtor in the form of higher interest rates. The principal economic effects of the Debt Recovery Act were likely to be lower interest rates on both secured and unsecured credit[75] and expanded land markets.

Did the Debt Recovery Act in fact improve credit markets in the colonies? The clearest example of contemporaries' perceptions of the Act's economic effect is a statute enacted in 1739 in Jamaica that explicitly responded to the Debt Recovery Act. The Jamaican statute lowered the legal interest, or usury rate, by 20%.[76] It stated that "[w]hereas by an act of parliament . . . entitled, 'An act for the more easy recovery of debts in his majesty's plantations and colonies in America,' creditors in the colonies are secured [in] their debts in a more ample manner than when interest was established in this island at [10% per year]," it was appropriate that in all "mortgages, bonds, and other specialities," the legal interest rate be reduced to "eight pounds for the forbearance of one hundred pounds for a year."[77] A 20% decline in the interest rate—spread out over thousands of secured transactions—would have had significant effects on imports and credit available for productive investment.

The Jamaican usury law is strong evidence that contemporaries believed the Debt Recovery Act "secured [creditors'] debts in a more ample manner," but statutes establishing maximum legal rates of interest were not always complied with when the legal interest rate differed substantially from the market interest rate. Moreover, in the colonial period, "interest rates" were likely to be expressed most often in terms of import levels. When creditors felt more secure about repayment, they would allow colonists to import more goods on the basis of the annual crop yields, and perhaps for a longer term.[78] Pinpointing the precise economic effect of the Debt Recovery Act by means of economic growth data or data on imports to the colonies is difficult, however, because economic trends such as import levels were affected by many different variables. These included conditions in the English and European markets for goods like tobacco, wheat, and rice; crop production, which depends on the weather; productivity advances; and, equally important, economic events in Great Britain, Europe, and Africa.

Moreover, the Debt Recovery Act was enacted during a period of economic recession, so the immediate economic effects are difficult to disaggregate from the growth one would expect in the aftermath of a recession. It is well known, however, that a period of great colonial economic expansion, driven by credit, began in the 1740s. The terms upon which credit was extended appear to have improved considerably in the period after the enactment of the Debt Recovery Act, as reported in studies not addressing the Act. For example, the economic historian Marc Egnal examined advertisements in the *Virginia Gazette* and found that "[i]n the 1730s the typical advertisement for land or slaves demanded payment in cash."[79] By the 1760s, similar advertisements offered credit terms of a year or more.[80] Egnal adds that "[s]tatistical series and planter correspondence illustrate the strong growth of credit after the 1740s."[81] Customs records reveal that imports to the colonies from England increased steadily from the 1730s and 1740s through the end of the colonial period.[82] For example, the colonies imported from England approximately £530,000 (pounds sterling) in goods in 1732, the year that the Debt Recovery Act was enacted, and more than double that amount, approximately £1,230,000, by 1749.[83] Over this period, colonial factors became willing to accept bills of exchange drawn for longer periods of time.[84] The terms of trade—the quantity of an imported good that could be purchased with a given unit of a colonial good—improved dramatically during the same period.[85] These imports led to increases in the standard of living and what historians such as T. H. Breen have referred to as a "consumer revolution" and an "empire of goods" by the 1750s.[86]

Slave imports expanded during the same period.[87] Although import levels and credit terms to the colonies were determined by many different economic factors, data on this expansion of slave imports in Virginia provide the best evidence of an immediate and direct effect of the enactment of the Debt Recovery Act in 1732. Slave imports to Virginia equaled 276 in 1730 and 184 in 1731; rising to 1,291 in 1732; and from 1733 to 1737, the numbers rose to 1,720, 1,587, 2,104, 3,222, and 2,174, respectively.[88] These data are not conclusive evidence that the Debt Recovery Act had important economic effects on colonial America, but they are suggestive of the effects. In a brief discussion of the Debt Recovery Act, the historian Jacob Price speculates that "the credit-based slave trade in many colonies could and did expand significantly in the ensuing decades" after the Act became effective.[89]

The Debt Recovery Act also likely expanded the market for land in America, although this result is difficult to measure. With respect to both unsecured and secured credit, courts in America could order judicial sales of real property (or in New England, in-kind transfers to creditors) with far greater ease. These court-ordered sales meant that more land was placed into circulation.

Foreclosure sales would not, however, represent the full extent of the impact of the Act on property markets. When the law offers all creditors the remedy of judicial sale of debtors' property, debtors are likely to be far more willing to sell the land, or some part of it, to satisfy their debts in advance of such a sale. Indeed, one would expect that, in most instances, debtors who owned land would choose to sell it separately to pay off creditors or to settle with their creditors outside of the court system, rather than endure a foreclosure sale. By selling separately or settling with creditors, debtors would avoid expensive court costs, lawyers' fees, and other transaction costs in the court-ordered auction process.[90] Changing the default rule to one permitting unsecured creditors to seize land would lead to an increase in voluntary sales of property.

THE DEBT RECOVERY ACT AND THE POLITICS OF EMPIRE

The Debt Recovery Act was an important parliamentary regulation of internal colonial affairs. The British colonial authorities viewed the Act as exemplifying the economic advantage of parliamentary oversight of colonial legislation. As the colonists became increasingly hostile toward parliamentary regulation and taxation during the 1760s, the question emerged as to how to interpret the Debt Recovery Act as a precedent. The Stamp Act[91] was resented, in part, because it represented taxation upon internal colonial matters and did not merely regulate external trade, which colonists accepted as within the scope of parliamentary authority. In a 1765 pamphlet responding to the Stamp Act crisis, William Knox argued that the Debt Recovery Act had severely impinged upon central liberties inherent in English common and statutory law.[92] Knox's motive was to make the Stamp Act seem less interventionist by comparison. According to Knox:

> [The Debt Recovery Act] abrogates so much of the common law as relates to descents of freeholds in America, takes from the son the right of inheritance in the lands the crown had granted to the father, and his heirs in absolute fee, makes them assets, and applies them to the payment of debts and accounts contracted by the father without the participation of the son. . . . [T]he power of parliament having been exercised to take away the lands of the people in America, (the most sacred part of any man's property) and dispose of them for the use of private persons, inhabitants of Great Britain, [who can] question the parliament's having sufficient jurisdiction to take away a small part of the products of those lands, and apply it to the public service?[93]

Alexander Hamilton later reflected upon the Debt Recovery Act as an exercise of parliamentary power that exceeded the bounds of legislative authority to which the colonists should have submitted. In his Practice Manual of the early 1780s (a manual he drafted about the operation of legal process in New York State, and the first legal treatise of American state law), Hamilton states:

> The English [fieri facias] affected only Chattels ours the Real Estate equally; this Extension of it was by Act of Parliament of Geo: 2d. particularly made for this Country, a memorable Statute & *which Admitted more then our Legislature ought to have assented to*; it was one of the Highest Acts of Legislature that one Country could exercise over another.[94]

It appears that Hamilton intended to emphasize that the Debt Recovery Act was a regrettable precedent for parliamentary regulation: it might have empowered Parliament to enact the offensive statutes leading to the American Revolution (such as the Stamp Act and the Townshend Act[95]). His description of the Debt Recovery Act as "one of the Highest Acts of Legislature," however, also reveals the importance placed upon creditors' remedies as a matter of economic, social, and political concern in the founding era. As we shall see, the new states were highly protective of their right to legislate in the area of creditors' remedies and were unwilling to cede authority to the federal government in the way that the colonies had, through tacit acceptance, ceded authority to Parliament and the Board of Trade in the colonial era.

PART III

Managing Risk in Colonial America

5

Managing Risk through Property

THE FEE TAIL

The Debt Recovery Act of 1732 mandated that throughout the British colonies all land, houses, and slaves would be available to be seized by creditors in the course of pursuing debt claims.[1] This law and similar laws previously enacted by individual colonies created a regime where a creditor had the power to use the courts to gain title to a debtor's land or slaves for even a small, unsecured debt, and where creditors would take precedence over heirs in inheritance proceedings. As a consequence, after 1732 in the British American colonies, colonists had access to credit on better terms, but were also exposed to greater financial risk.

The colonial economic world was marked by vast webs of debt. During periods of economic recession, debtors struggled to pay their creditors and creditors initiated litigation against debtors, often with a snowball effect due to the extent of mutual indebtedness within communities. The colonial economy was growing, but in a world of seemingly endless economic cycles, ricocheting back and forth from times of prosperity to times of recession and liquidity crises, the absence of legal protections from creditors made the population far more vulnerable to losing land and homes.

The situation for slaves was worse. Their owners' indebtedness in a world of financial cycles made slaves highly vulnerable to seizure or sale to satisfy debts. A creditor could use the process of law to have the court physically seize a slave and auction off that person for money to reimburse the creditor. More likely, the owner would preempt this process by negotiating with creditors to hand over slaves to satisfy his debts. Slaves were desirable to creditors because of their mobility and because slave markets were more liquid than land markets. The vulnerability of slaves to sale to satisfy creditors' claims, including individual slave children and mothers and fathers, was a particularly brutal hallmark of American slavery.

What legal mechanisms were available in colonial America to protect property from financial risk? How did these mechanisms impact the law of credit? This chapter describes how the legal device of holding property in fee tail was used in some colonies as a means of designating some forms of property as outside the reach of creditors. Historical scholarship on the fee tail during the colonial period has typically looked backward from the founding era, when states' decisions to abolish the fee tail became a symbol of the power of republican ideology and its hostility to legal forms that might support an aristocracy.[2] This chapter looks at the fee tail through a different lens: as a legal means to reduce risk.

The Fee Tail as a Way to Shield Property from Creditors

The basic form of ownership of land recognized in the United States is referred to as "fee simple absolute," or "fee simple." Fee simple ownership carries with it the right to sell, pledge as collateral, give, devise in a will, and use the land. In past centuries, the "fee tail" was an alternative form in which to own land. Landowners could put land in the form of fee tail by deed (during the property owner's life) or by a will (at the owner's death).[3] Fee tail or "entailed" property had several principal qualities. When the owner of entailed property died, the property automatically descended to the eldest living male son. In the event there were no sons, the entailed property was inherited by all daughters jointly. (They were referred to as co-parceners.[4]) Although it was much more common for sons to inherit land, a landowner could devise land in fee tail to both men and women in the family. If a daughter inherited land in fee tail, at her death it would go to her eldest son. When property was held in fee tail, it was protected from the claims of any creditors. Conveyances and mortgages of entailed land were ineffective.[5]

Historians currently lack a clear picture of how widely the fee tail was used in the British American colonies; the historical evidence suggests that it was in regular use in the wealthier areas of colonial Virginia and North Carolina, and possibly New York, that it was uncommon in the Middle Atlantic colonies, that it was rare in New England, and perhaps nonexistent in South

Carolina.[6] By exposing land to unsecured creditors' claims, the Debt Recovery Act may have encouraged the use of the fee tail in Virginia and a small number of other colonies after 1732 as the principal way to shelter assets.

In addition to other historical research, this chapter examines the private acts of the Virginia legislature removing or "docking" the entail on land or slaves; there were 133 private acts of the legislature removing entails between 1711 and 1773.[7] Removing or docking the entail converted the land or slaves to fee simple, which meant it could be sold. Virginia, along with North Carolina and Barbados, adopted the unusual requirement that owners in fee tail had to petition the legislature for a private act "docking" or removing the entail.[8] The private acts of the legislature in Virginia reveal insights about the terms of the wills that put property in fee tail and the petitioners' explanations for why they wanted the entail removed. They also offer information about who was inheriting land in fee tail: for example, twenty-six of the 133 private acts related to entailed land held by women.

The Virginia petitions reveal that the entail allowed landowners to diversify asset holdings. Thus, some land was kept alienable or as security for credit (fee simple land), whereas other land was maintained free of the risk of foreclosure (the entailed land). For example, a petition to the Virginia legislature in 1769 mentions a will devising lands to his son in fee simple "that if he thought proper, he might sell and dispose of the same toward the payment of a debt" and separately devises other land in fee tail, which would be immune from creditors' claims and kept within the family line.[9] After the Debt Recovery Act of 1732, entailed lands remained as islands of protected wealth.

Under normal circumstances, debtors have strong incentives to pay their debts. Debtors who fail to repay debts presumably will lose access to further credit. Those who owned land in fee tail and had large debts were likely to feel pressure to remove the entail to sell property to pay their creditors. So was it truly a protection? The Virginia petititions reveal that the main protection was timing: converting fee tail property to fee simple took place at the discretion of the fee tail owner. The fee tail thus provided protection during periods of temporary hardship, such as periods of severe recession, bad weather, or plant diseases affecting crop yields, or after accidents or deaths that reduced the family's income stream. In those circumstances, it served as a buffer against the loss of property through involuntary process of law.

In Virginia, the fee tail shielded assets from creditors' claims, often for decades, before the creditors closed in. By means of a will drafted in 1726, Benjamin Harrison inherited an 1,800-acre parcel, Joseph's Swamp, in fee tail as well as "other tracts of land, slaves, stock, and other personal estate" in fee simple.[10] Benjamin died in 1758, leaving his estate to his son. The Virginia legislature removed the entail on Joseph's Swamp in 1764, and the petition explained that his father had lost all of the fee simple property to creditors. His father, "in his lifetime contracted several debts, for the payment of which all his lands in fee simple, slaves, stocks, and other personal estate, were taken in execution, and sold." Benjamin's son explained that because the slaves had all been taken to satisfy debts, "for want of negroes and stock to cultivate the same [Joseph's Swamp is] of little use or profit."[11] As this case illustrates, the entailed land was shielded from creditors, in contrast to the other assets, until Benjamin's son petitioned to voluntarily remove the entail. This example also illustrates a central theme in the Virginia private acts to remove entails: the petitioners often expressed that their plantations were unproductive because they lacked slaves and needed to sell entailed land to buy slaves; or that they owned slaves and needed to sell entailed land to pay off creditors threatening to seize their slaves.

The act relating to John Spotswood's petition of 1764, for example, explains that he wanted to save his slaves from creditors by removing the entail on a factory for casting pig iron he had inherited. The slaves may have been skilled iron workers.[12] Spotswood explained that under his father's will he owed his sisters £2,000 sterling each plus interest and, "not being able to borrow money on the security of his [fee tail] lands to discharge the same," he took out loans by means of bills of exchange on British creditors: "to gain time, and devise some means of raising the money so recovered of him, which bills were returned protested, and now remain unsatisfied, besides which several creditors of [his father] having obtained judgments for their debts, to ascertain the same, forbore to sue out executions thereupon, and are yet unpaid such debts."[13] Similarly, a 1766 petition noted that Nathaniel West Dandridge was "possessed of sundry other slaves, as his *absolute property*, and being indebted in large sums of money, must sell those slaves, or they will be taken in execution, and sold for the payment of his debts, . . . unless he can be allowed to sell part of the [entailed] lands to enable him to pay his debts."[14] In each of these examples, the entailed land was shielded from creditors until the time when the owner chose to file a petition.

In Virginia, the loss of all other assets and the need to remove the entail to reorganize the family finances was a common justification for removing entails. A private act of 1734, for example, removed the entail on land so that "Anne and Elizabeth, and their poor families, may hereafter be comfortably subsisted," noting that they were "all in miserable circumstances."[15] A 1762 private act emphasized that the entailed land in question "is very barren, and yields but a small profit."[16] An act removing John Gregg's entail described his fee simple land, slaves, and personal estate as "insufficient for the payment of his debts" and the fee tail land as "very barren and poor."[17] Anna and John Armistead's petition requested that the entail be removed from Anna's land because otherwise "the slaves given [Anna's son John] by his father should be sold to pay [debts], which if sufficient for that purpose would render the remainder of his lands of little or no benefit to him."[18] The act removing the entail on Harry Beverley's land stated that he had to sell the fee tail lands, which "for want of slaves to work them are rather a burden," and by selling entailed land, "Harry may be enabled to support his family, and make provision for his younger children, and the estate will descend to the heir in a more profitable state."[19] Anne Hall petitioned to have the entail removed on land "for want of slaves."[20] James Roscow petitioned to remove the entail on land in order to purchase slaves, explaining that his problem was "having no slaves to cultivate" the entailed land.[21] Again, these types of cases, where the slaves had either been sold or taken to pay debts, and where the land might be barren, dominate the petitions.[22]

It was possible to lease entailed land and gain the rents as income, but these leases faced an uncertainty: the lease would terminate immediately at the death of the present owner. A 1765 Virginia law addressed the detrimental effect of the fee tail on the rental market for land, noting that "many large tracts of entailed lands remain uncultivated, the owners not having slaves to work them, and no persons inclining to take leases of such lands, because those leases are thought to be valid no longer than during the life of the tenants in taille."[23] The Act held all leases good for terms of up to twenty-one years, regardless of whether fee tail owners died during the lease period.

An incident involving the legislature of Antigua demonstrates the entail's role as a wealth-shielding device in trans-Atlantic credit relationships. Pursuing an unusual course of action that violated English law, a London creditor persuaded the legislature of Antigua to remove the entail on one of his debtors' estates, making the land available for him to seize by process of law. The governor of Antigua wrote to the Board of Trade requesting that it disallow the legislature's private act, rightly noting that this was an unprecedented use of legislative authority. According to the governor,

> [T]he method [of barring the entail] is very common, but the manner of obtaining it most extraordinary and unprecedented, for it is passed upon the application of a creditor to a person who never had a title to this

estate; . . . I apprehend there can be no instance shewn where any legislature ever interposed so far as to divest a tenant in tail and barr his issue . . .
unless it had been upon his own application or he had been privy or
consenting to it. . . . This is in my apprehension so extraordinary a stretch
of power in the Legislature, for it is actually taking upon themselves to
convey away the estates of the planters to whom they please, that it ought
to meet with the utmost discountenance from your Lordships.[24]

In this exceptional case, the Antiguan legislature removed the entail to
benefit a creditor without the owner's consent. The governor's letter reveals,
however, that under English law, the debtor holding entailed land should
have voluntarily petitioned to remove the entail. The legal protections to
entailed land offered in the common law courts provided a buffer against
short-term and unforeseen financial problems.

THE ENTAIL, SLAVES, AND CREDIT MARKETS IN VIRGINIA

Perhaps the most explicit example of the connection between the entail,
wealth shielding, and credit markets arose in the Southern colonies in the
determination of whether to characterize slaves as "real property" (land)
or as "chattel property." As mentioned in chapter 4, in 1727, the Virginia
legislature enacted a statute allowing slaves to be entailed for the purposes
of inheritance, that is, to "preserve slaves for the use and benefit of such
persons to whom lands and tenements descend . . . for the better improvement of the same."[25] To enhance credit, however, the law clarified that
entailed slaves could be taken to satisfy creditors' claims. This bifurcated
approach—considering slaves as land for inheritance, but as chattel property
with regard to creditors—is similar to the laws in other American and West
Indian colonies.[26]

In the late 1740s, the Governor's Council, along with the House of Burgesses, the representative assembly, tried to repeal the 1727 act in order to
abolish the fee tail for slaves completely. The Board of Trade disallowed the
repeal, with no explanation. Why did Virginians want to end entailing slaves?
The council and House of Burgesses drafted a report for the Board of Trade
in England explaining the problems brought about by entailing slaves. The
report emphasizes the inefficiency of having a plantation's slave population
expand but remain "annexed" to the same plot of land; the profitability of
moving slaves to new, uncultivated land; and the weaknesses of existing
institutions to properly notify creditors as to the status of the "collateral"
upon which they might extend credit. In the language of the report:

[The Assembly] saw that slaves could not be kept on lands to which they were annexed without manifest prejudice to the tenant in tail. Because over time they overstocked the plantations and often the tenant was the proprietor of fee simple land, much fitter for cultivation than his intailed lands, where he could work his slaves to a much greater advantage. But on the other hand, the frequent removing and settling them on other lands in other counties and parts of the colony, far distant from the county court, where the deeds or wills which annexed them were recorded, and the intail lands lay; the confusion occasioned by their mixture with fee simple slaves of the same name and sex, and belonging to the same owner; the uncertainty of distinguishing one from another, after several generations, no register of their genealogy being kept, and none of them having surnames, were great mischiefs to purchasers, strangers and creditors, who were often unavoidably deceived in their purchases, and hindered in the recovery of their just debts. *It also lessened the credit of the country; it being dangerous for the merchants of Great Britain to trust possessors of many slaves for fear that the slaves may be intailed. And should credit be destroyed in a trading country, as ours might be properly called, the consequence might be fatal.*[27]

In the report, "merchants of Great Britain" must be reassured, because an unwillingness on their part to extend credit would hurt the slave economy. The report emphasized that:

Virginia estates are attended with a certain large and yearly expence in furnishing these slaves with cloathing, food, and tools, paying their public poll taxes, and the quit rents of the lands. The profits arising from the crops of tobacco, and indian corn, are precarious, and often destroyed by gusts, droughts, and other casualties. But in such cases if the master cannot be trusted for necessaries, till he makes another crop, himself, family, slaves, and stocks, must be in miserable and starving circumstances.[28]

Because the Board of Trade disallowed the 1748 statute, the legal status of slaves as both land and chattel property remained in place until after Independence.

Barring Entails under English Law

In contrast to Virginia, which required a private act of the legislatures to remove entails, under English law going as far back as the fifteenth century, owners of entailed land could convert the land to fee simple with the help of lawyers.[29] The most widely used process to remove an entail was the "common recovery," which involved a complex series of conveyances.[30] The process was formalized and recorded by a court judgment in favor of the new owner of the land, who held the land in fee simple, free of the entail.[31] James Kent's 1830 treatise describing English and American practice states, "A common recovery removes all limitations upon an estate tail, and an absolute, unfettered, pure fee simple, passes as the legal effect and operation of a common recovery."[32] The common recovery involved compensating lawyers and others, but it was available to anyone. The other mechanism for removing an entail, obtaining a private act of Parliament, was more arduous and costly.

Because the entail could be removed, members of the English landed elite relied on different legal devices to secure land more permanently within their families. As described in chapter 3, many estates in England were bound by "strict settlements." The entail was often used in association with a family settlement agreement entered into at the time of a marriage that established charges on the land for the landowner's mother, wife, or younger siblings.[33] These commitments of income and trust devices, which the equity courts upheld, were far more powerful restraints than bare entails on landowners' abilities to subsequently sell or mortgage land.

IMPORTING THE COMMON RECOVERY TO THE COLONIES

In colonial America, in contrast to England, family settlements and strict settlements had far less impact on land use.[34] The flexibility of the entail was viewed as a remedy for any disadvantages that recognizing entails might otherwise have. A 1750 Pennsylvania statute confirming the validity of common recoveries in the colony, for example, stated that: "[T]he entailing of estates within this province *without a provision by law for barring them* would introduce perpetuities, prevent the improvement of such estates, disable the tenants-in-tail to make provision for the younger branches of their families, prove of general detriment to the province and be attended with manifold inconveniencies."[35] According to the preamble, the availability of the common recovery ensured that the entail would not conflict with the "improvement of . . . estates," suggesting that the entail could be removed either for the land to be used as leverage for credit—providing the funds for the improvements—or simply to provide incentives to invest in and develop the property. Allowing owners to bar entails in order to "make provision" for the younger members of their families suggests that the entail might be removed to give or devise land to a child other than the eldest son.

The flexibility underlying the Pennsylvania approach was common throughout the Mid-Atlantic and New England colonies. James Sullivan's 1801 treatise, *History of Land Titles in Massachusetts*, states that "Before the revolution, the [fee tail] was easily overturned by a common recovery."[36] A Maryland statute of 1782 notes that "common recoveries are considered as a mode of conveyance by which tenants in tail are enabled to convey and dispose of their lands and tenements."[37] Similarly, a New Jersey statute of 1784 notes that heirs can "su[e] out Recoveries, in order to dock . . . Entails."[38] Alexander Hamilton's legal papers provide an example of Kilian Van Rensselaer, who created an entailed estate inter vivos by conveying land in fee tail to his brother Henry in 1704. Henry's eldest son John inherited the property and docked the entail by common recovery in 1763. Then, in 1783, John drafted a will that left the property in tail to his grandson (which proved ineffective because New York had abolished the entail after the Revolution).[39] In this case, the entail remained on the land for fifty-nine years, but the common recovery process was available to the family when they chose to procure it.

REMOVING ENTAILS BY PRIVATE ACTS OF THE LEGISLATURE

Unlike Pennsylvania and other colonies, however, the legislatures of Virginia and North Carolina, and islands such as Barbados and Antigua, diverged from English law and required private acts of the legislature to bar an entail.[40] Why did some colonies adopt the legislative approval process? The colonies had few lawyers, and there were problems with importing English law in the absence of a sophisticated legal culture.[41] In 1727, the governor of Antigua explained to the English Board of Trade that, in reference to common recoveries (likely because of the lack of lawyers), "no method of that sort was ever put into practice" and "the Legislature very wisely and politickly considering the inconveniences that might arise from the want of it in a trading country, instituted the method of cutting off entails by private Acts of Assembly."[42]

The most likely explanation for reliance upon the legislative approval process in Virginia and North Carolina, however, is that the legislatures in these colonies determined that legislative approval provided advantages to local landowners. An act of the legislature established the strongest form of security that the removal of the entail would be free from later challenge. In addition, moving to the legislative approval process shifted conveyancing law away from the privacy norm that governed conveyancing practices in England: An act of the legislature widely publicized the removal of the entail. The legislative acts barring entails notified the creditor communities both locally and in London about status changes in colonial estates because the legislative acts of the colonies choosing this approach were subject to review and approval by the Board of Trade in London.[43] Creditors were likely to value information relating to whether the entail on their debtors' land had (or, equally important, had not) been removed, because removal signaled a landowner's desire to sell or mortgage the property. Thus, legislative approval provided certainty and publicity to the barring of an entail.

The colonies adopting a legislative approval process to bar entails took two distinct approaches. In 1677, the Barbados legislature enacted a statute to "enable every tenant in tail to bar the issue in tail."[44] The Barbados statute books are filled with private acts to bar entails, for the purpose of selling the property for cash or mortgaging it. As an example, in 1717 the legislature passed a private act to dock the entail on five properties and slaves inherited in tail by "Martha Lenoir . . . Daughter and Heir of William Cragg, . . . Merchant, deceas'd." According to the act, upon examination Martha explained that "she is very desirous to have the Entail on the said Land . . . and Negro Slaves, docked and barred, to the end that the same may be sold, and the Money arising by such Sale, placed out and improved for the better Increase of the said *Martha*'s Fortune."[45] The act held that "the said *Martha Lenoir* shall be adjudged and taken to be seized thereof, as of a good, pure, absolute, and indefeasible Estate of Inheritance in Fee Simple."[46] As another example, in 1715, the legislature passed "An Act to Dock the Entail . . . and to enable George Nicholas, Esq., and Susannah his Wife, to mortgage or sell the same, with the Negroes thereto belonging."[47]

Interestingly, docking the entail to allow Martha Lenoir to sell her land and slaves to increase her "Fortune" suggests a lack of regard for securing property within her family line to the benefit of male heirs. As a general matter, the Barbados private acts seem entirely routine.[48] The approach toward entails of the Barbados legislature is typical of the West Indies. The correspondence between the Board of Trade and the other West Indian colonies, for example, is riddled with references to colonial acts barring entails.[49] The Board of Trade typically rubber-stamped these acts.

VIRGINIA'S PROTECTION OF THE RIGHTS OF HEIRS

In the early eighteenth century, the Virginia legislature departed from English law and adopted an unwritten rule that it would only approve petitions to bar an entail when the landowner simultaneously agreed to entail other land or slaves of equal or greater value. In practice, this unwritten rule meant that entails could not be barred to disinherit the heir or for the purpose of acquiring credit or cash to use generally. Although the precise origins of this approach in Virginia are obscure, it may have been modeled on the strict entail law of Scotland (criticized by Adam Smith in *The Wealth of Nations*).[50]

The equal value limitation of the Virginia legislature only allowed landowners to remove entails when they committed to entailing other land or slaves of the same value. As an example, in 1765, the Virginia legislature docked (removed) the entail on lands held by John Gregg to allow him to pay off his taxes, but then required he buy other land and slaves that would be held in fee tail. The legislature explained that the justification of the act was that:

> the lands . . . together with all his slaves and personal estate, were insufficient for the payment of the [testator's] debts, and the maintenance and education of his children, . . . [and have] become rather a burthen to him than of any real benefit or advantage, and are moreover very barren and poor, and in arrears to the lord proprietor . . . for many years quitrents, which he is utterly unable to pay . . . it would be greatly to the advantage of the said John Gregg the son, and the heir of his body, *if he was permitted to sell the said entailed lands [and purchase] other lands fitter for cultivation, and the residue, after discharging the quitrents*
> . . . *in slaves to be annexed to the lands so to be purchased, and to descend, pass, and go therewith, to the heirs of the body of the said John Gregg.*[51]

As a similar example, in 1764, the Virginia legislature docked the entail on lands held by William Cary, explaining that "the said William Cary having no slaves to work the said land the same is of little profit to him, and it hath been represented to this assembly that it will be for the benefit of the said William Cary, and his issue, to sell the said entailed lands, and lay out the money in the purchase of other lands and slaves, to be settled to the same uses"[52] (settled meant entailed). Again, this "strict" version of the entail differed greatly from English law and the law of most other colonies. Although the Virginia private acts that docked entails describe landowners in circumstances that appear financially tenuous, the strict form of the entail adopted in Virginia, and replicated later in North Carolina, potentially could lock property within elite families through the generations.

There were, however, two ways that tenants in tail could avoid Virginia's strict system of entail. The first was by petitioning the legislature to convert assets held in land into wealth held in the form of slaves (such as in the private act docking the entail on William Cary's land, described previously). The second was under a statute enacted in 1734, described in the next section, which allowed owners of small plots to bar the entail at a low cost. When entailed land was sold and the profits were used to purchase slaves in tail, those profits were converted into an asset with no immunity from creditors. The tenant in tail might then strategically defeat the interests of the next male heir by borrowing against the value of the slaves. As stated in a 1748 report from the Virginia legislature to the Board of Trade, "an unthrifty or design-ing tenant, by running in debt or borrowing money, and then confessing judgment, and getting his creditors to sue out executions against the intailed slaves, might defeat their settlement [on the next heir]."[53]

Examining the 133 private acts to remove entails in Virginia reveals that twenty-five of the acts removed an entail on land in return for a commitment to entail slaves of equal value.[54] Forty-seven of the acts removed an entail on land on condition that new land and slaves were entailed. The overall effect of these acts (constituting 54% of the total) was to increase the amount of wealth held in the form of slaves (exposed to creditors) in relation to the wealth held in land (shielded from creditors). There was only one petition to remove the entail on slaves, for the purpose of selling them to buy land.[55] In addition, in fourteen cases of extreme hardship, the Virginia legislature allowed the petitioner to sell entailed land for cash to pay off debts, bringing the total number of moving assets into a more liquid form to 86% or 64.7%.

The Entail, Small Estates, and Female Owners of Slaves and Land

The prevailing view that the entail was a legal device used to perpetuate a propertied ruling elite presupposes that the entail was used primarily on large estates that descended through a line of eldest male heirs. In contrast, the evidence suggests that small landowners used the entail to shield wealth from creditors, and that estates in fee tail were frequently owned by women in colonial America.

THE ENTAIL AND SMALL ESTATES

As early as the mid-seventeenth century, property law reformers in England proposed ways to make the law of fee tail more responsive to the needs of owners of small estates. The most frequently proposed reform involved lowering the cost of removing the entail. John Cook wrote in 1651 that "a poore Farmer, or Cottager might leave some small portions to his yonger Children without paying one or two yeares purchase for the charge of a fine and recovery, what an ease might this be to men of small estates to passe them from one to another, and to cut off Intailes by a deed in writing without so much solemnitie and expence."[56] Similarly, in a 1694 treatise, Matthew Hale complained that removing an entail on 1 acre of land cost 50 s and proposed reducing this cost to 10 s.[57] That Hale would include in his treatise concerns about entails on 1-acre parcels suggests that they were in use by small English landowners, not just the owners of the larger estates. It is perhaps not surprising that the English enclosure movement of the late eighteenth century took place primarily by means of private parliamentary acts that removed entails.[58]

Virginia is the British American colony historians most frequently invoke to illustrate how the fee tail perpetuated a landed elite in the colonies. Nonetheless, Jefferson's 1776 Virginia Act abolishing the fee tail gave as one justification that "the method of defeating such estates, when of small value, was burthensome to the publick, and also to individuals."[59] Earlier, in 1734, the Virginia legislature enacted a statute for "poor people seised in fee tail of small and inconsiderable parcels of land."[60] The law offered a low-cost procedure for owners of entailed parcels worth £200 or less to converting their properties into estates in fee simple.[61] Under the statute, provided that the parcel in question was not contiguous with other entailed land, the entail could be removed by means of a "writ of *ad quod damnum*" from the secretary's office to the sheriff of the county commanding him to inquire whether the land was worth less than £200. If it was, then the sheriff could issue a new deed in fee simple and all remainder interests would be barred.[62] The statute describes that, for poor people, petitioning the Virginia legislature to remove entails was "so expensive . . . that they are not able to go through it; and therefore the docking intails by easier methods, will be a great relief to such poor people and their families, who, without it, must be confined to labour upon such small parcels of land, when, by selling them, they might be enabled to purchase slaves, and other lands more improveable."[63] North Carolina passed an act in 1749 introducing the same process for breaking entails on small estates, copying almost verbatim the text of the Virginia Act.[64] The survey of the data by historians Robert E. Brown and B. Katherine Brown led them to conclude that "in all probability [the entails] docked by writ of ad quod damnum were by far . . . more numerous" than entails docked by legislative act.[65]

Although the statute mentions relieving poor people of the burdens of the entail, the Browns' survey found that wealthy Virginians used the *ad quod damnum* process to remove entails when possible.[66] Richard Henry Lee, a member of the Virginia gentry, wrote in a letter, "You know I have got the entail on my estate from my father dockt by writ of ad quod damnum."[67] A member of the secretary's office stated that the process was used "to defeat entails on land, to enable them to sell and convey the same, in fee simple."[68]

Why would owners of small parcels devise their land in fee tail? The likely reason was to shield the land from financial and other risks. Small landowners, even more so than owners of vast estates, operated on a tight margin. Entailed land could not be seized through the process of law in the common law courts. The entail provided families with domestic security in an uncertain economic environment.[69] C. Ray Keim's study of Virginia found that family homes were more likely to be devised in tail, with the outlying land devised in fee simple.[70] Entailing the family home closely mirrors the safeguards on family wealth introduced in the property reforms of the 1840s. The homestead exemption laws widely enacted in the mid-nineteenth century protected the family homestead, to provide families with a minimum baseline of financial security. Entailing the family home had the same risk-reducing effect.

FEMALE OWNERS IN TAIL

The Virginia records also reveal that females were often owners of land in tail. There were 133 acts removing entails reported in the Virginia statute books between 1711 and 1773.[71] Out of the 133 private acts of legislation, twenty-six, or 19.5%, were addressed to women who owned entailed land or slaves.[72] A far greater number reveal that women owned the entailed land at some time, even though the current petitioner was a son or grandson.

Why were women owners of fee tail land? Some fathers and mothers devised entailed land or slaves outright to their daughters with no further explanation. William Thompson owned 300 acres in fee simple. Thompson's will of 1686 devised 300 acres "to his daughter Elizabeth, and the heirs of her body lawfully begotten" [meaning in fee tail].[73] The legislature noted that after Thompson's death, Elizabeth "entered into the same, and became thereof seised in fee-tail."[74] The text of the act in this case, and similar private statutes, places no great emphasis on the fact that a woman inherited entailed land. In fact, when Elizabeth Brooke inherited 578 acres in tail by means of a will written in 1725, it was reported that "some disputes [arose] in the family, concerning the will," but the devise to Elizabeth Brooke "w[as] confirmed" and the settlement was "recorded in the general court."[75] To provide another example, William Churchill's 1710 will devised 2,280 acres in tail to his son Armistead, but provided that if Armistead died without heirs, his daughter Elizabeth would inherit the 2,280 acres in tail, and if she died without children, his daughter Priscilla would inherit the 2,280 acres in tail.[76]

In other cases, it appears that parents had given birth only to daughters or that a son had died, leaving a daughter as the only remaining heir of the entailed land. As mentioned, under English law, when fee tail owners had no sons, daughters would inherit the fee tail land jointly, as co-parceners.[77] Virginia followed this practice. As an example, Daniel Parke's will of 1670 devised 1,678 acres to his son Daniel in fee tail.[78] Daniel (the son) inherited the land, but when he died, his only children were his two daughters, Frances and Lucy. Lucy became the sole owner of the 1,678-acre parcel in fee tail. Lucy gave birth to two daughters, one of whom died, leaving Wilhelmina to become the sole owner of the 1,678-acre entailed parcel.[79] Therefore, although the original devise was to Daniel, by process of law, the subsequent two generations of fee tail owners were female.

The colonial Chesapeake was plagued by high mortality rates, particularly for men. Blended families with stepchildren and combined resources were common. Landowners' wills often contained carefully crafted devises that used the entail to legally separate property estates in anticipation of future marriages and additional children.[80] It was a society with many widows, who were more likely to devise land to daughters.[81] In this setting, female landownership was not unusual.

Female owners of entailed land often married and, under coverture and by custom, their husbands gained managerial control over the land, but the land was protected entirely from the husbands' creditors. When the female owner of entailed land died, the land descended to her eldest son. It might be said that the female landowner was, therefore, only a custodian of land ultimately destined to continue in the male line. Nonetheless, as a practical matter, many women in colonial Virginia were legally owners of entailed land that could not be sold or mortgaged by their husbands and that could not be taken to pay their debts, much like the regime enacted under the Married Women's Property Acts of the 1840s.

The Browns' study found that some Virginia wills that devised land to one or more daughters in tail, also devised land to sons in fee simple.[82] The Virginia records, however, also reveal the opposite situation, with sons inheriting entailed land and daughters inheriting land in fee simple or monetary portions. Virginia testators clearly understood the tradeoffs between entailed land (offering wealth shielding) and fee simple land (offering alienability and testamentary freedom).

In sum, the incidence of female ownership of entailed property was highly significant. It is safe to presume that abolishing the fee tail had a dramatic effect on many women landowners as well as on owners of small parcels of entailed land.

Georgia: The Colonial Frontier

Georgia provides a direct illustration of the impact of entailing property on credit markets. Georgia was exceptional in that it was created for the purpose of serving as a military buffer to protect South Carolina from attack by Native Americans. The founders of the colony, the Trustees of Georgia, operating out of London, offered between 50 and 500 acres of land to anyone who would immigrate and accept their terms of ownership.[83] They required mandatory entail: all land was to pass from eldest male heir to eldest male heir. Allowing free alienation, they feared, would lead to land concentration that would reduce the buffering effect of a widely inhabited countryside. The Trustees also prohibited Georgia residents from owning or leasing slaves, because they felt that the number of slaves in South Carolina was a military threat and feared the threat would worsen if slaves were imported into Georgia.[84]

Immigrants to Georgia, however, found mandatory entail incompatible with economic survival because it prevented them from using land as collateral for credit. In 1738, the residents of Savannah petitioned the Trustees to provide a remedy for what they described as "our present Misfortunes, and this deplorable State of the Colony."[85] The central problem was that "Merchants in general, especially of *England*, not being willing to supply the Settlers with Goods upon Commission, because no Person here can make them any Security of their Lands or Improvements."[86] They asked that the "Constitution" of Georgia be revised to deal with two problems:

> I. The Want of a free Title or Fee-simple to our Lands; which, if granted, would both occasion great Numbers of new Settlers to come amongst us, and likewise encourage those who remain here, chearfully to proceed in

making further Improvements, as well to retrieve their sunk Fortunes, as to make Provision for their Posterity. . . .

II. The Want of the Use of Negroes with proper limitations; which if granted, would both induce great numbers of White People to come here, and also render us capable to subsist ourselves by raising Provisions upon our Lands.[87]

The Trustees in London were not responsive to these requests. Their response to the Savannah petition described "those who wanted a Power to mortgage or alien" their lands as merely "gratify[ing] the greedy and ambitious Views of a few Negro Merchants."[88] Moreover, the Trustees stated that "by giving them a Power to alien their Lands, the Colony would soon be too like its Neighbors, void of White Inhabitants, filled with Blacks, and reduced to be the precarious Property of a Few, equally exposed to domestick Treachery, and Foreign Invasion."[89] Thus, in Georgia, mandatory entail was intended to prevent the importation of slaves and to forestall land concentration for military reasons.

The Trustees pressed Georgia's residents to cultivate silk, which they thought would offer sufficient profits without demanding the plantation labor force required by the cultivation of rice, the profitable export of South Carolina. A group of Georgians who described themselves as the Malcontents tried to convince the Trustees of the failure of efforts to make silk and clamored for slavery. Moreover, as Betty Wood describes, slaves had been illegally imported since 1736 and "Georgia's local officials were forced to admit that slaves were being employed in the colony."[90] By 1751, the ban on slavery ended in Georgia by royal decree and rates of slave importation accelerated.[91]

After the Revolution, the demands of Georgia citizens for greater liquidity through abolition of the entail prevailed. Georgia is an example of a frontier society in the early stages of development, where residents expressed a desire to leverage their property to the maximum extent in order to import slaves and to accelerate the process of cultivation. By raising the abolition of the entail to constitutional status, the political leaders favored expanding credit conditions generally over recognizing the interest of individual property owners in having a means by which they could lower their exposure to economic risk. The Georgia Constitution of 1777 provides that "Estates shall not be entailed."[92] In historical accounts, Georgia's constitutional provision is often listed along with other state legislation in discussions of republican ideology, instead of a desire for credit and slaves.

THE ROLE OF THE ENTAIL

In sum, the historical evidence suggests that a central role of the entail was to shield wealth from creditors and to reduce immediate and unforeseen financial risk. While best known for its use by large landowners, the widespread appeal of entails is demonstrated by the number held by small landowners and the prevalence of female owners of entailed land. Fee tail estates in the colonies, however, present a puzzle: in an environment where Parliament enacted the Debt Recovery Act to defend the interests of creditors in Britain, and colonists in Georgia protested against entails as reducing their access to credit, why did the fee tail survive in several colonies until the American Revolution?

One likely explanation is that the role of slaves as collateral dominated economic markets in Virginia and North Carolina to such an extent that creditors in Britain, as well as local creditors, were relatively less concerned that land was legally protected from their claims. The 1727 Virginia law holding that entailed slaves would be treated as "chattel" to satisfy creditors' claims was thus a pillar of Virginia's credit economy. A second explanation is that, as mentioned, Virginia planters often held some land in fee simple (which was available to satisfy creditors' claims) and some land in fee tail (which was shielded from creditors' claims). So long as a landowner's debts did not exceed the total amount of the value of chattels, slaves, and the fee simple land, the debts would have been "secured" by the property that was not sheltered by the fee tail. Even if the presence of fee tail land reduced credit, the economy was growing on the basis of the property that remained in a liquid form.

There is a fundamental tradeoff between policies that protect creditors' interests, lower interest rates, and encourage taking on debt for further investment, and policies that minimize risk, increase interest rates, and stabilize the society. Each local community is likely to want to decide how much financial risk it wants to assume. Those Virginians leaving property to their children in fee tail likely preferred privileging economic stability over the long term. Moreover, by the mid-eighteenth century, Virginia planters often complained about the debt burdens they felt from creditors across the Atlantic in Britain. It is significant that the Virginia legislature passed a law abolishing the fee tail in 1776, once they had rejected the sovereignty of British rulers.

The entail should be viewed as a precursor to the property reforms of the mid-nineteenth century that enabled individuals to lower their exposure to financial risk. By entailing the family homestead, an individual shielded the home from creditors' claims in a manner permitted under the homestead exemption laws widely enacted beginning in the 1840s to protect landowners from financial risk.[93] Interestingly, allowing women to hold land that was protected from the creditors of their husbands was one of the principal ambitions of the Married Women's Property Acts of that period.[94] Historians have commonly viewed the mid-nineteenth-century property reform movement as a popular democratic response to the hardships many faced during the depression of 1838.[95] Understanding the uses of the fee tail suggests that these mid-nineteenth-century reforms are merely one element of a longer history in which Anglo-American property law offered means for interests in land to be shielded from creditors, to allow individuals to reduce risk, in an era before the rise of the welfare state and private insurance markets.

PART IV

The Stamp Act, Independence, and the Founding

6

The Stamp Act and Legal
and Economic Institutions

Could it now be supposed that any American chief justice, who in
the course of his office must have frequently pronounced decrees
of his court under the authority of this act of parliament for seizing
upon, and selling the freehold-lands inherited by the son from his
father for the discharge and satisfaction of a book-debt due from
the father to a British merchant . . . should doubt of the power
of parliament to dispose of the property of any inhabitant of the
colonies in the same manner as the provincial legislature of each
colony has authority to do?

—WILLIAM KNOX, *THE CLAIM OF THE COLONIES TO AN
EXEMPTION FROM INTERNAL TAXES IMPOSED BY THE
AUTHORITY OF PARLIAMENT* (1765)

In the search for ways to draw revenue from the colonies after the Seven
Years' War, Thomas Whatley, Britain's Secretary of the Treasury, asked
officials throughout the colonies to compile reports on the fees they collected for institutional services. Jared Ingersoll, Connecticut's future stamp
distributor, wrote in a letter to Thomas Fitch, Connecticut's governor, that
Whatley asked him to provide "information of the several methods of transfer, Law process &c made Use of in the Colony."[1] Ingersoll believed that when
London officials learned how heavily colonists used their institutions—based

on all the fees collected—Parliament would choose to impose only a minor tax on these services. In a February 11, 1765 letter to Fitch, Ingersoll wrote:

> I very well knew the information I must give would operate strongly in our favour, as the number of our Law Suits, Deeds, . . . & in short almost all the Objects of the intended taxation & Dutys are so very numerous in the Colony that the knowledge of them would tend to the imposing a Duty so much the Lower as the Objects were more in Number.[2]

Events proved Ingersoll wrong. After compiling the information on fees from all of the colonies, Parliament surprised the colonists by enacting the Stamp Act in 1765, which colonists saw as heavily taxing the institutional services offered in the colonies. Unlike taxes that Parliament had levied in the past, such as duties on imported goods that Parliament had imposed since the Navigation Act of 1660, the 1765 Stamp Act raised the cost to colonists of internal institutions. The Stamp Act imposed fifty-four duties on documents and legal instruments, including those required in obtaining land grants, securing and publicizing property rights (such as title deeds and mortgages in land and slaves), obtaining and enforcing credit agreements, and publicizing and advertising in newspapers.

Parliament's enactment of the Stamp Act is widely acknowledged as a starting point for the acceleration of tensions that led to the Declaration of Independence in 1776.[3] In the dominant scholarly accounts of the Revolution, the colonial opposition to the Stamp Act centered almost exclusively on ideological and constitutional objections to "taxation without representation." That is, individual colonists and colonial legislatures rose up against the Act because it violated fundamental constitutional rights by imposing an internal tax when colonists were not directly represented in Parliament.[4]

In contrast, this chapter emphasizes that "no taxation without representation" also referred to the colonial assemblies' demand that they approve any taxes. Colonial opponents of the Stamp Act abhorred the concept of English Parliamentary regulation of the fees and costs imposed on services performed by local institutions. They objected to the principle that a distant central authority had the capacity to impose costs on internal, local institutions.

The balance of power between representative assemblies, the crown-appointed governors and their appointed councils, and authorities in London was a central and constant struggle in the political world of colonial America. The institutions for recording land titles, executing land conveyances and mortgages, and resolving debt-related litigation were paid for by means of fees imposed for each institutional service. By the mid-eighteenth century, the representative assemblies' role in authorizing taxes and imposing fees had gained the general, unspoken acceptance of the colonial governors.[5]

The level of fees imposed for basic government services like recording a land title, or initiating a suit on a debt, was an issue that colonists took quite seriously. These institutional services were viewed as necessary and routine in colonial economic life. The political threat lay in the fact that colonial governors and their deputies might use executive authority to impose additional fees as perquisites of their offices or as a means of generating revenue for their salaries. The colonial assemblies defended the position that taxes and fees should not be imposed without their approval and confronted governors who were seen as usurping their power to tax.

This chapter focuses on the first colony, Virginia, as an example of events taking place throughout the colonies. The Stamp Act controversy was preceded in Virginia by two clashes between governors and the representative assemblies over the power to impose taxes and fees: an effort by Lord Howard to tax institutional services in the 1680s; and the explosive Pistole Crisis, a conflict in 1754 over the power of a governor to levy a fee for granting a land patent. The Pistole Crisis was a defining experience setting the stage for Virginians' reaction to the Stamp Act of 1765, which taxed a far greater number of institutional services. The chapter describes the Stamp Act and the contrasting visions of the colonial economy and its institutions advanced by the Stamp Act supporters in England and the Stamp Act opponents in the colonies.

No Taxation without Representation: Legislative Control over Fees and Taxes

The colonial assemblies assumed the power to tax in the early years of colonization. In one of its earliest formal meetings, in 1623, the Virginia General Assembly held that the Virginia governor would need to seek its approval to impose taxes, stating "That the Governor shall not lay any taxes or impositions upon the colony their lands or commodities other than by the authority of the General Assembly, to be levied and employed as the said Assemble shall appoint."[6]

Fees for institutional services were viewed as a tax. As the historian Jack Greene has emphasized, in most colonies the representative assemblies "came to regard fees as taxes and claimed the right to establish and regulate them by statute."[7] Royal instructions from London often purported to give the appointed colonial governors the power to set fees. But, as Greene shows, "the American lower houses denied the governors' authority to levy fees without their consent and almost always resisted any attempt to do so."[8]

Starting in the seventeenth century, colonial assemblies frequently enacted into law extensive schedules of fees documenting every institutional service and how much each would cost. The Massachusetts legislature, for example, established detailed fee schedules in 1692, 1743, 1744, 1747, 1751, 1753, 1757, 1776, 1778, and then after the Revolution in 1782, 1785, and 1786.[9] The Virginia legislature similarly enacted general schedules of fees in 1632, 1643, 1662, 1680, 1696, 1718, 1732, 1734, 1738, and 1745, with many more detailed laws relating to fees in other years.[10]

The level of the fees, of course, had a direct impact on all who relied on the institutions. There were ex ante and ex post effects of fees for institutional services. The fees levied to record titles and mortgages were direct costs paid by those acquiring land and lenders and borrowers. Ex ante (before the individual used the service), the level of fees would impact an individual's decision about whether, for example, to record a land conveyance. The statutory fee level likely influenced the total amount of land and slave sales and mortgages recorded in an economy in which land and slaves were primary assets.

In contrast, court fees on litigation posed an ex post problem for debtors and creditors. In the colonial era, court fees were imposed on the party losing the litigation. Court fees on debt litigation operated as taxes on debtors who were already unable to repay their debts (thus taking away from the assets available to creditors as well). During times of widespread economic recession, the volume of litigation ballooned, increasing the total amounts extracted for the payment of fees.[11] Thus, it is not surprising that fees for institutional services were a contested political issue in the colonies.

PRECEDENTS OF THE STAMP ACT IN VIRGINIA

By the early eighteenth century, the House of Burgesses, the Virginia assembly, had entrenched its authority over appointments and fees for different services, including land surveying.[12] In contrast, colonial royal instructions typically authorized Virginia governors to set fees with only the consent of their appointed council (that is, without needing the assembly's approval). No governor chose to exercise this power until the 1750s, with one exception. In the 1680s, Governor Francis Howard, Lord Howard of Effingham, imposed fees that operated much like the controversial Stamp Act of 1765, without the consent of the House of Burgesses: Howard imposed a fee of two hundred pounds of tobacco for fixing the public seal on land patents, probated wills, and other official documents, as well as thirty pounds of tobacco for recording land surveys.[13] The House of Burgesses opposed Howard's fees by appealing to the Privy Council, arguing that Howard's actions exceeded the scope of his authority. In September 1689, the Privy Council ruled that Howard's fees were illegal but did not adopt the argument of the House of Burgesses. To the Privy Council, the fees were illegal because Howard had not sought the consent of his appointed council before imposing them.[14]

Because the Privy Council did not rule that the governor needed approval from the assembly, the decision was not a resounding victory from the perspective of the colonists wanting greater control over institutions. As Greene has described in detail, however, in practice the Virginia legislature thereafter maintained control over institutional fees for the next sixty years, until 1752, when upon his arrival in Virginia, Governor Dinwiddie, with the consent of his council but not the assembly, assessed a fee of one "pistole" (a Spanish coin worth more than 16 shillings English sterling) on all land patents issued by his office with the royal seal. Dinwiddie quickly submitted the issue of the fee's legality to the Board of Trade, which gave its official approval.

Virginians were enraged. The opposition to the pistole tax focused on the fact that the fee was a tax imposed without the legislature's consent. As William Stith, a member of the Burgesses, wrote to the Bishop of London in April 1753, "[t]his Attempt to lay Taxes upon the People WITHOUT Law was certainly AGAINST Law, [and] an evident Invasion of Property."[15] The opponents of the fee championed the slogan *"Liberty & Property and no Pistole"*[16] and reported to their friends in London that the governor's fee gave "very general Disgust [and] Alarms to the whole Country."[17] They petitioned the Privy Council, which held a hearing on the legality of the fee in June 1754.[18]

Dinwiddie's supporters emphasized that the pistole fee was only imposed on land patents, not legal institutional services. William Murray, Lord Mansfield, who advocated on behalf of Governor Dinwiddie before the Privy Council, distinguished the pistole fee from the illegal fee imposed by Governor Howard in the 1680s because Howard's fee had taxed legal institutions.[19] According to Murray, Howard's fee had been unlawful, in part because it was imposed on "Probate of Wills, letters of administration, and various other things; which, your Lordships observe, were matters of Right, which the Subject was obliged, was compelled to comply with."[20] In contrast, the pistole fee was "a matter of Discretion; if the Subject does not incline to ask for a Patent, he is not compelled to take one out."[21] It is notable that Murray described institutional services as "matters of Right," with the inference that only local representative bodies could legally set their costs.[22]

Dinwiddie's advocates, including Alexander Hume Campbell, characterized the opponents of the fee as "Land Jobbers, a Species of Men, who, in accumulating Estates, pay no regard to the publick Welfare."[23] Indeed, Campbell continued, "[s]o inordinate and boundless is their Lust of acquiring Lands, that unless some effectual means are used to restrain it, it must in time produce the total destruction of that Colony."[24] In contrast, the House of Burgesses protested that the fee was "an Infringement on the Rights of the People, and a Discouragement from taking up Lands, and thereby . . . the settling the Frontiers of this Country, and the Increase of his Majesty's Revenue of Quitrents."[25] The Virginians repeatedly emphasized the need for inexpensive patenting of lands to encourage immigration. According to Robert Henley, who represented the House of Burgesses:

> A small Expence in taking up Lands is an Encouragement to Protestants to settle there from all parts of Europe; from Germany in particular; but can it be Imagined that any European will settle there, if the Governor proves this Arbitrary, if they find themselves Subject to the extravagant demand of a Governor?[26]

The Privy Council ultimately ruled in favor of Dinwiddie, although it carved an exemption from the pistole fee for plots of land under one hundred acres (presumably a size that immigrants would be likely to patent) and grandfathered those who had requested patents before Dinwiddie was appointed. The controversy foreshadowed the arguments that would reappear in the Stamp Act crisis.

The Stamp Act Crisis

The Stamp Act imposed fifty-four different duties on a wide variety of documents and legal instruments. Crucially, all of the duties had to be paid in the "Sterling Money of Great Britain," valued at "Five Shillings and Six Pence the Ounce in Silver," currency that was extremely scarce.[27] In 1764, Parliament's Currency Act banned all colonial governments from issuing any paper money, which reduced the volume of colonial money in circulation and raised the value of sterling.[28] Colonists repeatedly complained that they were entirely incapable of paying the stamp tax due to the shortage of hard currency in the colonies.[29]

Significantly for an economy dependent on the acquisition and transfer of land, the Act levied a substantial tax on land grants, the surveying of land, and the recording of land conveyances in colonial registries. Notarial acts, letters of attorney, procurations, mortgages, releases, and other legal instruments not specifically mentioned were all charged at two shillings and three pence per page.[30] Warrants, deeds, and grants were all to be taxed. As Justin duRivage has found, a modest 200-acre plot in Virginia, worth about six pounds Virginia currency, would have required stamps on the grant, the warrant to survey the land, and the registration of the land, amounting to slightly more than 4% of the purchase price.[31] The tax was progressive and it imposed a duty of two shillings, six pence tax on every 320 acres.[32] For land speculators, like investors of the Mississippi Company, who sought 2.5 million acres for free in exchange for surveying the land and retailing it to settlers, the Stamp Act would have significantly increased their costs. The Company would have paid the equivalent of about £1,562 Virginia currency as well as the cost of acquiring survey warrants for the individual tracts, which might have amounted to another £750.

The Stamp Act taxed all paper used on court proceedings, such as three pence per sheet on "any Copy of any Petition, Bill, Answer, Claim, Plea, Replication, Rejoinder, Demurrer, or other Pleading in any such Court."[33] It levied one shilling per page for "any Monition, Libel, Answer, Allegation, Inventory, or Renunciation" as well as for affidavits, bail documents, interrogatory depositions, rules, orders, and court warrants.[34] Bonds, which were used to secure the payments of debts, were likewise obliged to be printed on stamped paper.

The Stamp Act's cost depended on the amount of paper needing stamps. As legal disputes dragged on, the amount of stamped paper and the duties increased accordingly, which would affect a litigant's decision to use legal process. Due to the high volume of debt litigation occurring during times of economic recession, the Stamp Act represented a regressive tax on poor debtors. Taken together, these duties reflect an extractive policy program for colonial North America.

The First Congress of the American Colonies (consisting of delegates from nine North American colonies) held a meeting in New York City on October 7–25, 1765, in response to the Stamp Act. This "Stamp Act Congress" wrote a petition in 1766 to the House of Commons emphasizing that the small scale of landowning in the colonies was precisely the reason why low-cost institutional mechanisms for land conveyancing were essential. It stated "[t]hat from the Nature of *American* Business, the Multiplicity of Suits and Papers used in Matters of small Value, in a Country where Freeholds are so minutely divided, and Property so Frequently transferr'd, a Stamp Duty must ever be very Burthensome and Unequal."[35]

In contrast to tariffs, the principal revenue source of the Crown, both supporters and opponents of the Stamp Act understood that it was a measure to use taxation to deliberately change colonial institutions and to shift the trajectory of the North American economy. The Stamp Act's taxation of land conveyances and official legal documents threatened to disrupt the functioning of local colonial institutions, to suppress the recordation of land conveyances and mortgages, and to increase fees for litigation on the basis of credit transactions. To the extent that local institutions' central role was to publicize information about property rights and to process credit claims, those functions are impaired by excessive costs imposed on the participants. The Stamp Act crisis serves as a landmark effort to defend local institutions from excessive and inequitable taxation by an unrepresentative government to protect the relatively well-functioning colonial land and credit markets.

The Stamp Act Advocates' Economic Vision

As Steve Pincus and Justin duRivage have emphasized, Parliament enacted the Stamp Act in a broad effort to reform both Britain and its colonial regime. Following the accession of George III, Britain was ruled by governments that embraced the fiscal and economic logic of austerity, that is, reducing spending while increasing revenue from the colonies.[36] In the wake of the Seven Years' War, Britain had contracted a debt of more than £130 million, making it one of the most heavily indebted and highly taxed nations in Europe.[37] Led first by John Stuart, Third Earl of Bute, and then George Grenville, First Lord of the Treasury, these administrations used their influence in Parliament to pass new taxes and to increase the enforcement of old ones.

Upon taking office, Grenville described "a Commercial nation . . . exhausted of its wealth and Inhabitants, loaded with debts and taxes, the landed Interest distressed, and more peculiarly groaning under the weight of every additional Supply."[38] Grenville and his supporters were particularly alarmed by Britain's high rate of domestic taxation. Taxes on landed wealth weighed on all parts of the economy, including commerce and manufacturing.[39] Faced with the choice between promoting growth or imposing taxes, the Grenville administration's response was to pursue both fiscal austerity and greater authority. The Stamp Act's most prominent advocates were strongly committed to a vision of reform that reined in the colonial economy and taxed existing institutions. Their position won out over a competing vision, which would have promoted colonial commerce and expansion, to increase colonial consumption of exports from England, and to secure revenue for the Crown through greater colonial import tariffs.[40]

The Stamp Act was part of this broader project of economic austerity. Grenville and his supporters designed the Stamp Act as a means of protecting colonial officials by providing an independent revenue source. The Act would free governors from having to negotiate with colonial legislatures for funds and thereby strengthen executive authority. Both Georgia's agent to Parliament, William Knox, and Massachusetts's governor, Francis Bernard, urged policy makers in London to provide governors with sources of revenue that could not be held hostage by colonial assemblies.[41] Like the new duties on trans-Atlantic trade and improved customs enforcement, the Stamp Act promised to make Britain's colonies more governable.

The regulations the Stamp Act placed on the colonies would reduce land speculation by raising the cost of buying and selling real property. It was designed, Grenville explained, "to discourage by a high Duty the Grant of large Quantities of Land to one Person."[42] Grenville's deputy Whately also asserted that the Stamp Act would serve as "some Check to those enormous Grants and Conveyances which are so detrimental to the Colonies."[43] The Stamp Act also promised to reduce the volume of litigation. Indeed, in drafting the Act, Whately observed "the great Number of Law Suits in most of the Colonies" and the vast potential source of revenue that they offered.[44] In 1768, George Grenville was more explicit about the goals of the Stamp Act when he explained to William Knox that it had been intended as a way "to discourage a Spirit of unnecessary Litigation."[45] Some colonial officials agreed: as early as 1742, Pennsylvania's governor, Sir William Keith, proposed stamp duties as a means of putting "an entire stop to all those Complaints and disputes, daily arising between the people of the Colonies, and their Respective Governours" and of reducing the "immoderate Quantity of Paper Bills Struck in many of the colonies to the discouragement of fair trade."[46]

Both supporters and opponents of the Stamp Act recognized that its taxes, particularly those on legal and commercial transactions, would disproportionately affect the economies of the less wealthy Northern colonies over the wealthier Southern ones. Legal institutional services such as the recording of land grants, mortgages on land and slaves, and debt litigation played a central role throughout all of the colonies. But the impact of the taxes was proportionately higher, of course, where the values of the underlying assets were lower. An additional fee for recording a mortgage on a high-valued slave, for example, would have had less of an impact than the same fee in sterling imposed for debt litigation used to call in a small debt. English supporters of the Stamp Act were aware of the differential impact. Indeed, Thomas Whately, Britain's Junior Secretary of Treasury, made it very clear in a spring 1764 letter to his friend and Connecticut's future stamp distributor, Jared Ingersoll, that the Stamp Act was "preferable to a Tax upon Negroes, which would effect the Southern much more than the Northern Colonies."[47] And, as the Maryland lawyer Daniel Dulany observed in an influential pamphlet attacking the Stamp Act, "[a] larger Sum will be extracted from a Tobacco Colony than from Jamaica; and it will not only be higher in one of the poorest Colonies, and the least able to bear it, than in the richest."[48]

In response to these concerns, the Stamp Act taxed land transactions in the West Indian sugar colonies at a higher rate than on the mainland.[49] Stamps for land conveyances in the Caribbean (denoted as "all other parts of America") were twice as expensive as in North America. West Indian land was more valuable, however, which helps explain the perception that the tax fell most heavily on the relatively poorer, but more mercantile, northern colonies. There is considerable evidence that the Stamp Act's architects and advocates intended these disproportionate effects. They believed that parliamentary taxation of the colonies offered a means of implementing much needed institutional reforms, which were more necessary in the Northern colonies than in the Southern ones.

Opposition to the Stamp Act and the Defense of Colonial Institutions

While supporters of the Stamp Act believed that it would bring much needed institutional reform to Britain's colonies, radical colonists opposing the Act insisted that it spelled the end of colonial liberty and prosperity. Colonists argued that arbitrary taxation by an unrepresentative Parliament was both unconstitutional and foretold the end of secure property rights. If British legislators could take colonial property whenever it suited them, the expansion of commerce would suffer. In their view, the Stamp Act raised the cost of economic transactions, legal services, and transmission of information. They criticized the bill for placing a heavy burden on debtors. In a world in which North Americans were perpetually short of hard currency, particularly the pound sterling necessary to pay the Stamp Act duties, and in which the instruments of credit that provided desperately needed liquidity were themselves taxed, the Stamp Act seemed not just unconstitutional but a threat to colonial economy and society.

John Adams's landmark essay, *A Dissertation on the Canon and the Feudal Law*, emphasizes that it was "manifest from the Stamp Act" that "a design is formed . . . to introduce the inequalities and dependencies of the feudal system, by taking from the poorer sort of people all their little subsistence, and conferring it on a set of stamp officers, distributors and their deputies."[50] Adams also emphasized the impact the Act would have on the broader colonial economy. At a Braintree town meeting in 1765, he remarked that

> the duties are so numerous and so high and the embarrassments to Business in this infant Sparcely Settled Country so great that it would be totally impossible for the people to Subsist under it even if we had no Controversy at . . . all about the Right and authority of imposing it Considering the present Scarcity of money.[51]

To Adams, the Stamp Act

> would dreign the Country of Cash, Strip multitudes of the Poorer people of all their property and Reduce them to absolute beggary. And what the Consequence would be of so Sudden a Shock and Such a Convulsive Change in the whole Course of our business and Subsistance, to the peace of the Province We tremble to consider.[52]

American opponents of the Stamp Act and their radical Whig allies in Britain repeatedly argued that it was not only unconstitutional but that its very unconstitutionality threatened property rights that were absolutely necessary for economic prosperity. As Thomas Fitch, the elected governor of Connecticut explained, the Stamp Act made colonial "Liberties and Properties precarious," which could only have "that unhappy Effect of causing the Colonies to languish and decrease."[53] Secure property rights, the kind that came with colonial self-government, would, on the other hand, "tend to invigorate, enliven and encourage the People, and keep up in them a Spirit of Industry in all Kinds of Dealing and Business."[54] Radical colonists were convinced that confidence in secure property rights was absolutely necessary for investment and productivity.

While those opposed to the Stamp Act worried that it threatened colonial property rights in general, they also expressed serious concern that it would undermine colonial legal institutions that adjudicated those rights. As described above, Daniel Dulany observed that the tax would "produce in each Colony, a greater or less sum, not in proportion to its wealth, but to the multiplicity of juridical forms, the quantity of vacant land, the frequency of transferring landed property, the extent of paper negotiations, the scarcity of money, and the number of debtors."[55] For the Stamp Act's staunchest opponents, it threatened not only to price the poor and indebted out of the legal market, but also to make it more difficult and more expensive to adjudicate property rights.

In arguing against the Stamp Act, radicals on both sides of the Atlantic maintained that a tax that targeted legal transactions rather than wealth would prove particularly damaging to the colonies' most industrious population. Otis, for example, argued, "The burden of the stamp act will certainly fall chiefly on the middling, more necessitous, and labouring people."[56] Like other radicals, Otis based his argument on the fact that the Stamp Act would raise the cost of legal defenses, particularly those of debtors who had been sued for recovery of debts. Benjamin Franklin similarly told Parliament that

> [t]he greatest part of the money must arise from law suits for the recovery of debts, and be paid by the lower sort of people, who were too poor easily to pay their debts. It is therefore a heavy tax on the poor, and a tax upon them for being poor.[57]

Indeed, he rejected the argument made by supporters of the Stamp Act that it would reduce the number of lawsuits in the colony, insisting that because the costs of litigation "all fall upon the debtor, and are to be paid by him," the Stamp Act offered "no discouragement to the creditor to bring his action."[58] Dulany was likewise convinced that most of the stamp revenue would "be drawn from the poorest individuals in the poorest colonies, from mortgagors, obligors, and defendants."[59]

———

Advocates of the Stamp Act were convinced that Britain needed to raise new revenue in order to defray the costs of war and public debt and to provide a strong, guiding hand to ensure the colonial commerce was to the advantage of the Crown. To their opponents, the Stamp Act offered abundant evidence that parliamentary taxation would serve the economic interests of those who were represented—British taxpayers—at the expense of those who were not—American colonists. It threatened the security of property and did so in a way that struck at the heart of the colonies' burgeoning commercial economy. Raising the cost of credit, of litigation, and of acquiring and transferring property was not only inequitable, it promised economic ruin.

Had the Stamp Act survived the opposition in the colonies, it seems likely that the effects of the Act would have stopped short of the total ruin predicted by its antagonists. Ultimately, much of this disagreement boiled down to contrasting visions of the relationship between institutions and commerce. Thus, the fierce opposition to the Stamp Act—which set the stage for the broader Revolutionary movement—reflected more than an ideological and constitutional opposition to the structure of Parliament and British colonial law. Colonial protestors defended the achievement of the colonial legislatures and localities in creating an institutional framework that they believed represented the interests of participants in the colonial economy. The opposition to the Stamp Act, in part, derived from an assessment of how increasing the cost of legal and institutional services would affect colonial economic activities. Understanding this more nuanced history of the Stamp Act controversy reveals that the movement for Independence was, in part, a movement for local control over institutions that secured property rights and underlay the credit economy.

7

Property Exemptions and the Abolition of the Fee Tail in the Founding Era

The liberties of a country, depend upon the light and information possessed by the people.

—JAMES SULLIVAN, *THE PATH TO RICHES* (BOSTON 1792)

To contemporaries in the founding era, the role of property and inheritance was a central question that would define the new American society. The founding era was a period in which landed wealth still framed conceptions of the economic, social, and political order. At the time of the Revolution, every state but one required freehold property ownership for participation in the franchise based on the belief that land ownership conferred an independence necessary for political participation and led to the strongest form of attachment to the nation.[1] As the historian Gordon S. Wood describes, "Men were equal in that no one of them should be dependent on the will of another, and property made this independence possible. Americans in 1776 therefore concluded that they were naturally fit for republicanism precisely because they were 'a people of property; almost every man is a freeholder.'"[2]

The prevalence of landownership begged the question of how to define the relation of property ownership, credit relations, and inheritance: Was land simply a form of wealth like other chattel property? If not, to what extent should government policy isolate land from commercial risks? What was the proper role of inheritance in post-Revolutionary America? Now free from earlier parliamentary mandates, the context in which states enacted laws pertaining to property and the claims of creditors became increasingly complex. Each state had to decide how to balance the desire for credit and investment with the competing desire to safeguard landowners' independence and families' financial security. The policies governing creditors' remedies, inheritance practices, and judicial process were related to deeper issues about the nature of the society as a whole. State policies and court decisions in the 1780s and afterward reveal a pervasive lack of uniformity among the states and their constituents in their understanding of the most desirable economic and inheritance policies. These differences among the states became a powerful barrier to strong federal government authority in areas like bankruptcy policy and taxation.

The dominant ideological position of the founding era is what will be referred to as the "commercial republican" view—which emphasized the importance of the expansion of commerce to the creation of an American meritocracy. According to this view, the new American republican order contrasted sharply with English aristocracy, which linked social and political privilege to land ownership and inheritance. Commercial republicans defended the policy of making land available to satisfy debts, and the streamlined nature of legal process under Parliament's 1732 Debt Recovery Act, on the ground that the circulation of land would prevent the rise of a domestic aristocracy. In addition, as the system of slavery expanded and became more entrenched over the colonial period, it became increasingly incompatible with restraints on alienation of land like the fee tail. Slaveholders actively regulated the relationship between the number of slaves they owned and the amount of acreage the slaves cultivated, and often moved slaves to new parcels of land. Moreover, slaveholders wanted the ability to mortgage both land and slaves to obtain credit to purchase more slaves. The fee tail limited the ability of slaveholders to buy and sell land with ease, to better manage this calculus.

Most state legislatures enacted statutes affirming that the remedial regime existing prior to the American Revolution would remain in place without substantial modification. In some states, the Debt Recovery Act remained valid law. For example, a New Hampshire judicial opinion of 1828 concluded that the Debt Recovery Act "is still the law of the land here at this day."[3] Indeed, the early state legislation was even more explicit than analogous colonial legislation that its purpose was to signal to creditors that the state's law offered few opportunities for debtors to shield assets from creditors' claims. A North Carolina statute of 1777 that extended the Debt Recovery Act, for example, stated that it was directed toward "divers Persons residing in other States or Governments [who] contract Debts with the Inhabitants of this State," and that "by the Policy and Genius of our present Constitution, Lands and Tenements ought to be made subject to the Payment of just Debts, when the Debtor hath not within the Limits of this State Goods and Chattels sufficient to satisfy the same."[4]

In contrast, competing views gave support to the continued implementation of the old English protections to land, but without the concentrated landholdings that resulted from primogeniture. This position reflected a worldview reminiscent of the English perspective that land was a natural family endowment, and ideally a source of family prosperity through the generations. Thomas Jefferson's statements on debt suggest that he opposed the regime enacted under the Debt Recovery Act. His views are famously expressed in his 1789 letter to Madison, in which he claimed that it is self-evident that *"the earth belongs in usufruct to the living."*[5] A few lines down, he explains the comment by stating that:

> [N]o man can, by *natural right*, oblige the lands he occupied, or the persons who succeed him in that occupation, to the paiment of debts contracted by him. For if he could, he might, during his own life, eat up the usufruct of the lands for several generations to come, and then the lands would belong to the dead, and not to the living, which would be the reverse of our principle.[6]

The theory of property expressed in Jefferson's comment reveals his assumption that land, at least according to "natural right," involved not just the fee simple ownership of one person, but also the claims of family members. It is particularly striking that Jefferson chose to use the term "usufruct" (a right to use property, and to transmit it to the next possessor in substantially the same state) in the course of describing an individual's relation to his land. Americans in the founding era typically viewed American republicanism as rooted in the country's unique attribute of having widespread freehold ownership. Usufructuary rights have more in common with the traditional English approach toward land, in which a dominant mode of ownership was a life tenancy (with the remainder held in trust, often formalized in the strict settlement). Stating that a property owner violated his heirs' natural rights to property when he incurred debts that might "eat up" his heirs' interests and treated the land as though it "belonged" entirely to him was antithetical to the commercial republican fee simple worldview. The commercial republican view was that the right of the living freehold owner was total and included the right to alienate the property or to incur debts on the basis of the owner's property holdings. Writing in 1830, James Kent, for example, viewed America as distinct from England in its rejection of the societal dependence on inheritance.[7] As Kent remarked in his treatise, "[e]very family, stripped of artificial supports, is obliged, in this country, to repose upon the virtue of its descendants for the perpetuity of its fame."[8] Jefferson's statement that the "earth belongs in *usufruct* to the living" is thus deeply conservative. Jefferson opposed primogeniture on grounds that it led to an aristocracy and, therefore, an aristocratic form of government. Jefferson described the abolition of primogeniture as necessary to destroy "every fibre . . . of ancient or future aristocracy" as the basis of "a foundation . . . for a government truly republican."[9] But his letter to Madison suggests a desire to defend Virginia's policy of retaining the safeguards to land of the English law. Only by enacting legal buffers protecting property from the immediate claims of creditors would fee simple owners have the independence and security necessary for citizenship in a republic.

This chapter explores founding era property law and institutions. It examines the legacy of the Debt Recovery Act through state legislation, court decisions, and theoretical discussions. It then discusses the diversity of views in the founding era on the question of protections to land from creditors. It analyzes the abolition of the fee tail estate in land in many states, and the move toward greater transparency of institutions such as title recording.

Defining the Role of Land and Inheritance in Founding Era America

The Debt Recovery Act brought greater uniformity to the body of creditor remedies enforced throughout the British colonies in America and the West Indies and had a lasting legacy in founding era America. It was incorporated by many state legislatures and courts after the Revolution into the newly created state law. The enactment of new state statutes, however, invited litigation concerning how the courts would interpret the new statutory language. The most highly litigated issues under the state statutes that superseded the Debt Recovery Act related to, first, the procedural issue of whether executors of estates should be permitted to sell the deceased's land to satisfy creditors' claims without the formal participation of the heir and, second, the status under the new state legislation of the mortgagor's equity of redemption.[10]

The issues involved are illustrated by *D'Urphey v. Nelson*,[11] an 1803 opinion of the Constitutional Court of Appeals of South Carolina, which unequivocally denied the traditional privilege in that state. D'Urphey brought an action as heir to his father's estate. His father's land had been sold by the lower court to satisfy one of his father's bond debts. D'Urphey petitioned the South Carolina Constitutional Court of Appeals to hold void the deed of conveyance of the property issued by the sheriff, because his consent had not been obtained before the land was sold.[12] The Constitutional Court of Appeals, however, held that the Debt Recovery Act was still good law in South Carolina in 1803, and emphasized that it required lands to be seized and sold "*in like manner as personal estates.*"[13] According to the court, "the statute cannot be construed to make any distinction between lands and personal chattels, but they must be considered as equally liable for satisfaction of debts, and to be assets for that purpose in the hands of the personal representatives of the debtor."[14] It noted that the Debt Recovery Act was "certainly intended for the benefit of the creditor."[15] More dramatically, the court stated that due to the Debt Recovery Act:

> [T]he extreme anxiety observable in the common law of England to preserve the rights, and favor the claims, of the heir at law, has been entirely dismissed from our law. . . . And therefore there is no reason for giving notice to the heir . . . before issuing execution to seize and sell the land.[16]

Similarly, in an 1805 decision of the US Supreme Court, Justice John Marshall decided a case relating to Georgia law, and held that the Court reviewed "the construction given by the courts of Georgia to the statute of *5 Geo. 2.* making lands in the colonies liable for debts, and are satisfied that they are considered as chargeable without making the heir a party."[17]

A second issue under the new state legislation involved the question of whether mortgagors retained the traditional equitable right of redemption after a judgment at law. In ten states, through 1820, the courts sold real estate at auction without recognizing any right of redemption and without requiring that a minimum amount of the appraised value be obtained by means of the sale.[18] In New York, the legal case *Waters v. Stewart*, where Alexander Hamilton and Josiah Hoffman represented Stewart and James Kent served as judge, was a landmark in this area.[19] The facts in *Waters* are similar to the facts in *D'Urphey*. The appellants, Thomas Waters and his sister Sarah, were devisees of seventy acres of land, subject to a mortgage, under their stepfather's will. They brought an action in Chancery Court to redeem the property by paying the remaining mortgage debt. The equity-of-redemption interest, however, had been sold under the directive of a court of law to satisfy one of their stepfather's debts during the settlement of his estate. In the lower court's words, the issue at hand was "whether an equity of redemption in lands mortgaged in fee [was] subject to a sale [under] a *fieri facias*."[20] If the court of law lacked authority to sell the equity-of-redemption interest, then the sale would have been void and Waters and his sister would inherit the land and be able to redeem it from the mortgagee.[21]

To decide the case, the court was required to interpret the language of a 1787 New York statute that superseded the Debt Recovery Act. The statute stated that "all and singular the lands, tenements, and real estate of every debtor shall be, and hereby are, made liable to be sold on execution."[22] At issue was whether the legislature intended to include equity-of-redemption interests within the term "real estate," or whether the statute envisioned a regime more analogous to English practice, in which sales of land could take place only after formal foreclosure proceedings in the equity courts.

The lower court held for Stewart, the purchaser of the equity-of-redemption interest in the court-ordered sale. According to the lower court, the Debt Recovery Act had "in its operation, *so far as respected the interest of creditors*, completely converted real into personal estate."[23] The court disparagingly described traditional distinctions made between real and chattel property as "solicitude of the holders of landed estates, to perpetuate them within families, combined with the genius of the English government."[24] The court noted, however, that the "collision between the landed and commercial interest being merely *local*, as confined to Great Britain, and not so extending to its colonies[,] . . . the same impediments did not present to the passing of the [statute] for the more easy recovery of debts in the colonies."[25] It then noted that, since the enactment of the Debt Recovery Act, "sales of equities of redemption have been uninterruptedly made."[26] The court held that the language of the 1787 statute indicated the legislature's desire to continue the regime adopted under the Debt Recovery Act.

In their appeal before the Supreme Court of Judicature of New York, Thomas and Sarah Waters argued that the equity of redemption was an interest that only had legal validity in the equity courts—courts of law in England did not recognize equitable redemption rights. They also argued that without explicit legislative approval, such as by explicit inclusion of "equitable interests" as interests to be sold at execution sales, only equity courts could authorize sale of or foreclosure upon interests that simply were not recognized as relevant to legal actions.[27]

The court, however, upheld the decision of the lower court. With regard to the law, Kent's opinion adopted the argument made by Hamilton and Hoffman, the lawyers for Stewart, who had purchased the land at the execution sale. It held that since mortgage law had evolved to treat a mortgage as simply a lien on land, rather than a title interest in land, the mortgagor should be treated as having a legal interest, subject to the remedies applicable in courts of law.[28] Kent's opinion reasoned that the interest should therefore be viewed as "real estate" under the New York statute.[29] Kent noted that the New York statute at issue "adopted the same loose latitudinary terms as those in [the Debt Recovery Act]"[30] and that "there can be no doubt, I think, but that an equity of redemption will be comprehended in the expression."[31]

Yet Kent's opinion also emphasized two practical issues. First, it noted that courts of law had been selling land subject to mortgages in execution sales since the Debt Recovery Act and stated that the "long and established practice in favour of such sales . . . is of itself deserving of considerable weight."[32] Kent also noted the importance of offering low-cost procedures to creditors. According to Kent, "if judgment creditors are under a necessity in every case of resorting to chancery, for leave to sell the land of the debtor, it would create double suits and double expense, and would lead to much inconvenience and delay."[33] Kent emphasized that execution sales of real property were "agreeable to the general bent and spirit of the more modern decisions."[34]

Many other state legislatures enacted laws providing that land would be available to satisfy the landholder's debts, and state courts, in interpreting the new statutes, often came to conclusions similar to Kent's.[35] North Carolina's state legislation and judicial decisions, such as *D'Urphey* and *Waters*, reflected a broader ideological position that asserted that protections to land from the claims of creditors were undesirable remnants of aristocratic England that had no place in republican America. It is notable that the judges in both the *D'Urphey* and *Waters* opinions felt compelled to state explicitly that the laws at issue purposefully rejected the value system of the English landed class that privileged heirs. In doing so, these judges related protecting creditors' interests and a streamlined judicial process with dismantling aristocratic dynasties.

Over the years, the commercial republican position reinforced and extended this line of argument. In his famous Plymouth Oration of 1820, Daniel Webster, for example, emphasized the abolition of traditional protections to land from creditors as a legislative reform that had pushed American society toward republicanism. In describing the major reforms of colonial law that had set the stage for democracy, Webster stated that "alienation of the land was every way facilitated, even to the subjecting of it to every species of debt."[36]

As is reflected in these writings, the focus of the commercial republican thinkers was on using property law to protect against landed "monopolies" and the aristocracy that emerged in association with concentrated landholdings, and also to ensure that debtor-creditor law did not privilege the landowning class at the expense of non-landowners.[37] It is interesting that there is no hint of concern relating to the possibility that commerce might create inequalities of its own, inequalities that could influence, and potentially corrupt, politics. As Noah Webster stated in a 1787 pamphlet, "the inequalities introduced by commerce, are too fluctuating to endanger government."[38] The commercial republican view narrowly focused on the belief that subjecting land ownership to the risks of commercial life would prevent the rule of an American aristocracy on the English model.

Founding Era Opposition to the Debt Recovery Act Regime

The commercial republican position was highly contested. In the late 1780s, debtors' movements such as Shays's Rebellion in Massachusetts led state legislatures to enact laws temporarily relieving debtors of the severity of the remedial regime that treated land as legally equivalent to chattel property.[39] Some form of debt relief legislation was enacted in the 1780s in Virginia, Pennsylvania, Maryland, Massachusetts, New Hampshire, North Carolina, and South Carolina.[40]

The debt relief legislation of the 1780s expressed a sentiment that would gain greater force over time in American history: that the regime of the Debt Recovery Act subjected landowners to an undesirable level of financial risk. During times of economic recession, a great number of people were likely to experience the threat of losing their land and homes due to their inability to pay their debts. The loss, or potential loss, of land ownership in this period, and the fear that independent farmers would become wage laborers, was a matter of serious social and political concern.

Moreover, some state court judges were highly respectful of traditional English legal distinctions between real and personal property. In *Baker v. Webb* (1794), for example, the North Carolina Superior Court addressed the same issue as that of *D'Urphey v. Nelson*: did the heir have a right to be a party to a suit in which his landed inheritance might be sold to a creditor of his father?[41] One of the judges stated that "[t]he whole weight of this labored case, seems reducible to this question, what is the true construction of the *5th Geo. II. ch.7.* [the Debt Recovery Act]?"[42] Did the Act abolish all distinctions between real and personal property, and therefore between law and equity?

Unlike the judges in *Waters v. Stewart* (New York) and *D'Urphey v. Nelson* (South Carolina), the North Carolina court in *Baker* held that the Debt Recovery Act was compatible with fundamental legal distinctions between land and chattel and between law and equity. The court held that, at the death of a landowner, his land immediately descended to the heir at law.[43] The land never came into the hands of the executor of the estate. The Debt Recovery Act had transformed the law to create a cause of action on behalf of the deceased's unsecured creditors against the heir with respect to the land. It did not, however, eliminate the traditional privilege of the heir to be a party to a lawsuit in which he might be denied his inheritance.[44]

Baker v. Webb is interesting not only for interpreting the Debt Recovery Act more conservatively than New York or South Carolina courts had. Haywood, the lawyer for the heir challenging the execution sale of his father's real property, framed the issue as implicating nothing less than the fundamental significance of land ownership to American political life. Were traditional protections of land a relic of feudalism and aristocracy? Or, in contrast, were protections of land necessary to maintain the independence and attachment of the citizenry and therefore equally essential to preserve a republican form of government?

Speaking of the traditional privilege of heirs to be parties to proceedings in which their landed inheritance would be taken, Haywood contended:

> This rule is not any relick of the ancient feudal system. It is founded in the soundest policy, equally applicable to the condition of this country as to that of England. . . . The more freeholders there are . . . the greater is the public strength and respectability—and the method the law has taken to encrease their number, is by placing freehold property as far out of the reach of creditors as was consistent with that other maxim of justice and good policy, that all just debts ought to be paid when the debtor has any property wherewith to pay them. These we think are sufficient reasons for the preference the law has given real over personal property; and notwithstanding the construction contended for, I believe it has always been understood since the passing of this act, that the rule of law is so.[45]

Haywood claimed that protections from creditors increased the number of freeholders in the society. Heirs' traditional procedural privileges strengthened the republican nature of the society by increasing the likelihood that freehold estates would descend through the generations.

In contrast to North Carolina, where the Debt Recovery Act was given a qualified acceptance into the body of remedial law, the legislatures and courts in Virginia, Pennsylvania, and Delaware never fully implemented the Act. Indeed, after Independence, Virginia rejected a proposal to reenact the Debt Recovery Act and instead maintained the traditional English remedial regime until 1849.[46] Pennsylvania and Delaware maintained the remedial regimes they had adopted in the colonial era: their policy was to sell a debtor's land at auction only if the judgment exceeded seven years of earnings off the debtor's land. These policies remained good law through at least 1920 in Pennsylvania and through 1925 in Delaware.[47] In Virginia, Pennsylvania, and Delaware, the writ of *elegit*—giving a creditor a right to the income from land, but not a title interest—remained an important creditor remedy throughout the nineteenth century.[48] These states' policies reflected the perspective that land was a natural family endowment, and ideally a source of family prosperity through the generations. Thomas Jefferson's comment that no natural right permits burdening the family property with debts, although derived from English conceptions of natural law, might also be viewed as an intellectual development emerging after more than fifty-five years under the regime of the Debt Recovery Act. Virginia planters, under Parliament's Debt Recovery Act, had experienced decades of a legal alternative to the property laws of England and chose to adopt English law when it came to protections of land from creditors' claims.

Some Virginians opposed Virginia's body of laws on grounds that its property exemptions were economically detrimental. One Virginian's letter of November 14, 1787, published under the name "A True Friend," argued that Virginia's protection of land from creditors harmed Virginians and the Virginia economy.[49] The author suggested that Parliament's role in monitoring colonial legislatures to advance English economic interests was crucial to Virginia's economic development, and he expressed fear about the absence of Parliament as a check on local legislatures.[50]

According to the letter, Virginians remained "in the chains of British slavery"[51] because state laws protecting land drove capital elsewhere, even though "[w]e have the best mortgage to offer, which is immense and fruitful lands." Virginians thus:

[H]ave enjoyed none of the great advantages, which independence promised us. . . . For this axiom is certain, *nothing is lent those that have nothing, and credit is offered, at its lowest rate, to those that offer the best securities.* Therefore as long as the law will subsist in Virginia that the creditor cannot seize, lay attachment and sell the land of his debtor, at the epoch the debt fall due, it is as we had nothing, and as long as it will be by the tediousness of the courts of justice almost impossible to force the debtor, we shall not find money lenders, none but usurers will offer, that will ruin us.—Specie of course will turn its course towards other states that will have better and more political laws.

America (and principally Virginia) is of necessity a borrower. The extent of her lands which demand great advances to grub them up, her commerce just rising of which the first funds ought to be laid, and her manufactures of chief wants which ought to be established, require assistance and credit. When we were under the tuition of Great-Britain, she presided over our laws, and in a manner digested them. We could pass no act tending to hurt, or annihilate the rights and interests of British creditors; consequently they did not fear to advance considerable sums, on which they drew an annual interest higher than the rate in England, besides the profits arising from a trade in which the balance was always in their favor, and which has brought us five millions of pounds sterling in their debt. Those services and advances, though so dearly bought, were however indispensable, and augmented in a greater proportion the mass of the produce of population, and of our territorial riches. By running in debt with the mother country, America increased really in power. We may from thence judge how much more rapid and prodigious her progress would be, was she, (as she might) by her union and unanimity, to purchase at this moment her assistance cheaper, and in a way less burdensome for her. It would be then only she would enjoy the advantages of her liberty and of her independence.[52]

As this letter suggests, some Virginians thought that the economic implications of rejecting the principles of the Debt Recovery Act would be severe.[53]

Reforming Institutions: The Abolition of the Fee Tail

During the late eighteenth and early nineteenth centuries, Virginia, along with New York, Georgia, North Carolina, Kentucky, and later Missouri and Mississippi, abolished the fee tail. What was the difference between property exemptions and the fee tail? The property exemptions in English law, which the Debt Recovery Act removed, prevented courts from selling a debtor's land to satisfy unsecured creditors. They did not prohibit creditors from foreclosing on land that had been voluntarily pledged as collateral. In contrast, the fee tail allowed property owners to entirely shield their property from creditors for the benefit of the next heir: entailed land could not be pledged as collateral or used to satisfy debts. Abolishing the entail was both symbolic and important because it removed the strongest tool landowners and slaveowners had to shield their property from creditors.

For historians and property law scholars, the abolition of the fee tail by many states during the American Revolutionary period serves as a principal symbol of the power of republican ideology during the founding era. The prevailing history is based on a narrative most prominently put forth in Thomas Jefferson's *Autobiography* of 1821. Jefferson introduced the bill to abolish the entail in Virginia in 1776. (A loophole was found in the text of the 1776 statute, and the entail was abolished by a more expansive statute enacted in 1785.)[54] Nearly fifty years later, Jefferson's *Autobiography* claimed personal credit for the abolition of the entail in Virginia as a principal achievement of republican transformation: to Jefferson, it prevented rule by an "aristocracy of wealth," instead making "an opening for the aristocracy of virtue and talent" and laying "a foundation . . . for a government truly republican."[55]

Historians tend to accept Jefferson's characterization of the abolition of the entail as a great symbol of the anti-aristocratic ideology of the American Revolution.[56] For many decades, however, historical scholarship was heavily influenced by work from C. Ray Keim, presented first in a 1926 PhD dissertation and published in 1968. Amidst a rich description of the practice of entailing property, Keim documented that only a small percentage of Virginia wills and deeds created estates in fee tail. Keim concluded that entail "was not a general custom" among small property holders, and that only in the Tidewater region did the practice have a "somewhat general use even among the great planter class."[57] Keim's essay led to a consensus view that the abolition of the entail was highly important symbolically, but did not radically alter existing land practices.

The principal work questioning the dominant consensus was that of Bernard Bailyn, who emphasized the incompatibility of entail and slavery as an explanation for why the entail was not likely to have been used in the slave South. According to Bailyn, in colonial Virginia, "[a] mobile labor force free from legal entanglements and a rapid turnover of lands, not a permanent hereditary estate, were prerequisites of family prosperity."[58] Bailyn's interpretation relied on primary materials from Virginia as well as C. Ray Keim's data that only a small percentage of land was entailed.

In 1998, however, Holly Brewer revealed that Keim's work suffered from a serious methodological flaw: Keim overlooked the fact that once land was entailed, there was no need to "re-entail" the land in subsequent conveyances. Keim thus vastly undercounted the amount of land that was held in fee tail in Virginia.[59] Brewer's account, which showed a much more significant use of the practice, seems to confirm Jefferson's evaluation of Virginia's 1776 act as an important hallmark of republicanism.[60] Brewer notes that the greater quantity of fee tail land calls Bailyn's thesis into question.[61]

This book suggests that the role of the entail as a wealth-shielding device complicates the anti-aristocratic account. As chapter 5 described, a principal function of the entail in the colonies was to reduce risk. It was used to shield small estates as well as large estates from financial risk. Indeed, the entail might have buffered against land consolidation. Moreover, women were often owners of land in fee tail. The impact on small owners and women transforms the Jeffersonian account of the American Revolution. The abolition of the entail in the founding era exposed many property owners, large and small, men and women, to greater economic risk.

If the entail had a useful role in risk management in colonial America, why was it abolished? The dominance of the Jeffersonian, anti-aristocratic characterization of the entail has led historians to overlook that during the 1770s and 1780s, only some state legislatures abolished the entail. Other state legislatures *reformed* the entail, but retained it. It was retained in Pennsylvania where, according to Gordon S. Wood, "[m]ore than any other colony in 1776 the Revolution . . . was viewed as a social conflict between people and aristocracy."[62] Landowners could entail land in Pennsylvania until 1855.[63] The history of which states merely reformed the entail and which states abolished the entail, and understanding the purposes of those different approaches, is essential to understanding founding era republicanism.

At the heart of founding era reforms to property law was a desire for the transparency, security of property rights, and the reliability of title and mortgage records. Concerns about the entail often were concerns about transparency. States reformed the entail by requiring recordation, by limiting entails to one generation, and by lowering the costs of converting entailed land to fee simple. These reforms suggest that one of the most important legacies of the founding era in the realm of property was the advance of an institutional revolution toward a property and credit system rooted in a low-cost ability to publicly transmit information about property assets, and the priority of claims against those assets.

Why did some states abolish the entail entirely? Abolishing the entail certainly held symbolic importance as an anti-aristocratic measure, particularly in North Carolina and Virginia, which practiced an unusually strict version of entail law. One aspect of the republicanism interpretation is clearly correct: Political leaders in the founding era wanted to eradicate all vestiges of hereditary privilege. Various state constitutions and, ultimately, the US Constitution, prohibited titles of nobility. The opposition to government-sanctioned privileges based on birth and not on merit was deep and intense.[64] The structure of the fee tail—son to eldest male heir, daughter to eldest male heir—was reminiscent of English birthright and repugnant to republican ideals.

It is clear from the historical record that abolishing the entail had symbolic importance in advancing republicanism in the founding era in Virginia and North Carolina. North Carolina's law abolishing entails is the most striking evidence that the intention was to equalize wealth. It states that "entails of estates tends only to raise the wealth and importance of particular families and individuals, giving them an unequal and undue influence in a republic, and prove in manifold instances the source of great contention and injustice."[65] Virginia's 1776 law abolishing entails similarly explains as one reason for the act that "the perpetuation of property in certain families, by means of gifts made to them in fee taille, is contrary to good policy."[66] In addition to Jefferson's 1821 autobiography, legal thinkers such as James Kent and St. George Tucker interpreted abolishing the entail as a measure taken against inherited privilege.[67]

However, republicanism and the abolition of the entail cannot be truly understood without an understanding of their connections to slavery.[68] The states that completely abolished the entail were those relying most heavily on slave labor: Virginia, Georgia, North Carolina, New York, Kentucky, and later Missouri and Mississippi (South Carolina never recognized the fee tail). Thus, consistent with Bernard Bailyn's interpretation, the abolition of the entail increased the effective use of slave property in cultivation and as a source of credit and made slavery more profitable.

THE FOUNDING ERA INSTITUTIONAL REFORM TOWARD GREATER TRANSPARENCY

In the founding era, where the entail was reformed rather than abolished, the reforms were part of a broader movement to eliminate English conveyancing practices, to lower fees, to increase transparency in credit markets, and to enhance the reliability of the land title registration system. States, such as Pennsylvania, that reformed the entail after the Revolution, addressed two of its principal problems: (1) the entail increased the costs of credit because the entailed status of land was not likely to be readily apparent to outside creditors and purchasers; and (2) the high costs of the common recovery, the English conveyancing procedure used to remove entails from land.[69] In sum, the reformers wanted the entail to be used more inexpensively, flexibly, and transparently.

The cost to credit markets of the lack of transparency of the fee tail had long been recognized as an important problem. Blackstone and others more generally criticized the fee tail estate for its negative impacts on credit markets related to land. According to Blackstone, before the fee tail could be barred by a common recovery, "creditors were defrauded of their debts; for, if tenant in tail could have charged his estate with their payment, he might also have defeated his issue, by mortgaging it for as much as it was worth: innumerable latent entails were produced to deprive purchasers of the lands they had fairly bought; of suits in consequence of which our antient books are full."[70] Similarly, the Virginia act abolishing the entail provided as a primary justification that the entail "tends to deceive fair traders, who give a credit on the visible possession of such estates."[71]

How did the entail affect credit markets? Entails were not recorded in a single location. Land could be entailed in wills (probate records) as well as in deeds (land records). Purchasers and creditors might need to search the entire body of records, because entails ran with the land and, as an example, an entail created in 1660 would still be valid against a mortgage creditor in 1760. To find the removal of an entail, one would need to look for either records of a common recovery in the court records or a legislative act. In most colonies, to verify with certainty that land and slaves were not encumbered by entails, creditors or purchasers would have to search the entire body of land records and probate records and, depending upon the colony, either the records of the court of common pleas or the legislative acts.

States in the Middle Atlantic and Northeast reformed the entail in the founding era: by requiring the recordation of conveyances that entailed land; by limiting the duration of an entail to the current generation; and by substituting a streamlined deed approach for the English common recovery. Each of these reforms made land title records far more reliable and useful. Requiring recordation of all conveyances that entailed land ensured that the interest of subsequent purchasers or mortgage lenders could no longer be undermined by undiscovered devises or conveyances.

Second, New Jersey's and Connecticut's laws limiting entails to one generation boosted the reliability of the land records.[72] Under English and colonial law, the entailed status of land carried through the generations until the entail was formally removed. It was, therefore, possible to produce a will from decades earlier proving an interest in tail by someone who was not in possession of the land. Limiting the entail to one generation eliminated that problem, while shielding the land, unless and until the owner chose to remove the entail.

Third, the Pennsylvania, Massachusetts, Maryland, and New Jersey statutes allowed owners in fee tail to convert entailed land into fee simple by a simple deed process.[73] These statutes eliminated the need for the costly English common recovery. As the 1784 New Jersey statute reforming the entail stated, "Heirs are put to great Expence in suing out Recoveries, in order to dock such Entails."[74] Similarly, Maryland's entail reform of 1782 addressed the "heavy expence and great inconvenience" of common recoveries.[75]

The movement to legally reform the entail in states such as Pennsylvania, Massachusetts, Maryland, New Jersey, and Connecticut has been overlooked in historical accounts emphasizing the anti-aristocratic symbolism of the abolition of the fee tail. In these states, the primary founding era reform movement was directed toward lowering costs and increasing transparency in the legal institutions established to clear title and to promote land and mortgage markets. These reforms, however, were entirely consistent with "commercial republicanism." Recording title, conveying land, and obtaining credit on the basis of public land records promoted a society based not on family reputation or patronage ties, but on the basis of recorded assets.

THE ABOLITION OF THE ENTAIL IN THE SOUTH

Despite the egalitarian appeal of abolishing the entail, the broad popular support for the reform is better explained by its economic benefits. Impediments to liquid land markets imposed unique costs to a plantation agricultural system based on slave labor. It bears repeating that the entail was only abolished in Virginia (1776, 1785),[76] Georgia (1777),[77] New York (1782, 1786),[78] North Carolina (1784),[79] Kentucky (1796),[80] and later, Mississippi (1812)[81] and Missouri (1816),[82] and that South Carolina never recognized the entail.

Colonists were deeply concerned about the impact of the entail on credit markets. As described, Virginia abolished the entail with respect to creditors' claims on slaves in 1727 because to do otherwise, according to the legislature, "may destroy the credit of the country."[83] The 1727 entail law, however, raised a new set of problems in relation to a central feature of Southern land use practices. Increasing investments in slave labor led to an emphasis on intensive staple crop production associated with high rates of land exhaustion. With regard to tobacco, for example, the historian James H. Soltow has noted that "the exhausting nature of tobacco cultivation generally required abandonment in three or four years. Exhausted land returned to timber regained some of its fertility in twenty years or so, but it was less productive than new lands."[84] Agricultural manuals from the late eighteenth and early nineteenth centuries emphasized that tobacco grown on fresh lands was of better quality, which meant that tobacco cultivation typically involved moving slaves to clear and cultivate new land on a continual basis. According to *American Husbandry*, a book on colonial agricultural practices published in 1775 for the benefit of Londoners invested in the colonies, "There is no plant in the world that requires richer land, or more manure than tobacco; it will grow on poorer fields, but not to yield crops that are sufficiently profitable to pay the expences of negroes &c. . . . [T]his makes the tobacco planters more solicitous for new land than any other people in America, they wanting it much *more*."[85]

Similarly, a pamphlet from 1800 noted that in Virginia, "*new* ground . . . may be there considered synonymous with *tobacco* ground. . . . for a Virginian never thinks of reinstating or manuring his land with economy until he can find no more *new* land to exhaust, or wear out, as he calls it."[86] In 1761, the Virginia legislature removed an entail on land because the land was "cut down, and the soil exhausted" and the owner could then entail other land which "being fresh, might be worked with slaves to a greater profit for the estate."[87] Slaveowners constantly moved their slaves to new areas where the slaves cultivated new land to greater profit. The mobility of plantation labor forces, however, increased the cost of the fee tail and increased the effect of uncertainty over the status of land and slaves—that is, entailed or not—and resulted in a dampening effect on credit liquidity. It is likely the entail was abolished because of its costs to vital credit markets and land markets where institutional solutions did not present themselves.[88]

As mentioned, Jefferson's 1776 statute describes as one reason for its enactment that the expenses of removing entails on estates "of small value, was burthensome to the publick, and also to individuals."[89] In Georgia, colonists opposed the form of entail law in operation because it prevented the land consolidation that some residents desired. Empirical studies have shown that after the Revolution, in the Southern states where the entail was abolished, the profitability of slavery led large slaveholders to outbid non-slaveholders in land markets, which led to substantial inequality and, according to the economic historian David Weiman, to "'pre-emptive' displacement [of yeoman households] to more marginal soils."[90] The current historical literature has overlooked that the abolition of the entail might have accelerated the land consolidation observed after the American Revolution.

The wealth-shielding aspect of the entail is equally important to our understanding of Anglo-American property law. It is extremely important to recognize that today's body of property law contains within it an important example of wealth shielding that originated centuries ago. The entail enabled individuals to select particular assets to be immune from creditors' claims, despite the lack of transparency and additional costs to credit markets. Abolishing the entail in the South subjected all landowners, small and large, male and female, to greater financial risk, and its connection to the economy rooted in slave labor is highly conspicuous.

8

Property and Credit in the Early Republic

In gaining independence from British rule, the colonists rejected the extractive taxes and trade policies that they felt would suppress economic growth. Parliament's Currency Act of 1764 prohibited colonial governments from enacting currency policies to stimulate credit markets by expanding liquidity. The Stamp Act of 1765 would have extracted wealth by taxing institutions fundamental to the colonial economy, while the Townshend Acts and Coercive Acts imposed further taxes and threatened colonial autonomy and prosperity. Independence ended these threats but posed the question of what role the new federal government would play in regulating state legislatures and how much power it would have to standardize state laws on property rights, the credit markets, and the economy.

James Madison proposed in the Constitutional Convention that the federal Congress should have the power, as Parliament had before, to veto, or negative, any state laws. He recommended to George Washington the inclusion of a "negative *in all cases whatsoever* on the legislative acts of the States, as heretofore exercised by the Kingly prerogative."[1] Madison's proposal was rejected. Instead, the US Constitution included the Contracts Clause, which holds that: "No State shall . . . pass any . . . Law impairing the Obligation of Contracts." The Contracts Clause was intended to prevent the most extreme debt relief measures, like those that colonial legislatures implemented to provide temporary remedies in periods of economic hardship, from damaging property interests and credit markets. Fundamentally, however, the popularity of strong state-level governance remained high.

Property Exemptions and Federalism

The issue of exempting land from creditors' claims was debated in relation to national, as well as local, policy. The dueling imperatives of expanding access to credit and protecting debtors during recessions remained a source of contention in the early Republic. The Debt Recovery Act model, of course, was one of a uniform policy toward property exemptions determined at the highest levels of legislative authority. Ceding responsibility over creditors' remedies to the state legislatures reflected both a rejection of the parliamentary model of centralized control and a recognition of the economic and cultural discrepancies between states in the founding era. In the new United States, not only did states retain legislative authority over their own court procedures and remedial regimes, but the states also insisted that the federal courts recognize and implement the local state execution processes in the cases that they decided.[2] In 1790, President George Washington advised Congress to consider "whether an uniform process of execution, on sentences issuing from the Federal courts, be not desirable through all the States."[3] But opposition to a federal policy on remedies for creditors was strong enough that one was not enacted for much of the nineteenth century, meaning that the federal courts were required to implement the relevant state remedies in federal court litigation.[4]

The question of whether land would be available to satisfy unsecured debts emerged with respect to two other issues of national policy. One issue was what laws should apply to the Northwest Territory. Congress adopted Pennsylvania's policy of allowing sale of the debtor's property only if the debt exceeded seven years of the property's earnings.[5] Protecting land from seizure for small debts was thought to attract settlers to frontier areas.

The issue of whether land would be available to satisfy debts was also central to the debates over the nation's first bankruptcy legislation. In accordance with all of the legislation proposed before Congress, a bankrupt's lands would be seized and sold as a condition of obtaining a fresh start. As early as 1792, Thomas Jefferson questioned the desirability of a federal policy involving "seizing and selling lands." He noted that "[h]itherto, we had imagined the General Government could not meddle with the title to lands."[6] He emphasized that bankruptcy legislation providing for the sale of land was suited for a commercial or mercantile society, but not one based on agriculture. Jefferson asked:

> Is Commerce so much the basis of the existence of the U.S. as to call for a bankrupt law? On the contrary are we not almost merely agricultural? Should not all laws be made with a view essentially to the husbandman? When laws are wanting for particular descriptions of other callings, should not the husbandman be carefully excepted from their operation, and preserved under that of the general system only, which general system is fitted to the condition of the husbandman?[7]

In the debates over the Bankruptcy Bill of 1798 (the first bankruptcy bill that was seriously considered), the Federalists, however, were dedicated to a legal regime where property exemptions were minimal and where credit terms were improved to promote economic development. For example, James A. Bayard, a young Federalist, described state law making land immune from the payment of debts as "a remnant of the feudal system, of the principle of the ancient aristocracy of England, which was imported hither from that country by our ancestors."[8] To Bayard, the "principle goes to the root of commercial credit; because a merchant must know, that if he gives credit to a large amount, that the whole of that money may be vested in land by his debtor, and then he cannot touch it. . . . Commerce, and a law like this, cannot live and flourish on the same soil."[9] The Republicans, in contrast, wanted a general exemption from the statute for all agrarian debtors. Albert Gallatin, the most prominent Republican in Congress, argued that protections on land, such as Virginia's adoption of English law on remedies or Pennsylvania's limitation on execution sales to debts larger than seven years' worth of earnings, were necessary "in order to prevent the sacrificing of land at a rate so much below its value as it must sometimes be sold for, if it were always liable to be sold for debt, as personal property."[10] A Bankruptcy Act allowing execution against a bankrupt's land was enacted in April 1800, but it was repealed three years later under the Jefferson administration.[11] Tension between states over property exemptions was a central reason for the failure of bankruptcy legislation for much of the nineteenth century.[12]

Property Exemptions in Early Nineteenth-Century History

The subsequent decades saw a building up of protections to land ownership at the state level. Over the course of the nineteenth century, economic recessions were routinely followed by law reform movements that expanded protections for debtors' assets from the claims of creditors.[13] In the 1820s, even as politicians like Daniel Webster were praising laws that boosted creditors' abilities to seize land from debtors, the popularity of reforming such laws was growing. The preference for exempting some property from seizure was increasing among those who believed that subjecting all forms of property to commercial risk jeopardized democracy—or at least the livelihoods of families within the democracy—by creating conditions in which a mere economic downturn might lead a family to be forced out of the landowning class and into the ranks of the indigent.

During the early nineteenth century, state legislatures enacted laws exempting various types of personal property from the claims of creditors. A New Hampshire law of 1807, for example, listed the items that were protected from creditors:

> wearing apparel necessary for immediate use, one comfortable bed, bedstead and bedding necessary for the same, the bibles and school books in actual family use, together with one cow, and one swine, or in case the debtor be a mechanic, tools of his occupation to the value of twenty dollars in lieu of said Cow shall be altogether exempted from attachment and execution.[14]

The first major wave of reform laws, however, consisted of enactments in the aftermath of the recession of 1817 to 1818.[15] In those years, many states enacted more temporary stays on execution as well as "appraisal laws," which required that land only be sold if the price constituted a specified percentage (say two-thirds) of the property's value, as determined in an appraisal.[16] Many state legislatures also expanded the amount of personal property that was exempt from unsecured creditors' claims[17] and enacted statutory periods during which mortgagors and other debtors could redeem their property after creditors obtained judgments in a court of law. The Revised Statutes of the State of New York of 1829, for example, introduced a statutory period of redemption of fifteen months, during which mortgagors could redeem their property after a judgment at law.[18] Notwithstanding these legal reforms, the colonial era Debt Recovery Act still had a profound impact during this period. Indeed, legal scholar James Kent's treatise of 1830 states that the absence of any right of redemption in eight states (New Jersey, Maryland, North Carolina, Tennessee, South Carolina, Georgia, Alabama, and Mississippi) was due to the influence of the Debt Recovery Act of 1732.[19]

Further reforms occurred when the Panic of 1837 led to a widespread movement among state legislatures to go beyond former laws and to provide means by which homeowners could register and record their property as entirely exempt from the claims of creditors.[20] In the 1840s, almost every state enacted a law allowing married women to hold and register property in their own names—property that would be exempt from the claims of their husbands' creditors.[21] Then, over the next few decades (and particularly in the 1850s), state legislatures sheltered land from creditors' claims through homestead exemption laws based either on a minimum number of acres (typically ranging from 40 to 160 acres) or on a set monetary value of land.[22] States enacted laws providing for periods of time during which mortgagors could redeem their property after foreclosure. These laws—a partial return to the estate protections of early modern England—remain on the books today in some form.

But for more than a century, from 1732 to the 1850s, American property law offered few protections from commercial risks outside of the voluntary use of fee tails in Virginia, North Carolina, and other instances. Joseph Story explained this legal development as "a natural result of the condition of the people in a new country, who possessed little monied capital; whose wants were numerous; and whose desire of credit was correspondingly great."[23] Story is likely correct that the economic conditions of the colonies, the lack of internal capital sources, and the desire for credit might explain why colonial opposition to the Debt Recovery Act was not stronger. But Story's explanation does not capture the profound effects of the Debt Recovery Act on American economic, social, and political life.

The most important effect was to diminish the role of landed inheritance in American society by privileging the claims of creditors over heirs when debtors died. In England, land descended automatically to the heir free of the deceased's unsecured debts. In contrast, in America under the Debt Recovery Act regime, the inheritance of land occurred only when the deceased's debts were small enough to be satisfied out of the deceased's personal property. The profound impact of the Debt Recovery Act on inheritance is clearly expressed in writings assessing the Act after the American Revolution: in the 1803 South Carolina case of *D'Urphey v. Nelson*, in which the judge referred to the Debt Recovery Act as an explanation for why "the extreme anxiety observable in the common law of England to preserve the rights, and favor the claims, of the heir at law, *has been entirely dismissed from our law*"; in a lower court opinion in the New York case, *Waters*, which described exempting land from debts as a result of the "solicitude of the holders of landed estates, to perpetuate them within families, combined with the genius of the English government," which was "*local*, . . . confined to Great Britain, and not . . . extending to its colonies"; and in the Federalist congressman James Bayard's description of the exemption of land from creditors' claims as a "remnant of the feudal system, of the principle of the ancient aristocracy of England."

These tensions between expanding access to credit and protecting private property from creditors, between laws allowing the entailing of plantation land and slaves and those prohibiting the same, were important components of founding era debates over the legal preconditions of a republic. American republicanism was the outgrowth of earlier transformations toward truly "colonial" laws: laws developed in a colonial framework and suited to meet the ends of colonial imperatives. The ideology of the founding era was more than simply the combination of Enlightenment philosophy with hostility toward English rule during the run-up to the American Revolution: It was an expression of how far American social, economic, and political life had diverged from that of the English.

This book also ties the American dismantling of English inheritance law to slavery. In enacting the Debt Recovery Act, Parliament was centrally concerned with the laws of colonies that relied on English credit to import increasing numbers of slaves. The American adoption of English laws exempting property from debt was most threatening to creditors when that "property" was human beings. Slaves could be hidden from creditors or be sold and converted into land safe from seizure, or a colonial legislature might enact a law defining slaves as "land" and therefore as exempt from creditors' claims. The Debt Recovery Act promoted the slave trade by explicitly repealing all colonial property exemptions to land, houses, and slaves and by requiring colonial courts to administer streamlined processes for seizing each of these assets. In response to abolitionist protest, in 1797 Parliament repealed the Debt Recovery Act with respect to slaves in all of the remaining British colonies. In America, however, the Debt Recovery Act regime for slaves remained a fixture of the law. Indeed, after the American Revolution, when republicanism was at its strongest, America was moving toward a regime of pure "chattel" slavery.

Another important consequence of colonial era laws and institutions was to expand the commodification of land. Streamlining the process for recording titles and mortgages and simplifying the procedures associated with the sale of land by execution made it easier and less costly for both unsecured and secured creditors to seize land, and laid the foundation for more liquid land markets.

During the eighteenth century, the English exemptions of land from creditors' claims led, in Britain, to a categorical division between landholders, whose wealth was protected from immediate financial risks, and "merchants" and "traders" who by definition became people whose assets were subjected to greater financial risk. In 1732, Parliament introduced bankruptcy legislation that offered a fresh start to people legally defined as "traders," who were willing to give up their land to satisfy debts in the proceedings.[24] In 1807, Parliament enacted a more expansive statute stating that all land of persons defined as "traders" would be available to satisfy their unsecured debts both during life and at the time of death.[25] In America after the Revolution, the vast differences in local preferences on the issue of creditors' remedies expressed themselves not through occupational categorization, but instead through interstate variation and hostility toward federal government policies that might have imposed a uniform regime reminiscent of the Debt Recovery Act. Federalism emerged, in part, in response to the hostility toward Britain's colonial policies. The legacies of these policies—and of the reactions to them—still affect American economic, social, and political developments today.

9

Property, Institutions, and Economic Growth in Colonial America

For many decades, scholars have focused on institutional foundations and property rights as central determinants in countries' economic and political well-being. This chapter places the book's description of how property rights were defined, enforced, and managed in the British American colonies within the economic history literature. As scholars have identified, property rights are central to both political and economic life. With regard to political life, property rights help define an individual's authority over her person and belongings (land, creative works, possessions, etc.) vis-à-vis her relationship to the state. A democratic form of government presupposes a citizenry that enjoys spheres of individual autonomy made secure by the legal protection of property rights. Political-related property rights include protections of property from state confiscation, legal requirements for searches and seizures of property and, more broadly, voting and other constitutional rights.[1]

Property rights are also fundamental to a market economy, for different but at times overlapping reasons. Property rights grant "decisionmaking authority over access and use" of valuable resources.[2] Within a market-oriented culture, property rights structure incentives toward investing labor and resources in value-enhancing ways.[3] Private property allows communities, families, individuals, or firms to "reap what they have sown": to decide how resources are invested in and used; to decide the timing of extraction or sale in the market; and to gain the profits achieved on the basis of those decisions and investments.[4] Within a market-oriented society, property rights work in the aggregate: where property rights are protected, the cumulative effects of families', individuals', and firms' value-enhancing investments in their property raise the society's total wealth. Of course, most, if not all, societies have social, political, and economic systems that exclude or disadvantage certain groups while privileging others. In early America, the conquest of Native American land, slavery, and rules denying property rights to married women are examples of how property rights protection was used to concentrate economic and political power in the hands of some members of the society at the expense of others; at the same time the more equal land ownership among free Whites created a perception of relative equality within the government system.

In addition to protecting property rights, a legal system can promote economic exchange by clarifying and publicizing property rights. The legal scholars Thomas Merrill and Henry Smith emphasize that a principal purpose of property law is to reduce information costs relating to property entitlements.[5] Merrill and Smith note that most legal systems limit property rights to a set number of standardized forms ("fee simple," "lease," etc.). When a legal system recognizes idiosyncratic property forms, creditors and purchasers must expend increased search costs to determine the nature of the property interests in question before lending money on the basis of the collateral or buying the property. In contrast, clarifying property interests through standardization lowers information costs, spreading benefits in the market.[6]

Responding to Merrill and Smith, Henry Hansmann and Reinier Kraakman noted that information costs in property markets are driven more by the problem of verification of ownership rights than the relative simplicity or complexity of the property forms themselves. They assert that recording systems and other institutional devices to publicize rights are essential in reducing information costs.[7] Thus, legal definitions of property rights and institutional frameworks for publicizing property interests work together in a market economy: transactions costs are reduced and market activity enhanced when property rights are clearly defined and when title and encumbrances are made transparent through institutions. Chapter 2 describes how colonial governments adopted title and mortgage recording to publicize interests in property.

Within the field of economic history, the line of inquiry relating the importance of property and institutions to economic growth is most prominently associated with the work of Douglass C. North. North's *Institutions,*

Institutional Change, and Economic Performance (1990) asserts that by analyzing history through the lens of institutions, which he defines broadly as structural and cultural constraints, one can better understand a society's ability to adopt institutions that protect property rights promoting economic growth.[8] In the spirit of North, the economists Darren Acemoglu, Simon Johnson, and James Robinson have emphasized that "Countries with better '*institutions*,' more secure property rights, and less distortionary policies will invest more in physical and human capital, and will use these factors more efficiently to achieve a greater level of income."[9]

Measuring the impact of institutions on economic growth, however, presents substantial challenges. There is an endogeneity problem: Are property rights and institutions a product of a wealthy society, or are they what explains the creation of wealth? Looking for an exogenous variable, economists such as Rafael La Porta, Florencio Lopez-de-Silanes, and Andrei Shleifer focused on former colonies where European law was transplanted and documented strong correlations between modern-day economic measures of prosperity and a country's "legal origin." Legal origin in this literature refers to whether a country's legal system is based on the British common law or whether it is rooted in the French, German, or Scandinavian civil law. The former colonies of Britain, which instituted the common law, have had greater economic growth, and have stronger protection of property, than countries whose colonizer had a legal system rooted in the civil law.[10]

Acemoglu, Johnson, and Robinson advanced the legal origins literature by demonstrating that where colonists physically settled, rather than simply oversaw the expropriation of wealth, the legal regime led to greater economic growth over the long term. They examined settler mortality rates to approximate, inversely, the extent of law and institutions brought by the colonizers. The theory is that in settler societies, colonists "tried to replicate European institutions, with strong emphasis on private property and checks against government power." Where mortality rates were high, fewer Europeans settled and colonial powers were more likely to engage in extractive and exploitative forms of imperialism.[11] In a separate article, Acemoglu, Johnson, and Robinson find an "institutional reversal" that European colonialism led to the introduction of institutions of private property in previously poor areas. In contrast, colonies with preexisting profitable extractive industries, such as mining, failed to introduce institutions of private property that would disperse wealth throughout the society.[12]

This book describes how British American colonial legal institutions and debtor/creditor law departed from the institutions and property laws of

England. A new "colonial law" emerged that reflected the transplantation of English law, laws enacted by colonial assemblies, and continued oversight and legal regulation by Parliament and the Crown. In this sense, British law of the seventeenth and eighteenth centuries offered what Joel Mokyr has described as *meta-institutions*, that is, institutions that make possible a "high capacity for endogenous institutional change" because they "change and set the formal rules under which other institutions operate[]."[13] Mokyr emphasizes the British Parliament's role as a meta-institution domestically within England, but his argument applies equally to the British American colonies of the seventeenth and eighteenth centuries. European colonists brought with them a connection to European culture and updated their cultural beliefs as they absorbed Enlightenment ideas that developed in Europe after 1680. Enlightenment culture accepted "that it was the role of the state to enhance prosperity and growth and to encourage the formation and dissemination of useful knowledge."[14]

In the case of colonial governments, a system of federalism emerged where the colonial representative assemblies actively reshaped the legal regime to meet their local interests. At the same time, the British Crown provided not only military defense, but also oversight of colonial lawmaking. British oversight took place in several ways: by parliamentary law; through the crown-appointed colonial governors and the Board of Trade, an English governmental body constituted to supervise colonial matters; as well as by the Privy Council, the final court of appeal for colonial cases.[15] Historians have long recognized that British oversight of the colonies was limited until the 1760s. The Debt Recovery Act of 1732, which enacted a regime of creditors' remedies throughout the colonies, is an important counterpoint to the otherwise relatively loose oversight that allowed colonial representative assemblies the ability to enact new laws on behalf of their landowning and slaveholding constituencies.

At the foundation of the market economy in colonial America were formal legal institutions and a body of laws that protected property interests when individuals used their property for exchange in the market or as collateral for credit, as well as, in many colonies, a system of property that commodified both land and human beings (slaves). The colonists streamlined specific legal institutions, such as the common pleas courts and affiliated recording mechanisms, that allowed property owners to confirm and publicize titles, to convey property, and to record mortgages. Moreover, the same institutions provided creditors with remedies against debtors in the event debtors defaulted on agreements. The justices of the peace and other officials applied bodies of English common law, colonial-enacted statutory law, and parliamentary law such as (1) laws defining the assets—including land and slaves—that were available, through legal process, to be taken by mortgage creditors and unsecured creditors in satisfaction of debts; (2) inheritance laws that established priority over assets between creditors and family members when a debtor died; (3) laws and property forms (fee tail) that served to enable individuals or the society to manage financial risk.

The historical work here is related to the conceptual argument put forward in Katharina Pistor's *The Code of Capital* (2019), which asserts that capitalism is based on a "legal code" that allows individuals to use assets to generate wealth.[16] Similarly, the economist Hernando de Soto has attributed global wealth disparities to the ability of ground-level legal institutions to protect property rights and encourage entrepreneurialism. De Soto's *The Other Path* focuses on the institutional changes necessary to bring the tremendous entrepreneurial activities taking place in the informal economy into the formal sector. [17] De Soto's *The Mystery of Capital* makes two distinct arguments about property and institutions, the second of which is related to the subject of this book.[18] De Soto has famously advocated for policies formally recognizing private property rights in individuals squatting on land previously held by the state. *Mystery of Capital* includes a chapter titled "The Missing Lessons of U.S. History," which focuses on the "early American tradition of squatting" and the legal mechanisms adopted to formally recognize and validate informal claims to property.[19] The second argument made in *Mystery of Capital* relates to the reform of legal institutions necessary to allow property to be used to access capital. To de Soto, economic prosperity depends upon local policies that allow individuals to convert assets into fungible and liquid wealth. *Mystery of Capital*'s prescription for economic growth involves building institutions that confer clear title to property, that enable assets to be used as collateral, and that enforce credit agreements, so long as the institutions do not impose bureaucratic hurdles and fees that push market participants into the informal sector.[20] De Soto's work has been criticized for its perhaps mistaken assumption that formal title systems will be supported by state and economic institutions that allow the citizenry to gain the economic benefits of formalization.[21]

This book places in historical context the enactment of laws and the establishment of legal institutions underlying property rights in colonial America. It describes how local representative assemblies, with oversight from British colonial authorities, developed institutions that offered processes for confirming titles to land and extending property as collateral for debts, which are a central foundation of modern economic life.[22]

Did the adoption in the British colonies of formal legal institutions and a body of laws that promoted credit markets lead to economic growth? The legal origins and other economic history literature, described above, suggest that the answer is likely to be "yes" over the long term. The contemporary sources that form the basis of this book indicate that colonists believed laws promoting credit markets were essential to the economy. The next section, however, discusses the complexities in making causal claims about the effect of property law and legal institutions in colonial America on economic growth. First, slavery was central to colonial American economic history and complicates the understanding of the colonial past and its legacies. Second, it examines the current economic history literature on growth rates in colonial British America that provides insufficient data to support a causal claim that legal institutions affected growth. Finally, it discusses the central tradeoff, from an economic standpoint, of a legal regime that is centered on maximizing the remedies available to creditors. The focus in British colonial America on protecting creditors' immediate economic interests with few protections for debtors increased the financial risk in the society. To fully understand the impact of laws and institutions relating to credit markets, it is important to consider the tradeoff between growth and the problems that stem from financial risk.

The Complexities of Colonial Law and Institutions in Economic History

PROPERTY LAW, LEGAL INSTITUTIONS, AND SLAVERY

The centrality of slaves as a form of property is ubiquitous throughout the historical legal records of many colonies in British America. Colonial administrations created a law of slavery, defined slaves as property, provided recordation of slave mortgages, and used legal institutions to sell and auction slaves to satisfy debts. One cannot understand the history of property law and legal institutions in colonial British America without accounting for slavery. More work is needed, but existing evidence suggests that slaves might have constituted the collateral in mortgages that account for more than half the total funds extended in some colonies.[23] The historical evidence also suggests, for example, that slavery led to the institutional "innovation" of the first chattel mortgage laws in the country. Mortgage law traditionally applied to land, but as described in chapter 2, Carolina's recording statute of 1698 stated that "the Sale or Mortgage of Negroes, Goods or Chattels which shall be first recorded in the Secretary's office in *Charles-Town*, shall be . . . held to be the first Mortgage."[24] Yet, the profound harms of slavery to slaves as individuals, and to the society overall, make the colonial body of laws promoting the use of property as collateral run against standard whiggish narratives of economic history.

Beyond the harm to individual slaves, the long-term growth trajectory of economies relying on slave labor was poor. As Gavin Wright has described in *Slavery and American Economic Development*, slavery often emerged in areas with the highest land values. Slavery was most profitable in areas with the best soil for growing lucrative staple crops.[25] Slavery was often associated with mono-culture staple crop production, which led to land exhaustion, meaning that slaveholders often sought out new land and migrated to new regions in search of the greatest profits.[26] Although there are numerous examples of slaves working in diverse jobs such as iron mills and shipping, over a large range the economic development brought on by reliance on slave labor was often highly specialized in staple crop production. These regions lacked the commercial diversity of areas reliant on free labor, lacked equivalent infrastructure development such as roads and bridges, lacked equivalent public education, and impoverished large portions of the population.

Slaveholders amassed great wealth: If one includes the value of slaves as part of the per capita property, the South had far higher wealth per capita (per free capita) than the North in 1860. But, omitting the slaves as property, the South had lower wealth per free capita than the North.[27] As Wright has emphasized, regions in America relying on slave labor failed to adopt the types of institutions that would attract immigrants.[28] The economic history is complex, but even beyond the systems of racial subjugation that persist today, the laws and institutions promoting slavery weakened the economic health of many states over the long term.

DID THE COLONIAL LEGAL REGIME LEAD TO ECONOMIC GROWTH?

Contemporary sources consistently reveal the perception that credit terms were improved and economic conditions were advanced by laws expanding the property available for creditors to take in satisfaction of their debts.

As described in chapter 4, for example, in 1739, Jamaica enacted a law that responded to the Debt Recovery Act by lowering the legal interest (usury) rate by 20%, from an interest rate of 10% to 8%.[29] The law stated that

> [w]hereas by an act of parliament . . . entitled, "An act for the more easy recovery of debts in his majesty's plantations and colonies in America," creditors in the colonies are secured [in] their debts in a more ample manner than when interest was established in this island at [10% per year], it was appropriate that in all "mortgages, bonds, and other specialities" that the legal interest rate be reduced to "eight pounds for the forbearance of one hundred pounds for a year.[30]

Without further evidence it is not clear what role the usury rate played in trade relations, but even the perception among legislators that the Debt Recovery Act brought about a 20% decline in the interest rate reflects that there was likely a significant effect of the act—spread out over thousands of secured transactions—on credit available for productive investment. Other colonial sources also suggest that contemporaries thought creditors' remedies expanded commerce. To give merely one example, after the 1776 Declaration of Independence, North Carolina enacted a law to reassure foreign creditors that they would be able to use legal process to seize land in satisfaction of their debts. North Carolina's statute of 1777 announced that it was written for "divers Persons residing in other States or Governments [who] contract Debts with the Inhabitants of this State." It clarifies that "by the Policy and Genius of our present Constitution, *Lands and Tenements ought to be made subject to the Payment of just Debts*" when debtors "hath not within the Limits of this State Goods and Chattels sufficient to satisfy the same."[31]

Why would the North Carolina legislature enact a law telling out-of-state creditors about the scope of remedies available in its courts? The state legislators clearly thought that the promise of expansive remedies would increase the credit offered to its inhabitants. As described throughout the book, voluminous sources confirm that colonists perceived a clear connection between laws, institutions, and the costs of credit. In 1833, Supreme Court Justice Joseph Story's *Commentaries on the Constitution* described how the New England colonies defined land as "chattel," and how the Debt Recovery Act expanded the reach of creditors' claims to include virtually all property owned by debtors. To Story, these laws had made land "a substitute for money," which he explained as "a natural result of the condition of the people in a new country, who possessed little monied capital; whose wants were numerous; and whose desire of credit was correspondingly great." He added, "the growth of the respective colonies was in no small degree affected by" this legal transformation.[32]

Jacob M. Price and Russell R. Menard similarly have contrasted the "Anglo-Saxon or creditor defense model" of legal remedies against the land with the "Latin model" used in Brazil where, under Portuguese rule, landed estates were protected from creditors' claim.[33] Menard attributes the rise of centralized plantation slavery in Barbados, but not in Brazil, to the fact that broader creditor protections encouraged greater financial investment.[34] If one adopts wealth maximization as the criterion to evaluate a legal regime, it is likely that the policy that lowers interest rates will achieve the greatest wealth in the long run, provided it does not create economic upheaval and social instability.

The current economic history literature concludes that free colonists' standard of living was high on average relative to Britain, however, the high standard of living is not reflected in rates of growth. Alice Hanson Jones's 1980 study of probate records near the time of Independence moved her to conclude that personal wealth levels reveal a standard of living that was "probably the highest achieved for the great bulk of the population in any country up to that time."[35] Robert Allen, Tommy Murphy, and Eric Schneider examined wages in relation to cost of living and found that laborers in Philadelphia had approximately 25% higher wages than laborers in London.[36] Peter Lindert's and Jeffrey Williamson's large-scale project to examine income distribution suggests that incomes per capita in the British American colonies were higher than in England by 1774 and were more equally distributed.[37] These studies suggest that laborers were paid well and income levels among the free White population compare favorably with Britain.

Per capita economic growth rates, however, are a different matter, although there is consensus that the economy expanded consistently starting in the 1740s. In a review of the current economic literature, Joshua Rosenbloom concludes that "after overcoming the initial challenges of settlement the pace of aggregate economic growth was quite small."[38] John McCusker's and Russell Menard's *Economy of British America* estimates that the per capita income in the colonial economy was in the range of 0.3% to 0.6% per year, and that growth in the colonial era likely occurred in two "spurts": the first as settlers initially moved to each colony and developed farms, and the second beginning in the 1740s and lasting until the Revolution.[39] They found that average annual per capita exports from Great Britain to the continental colonies rose from £0.9, in 1699–1704, to £1.20, in 1767–1774.[40] Import and export rates are a proxy for transatlantic credit markets in the colonial era. The colonies lacked banks or other financial institutions. Extending "credit" often consisted of transferring goods or other property (say, manufactured items from England), with repayment in other goods at a later time (say, items for export like tobacco). The sustained growth of imports and exports after 1740 is notable. An important reason why growth in the colonies is difficult to measure, however, is that most of the economy produced for local, domestic markets, and credit markets were correspondingly local. Peter Mancall and Thomas Weiss estimated that colonial exports amounted to about 10% of economic activity throughout the eighteenth century.[41] And Mancall, Rosenbloom, and Weiss estimated that even in the lower South, where production for export was a more significant part of the economy, foreign exports only amounted to 20–25% of gross domestic product.[42] The existing data likely do not offer a good measure of the extent of commerce.

Per capita figures must be considered in light of high rates of population growth during the colonial period, although the impact of immigration on growth is unclear given the existing evidence. Population growth distorts the correlation between per capita wealth and economic expansion when newly added members of a society have lower than average incomes (for example, immigrants and newborns). Factoring in high levels of population growth means that the average total economic growth figures are not inconsiderable, especially for a developing economy.[43] In the case of colonial British America, however, Ran Abramitzky's and Fabio Braggion's research on indentured servant contracts concluded that immigration to the American mainland colonies was "positively selected" for people with high human capital who could contribute to the economy.[44] Immigration is therefore unlikely to explain low economic growth rates.

What impact did the Debt Recovery Act have on the colonial economy? As chapter 3 shows, most colonies had modified the English law to some degree prior to 1732, so it is necessary to examine the history of each colony's laws to understand the legal changes required under the Debt Recovery Act. More generally, it is difficult to measure the impact of the Debt Recovery Act, or any law, on the economy. The existing figures on import levels would not capture the effect of the Act because changes in other factors, such as, for example, the demand for tobacco and other exports, would likely outweigh the impact of the legal regime. These data caution against causal claims about colonial legal regimes and economic growth. The current legal origins literature, described above, suggests strongly that the former colonies of Britain have had higher economic growth over the long term than colonies of other European powers. Again, contemporaries believed these laws and institutions were essential to obtaining better terms of credit, an underpinning of the economy. The purpose of this book is to offer a legal history of credit, to present research on the history of laws and legal institutions that formed the foundation of the colonial market economy and served as one of the origins of capitalism. The hope is that the legal history offered here may help further work by economic historians.

THE PROBLEM OF FINANCIAL RISK

A final complexity in analyzing the impact of the colonial legal regime on growth is that laws and institutions designed to mazimize credit and liquidity increase the level of financial risk in society. The pervasive use of property as collateral for credit introduces the possibility of widespread foreclosures and a lack of social stability. One issue in examining the risk created by a legal regime relates to temporal considerations. Ex ante, an individual or the society might want laws that maximize the extension of credit and that lower interest rates. Providing expansive protections for creditors against debtors' default and creating conditions for competitive lending markets might be enacted as popular measures to achieve those ends. Later in time, ex post, the society's financial conditions might decline. When individuals are unable to repay debts on a widespread basis, popularity of property or homestead exemptions (which legally exempt certain property from the claims of creditors), measures to delay debt collection or foreclosure, as well as other debtor protections, might gain popularity, even in places where creditor-protective measures were preferred ex ante.

In a notable example from the nineteenth century, the economists Rachel Kranton and Anand Swamy found that when the British introduced new laws and civil commercial courts in the Bombay Deccan in India, an immediate effect was that interest rates declined, allowing landowners to have far greater access to credit. In a subsequent economic downturn, however, the foreclosures on land—newly offered as a remedy by the British courts— led to civil unrest and were a cause of the Deccan Riots against the British in 1875.[45] Debtor protection measures likely make good economic sense when the defaults are a result of widespread recession (rather than individual delinquency). Thus, the economically optimal policy might be to enact "creditor-friendly" and "debtor-protective" measures at different times in the same legal jurisdiction.

Analyzing the tradeoffs between protections to creditors—which lower interest rates ex ante, and protections for debtors—which ameliorate recessionary conditions ex post, is highly complex. Each local community is likely to want to decide how much financial risk it wants to assume. Chapters 3 and 4 describe in detail the legal history of property exemptions in colonial British America. In Britain in the seventeenth and eighteenth centuries, landowners could voluntarily mortgage their land, which offered the remedy of foreclosure (loss of title), but they could not lose their title to land through the legal claims of unsecured creditors. A central question in the British colonies was whether English protections on land from unsecured creditors would be adopted and apply to colonial land and slaves. Prior to 1732, each colonial administration was able to enact its own policies with regard to the status of land and slaves in the colonies. As chapter 3 describes, beginning in the seventeenth century, several colonies modified English law by defining land as a chattel—and therefore subject to unsecured creditors' claims. Other colonies retained English law and protected title interests to land from unsecured creditors. Then in 1732, Parliament enacted the Debt Recovery Act which held that, throughout all of the British colonies, all land, houses, and slaves could be taken involuntarily by legal process to satisfy all unsecured debts. Moreover, the law was mandatory and colonial legislatures could no longer enact new legislation on the subject. In essence, as a matter of the general law (fee tail aside) there were no more than minute property exemptions from unsecured creditors in the British American colonies after 1732.

In the founding era, each state had the opportunity to set its own policies with regard to the remedies available to creditors. Beginning in the 1840s, homestead exemption laws were widely enacted throughout the states to protect landowners from financial risk. When the first federal bankruptcy laws were enacted in the nineteenth century, differences between states on the nature of the property exemptions from creditors' claims were one issue preventing a uniform, national policy. Even today, our federal bankruptcy law defers to state law to define property exemptions. Thus there may be no perfectly "right" answer in balancing the tradeoff between lower interest rates and measures to reduce financial risk. The existing economic history scholarship has not engaged sufficiently with measures that remediate against risk.

—

Yet, one pillar of the capitalist economy we inherited from the past are credit markets that allow the use of property as collateral to access funds for investment. The colonial creation of functioning legal institutions that protected property titles, that made interests in property transparent, and that allowed individuals to pledge their property as collateral for debts, set the stage for the rapid economic advance of the United States. At the same time, the introduction of slavery associated with the same laws brought four centuries of stark injustice toward initially hundreds of thousands of Africans suffering the slave trade, and millions of descendants. The Debt Recovery Act was a foundation for a future capitalist economy and, by requiring courts to hold slave auctions to satisfy creditors' claims, brought legal formality to colonial practices of racial subordination. The laws and legal institutions of the colonial era that allowed individuals to vastly expand the liquidity of the economy remain at the foundation of today's economy.

10

Conclusion

The history of the laws and legal institutions underlying the colonial credit economy speaks to the history of our democracy and capitalist society. The rise of representative government was closely connected with the ownership of property—both land and slaves—in the history of the United States. In colonial British America, democracy originated in assemblies of property owners often at odds with the policies of royally appointed governors. These first representative legislatures viewed the protection of property interests as a principal role of government.

In the colonial era, the policy of the British authorities was to distribute land to settlers in small parcels, in order to maximize the land under cultivation and thereby increase the wealth of the realm. Encouraging immigration from Europe and the importation of slaves were explicit policy goals. It was feared that granting land in large parcels might lead to land being held in reserve, delaying cultivation. Cash crops helped Britain's balance of trade; landowners who cultivated crops could afford to consume more imports from England. But in granting small parcels and promoting slavery, the Crown appears to have been indifferent to the political repercussions on colonial society. By creating a nation of landowners and slaveholders, these colonial policies unwittingly laid the foundation for a republican society, radically different from England. The emphasis on property ownership also led to the focus on individual rights. As Joseph Story explained, early Americans' "jealous watchfulness of their rights and . . . a steady spirit of resistance against every encroachment" was a character trait flowing from the fact that the "yeomanry are absolute owners of the soil, on which they tread."

The laws and legal institutions developed in colonial America for protecting property rights were an essential foundation underlying the credit system. Security of title was the linchpin of the economic and political system. The simplicity and relatively low cost of American conveyancing allowed landowners to buy and sell property as a liquid asset. Allowing individuals to use their property as assets from which to draw credit led to the creation of wealth that could be used for further development or spent on consumption that increased the nation's wealth. In the eighteenth century, the paper money and debt instruments issued by the Bank of England expanded Britain's liquid wealth. In Britain's American colonies, legal institutions such as the common law courts, title recording devices, and a body of laws that clarified the terms of credit and the remedies of creditors laid the foundation for the expansion of credit, and capitalism, in the nascent United States.

At the same time, the credit system promoted the growth of slavery. Property held in slaves was a central underpinning of colonial American credit markets; mortgages on slaves were used to purchase yet more slaves. The rate at which slaves were shipped to the colonies was highest in the two decades before the Revolution. As Edmund S. Morgan explained in *American Freedom, American Slavery* (1975), "[t]he rise of liberty and equality in America had been accompanied by the rise in slavery." When Thomas Jefferson wrote in the Declaration of Independence that "all men are created equal," he owned more than one hundred slaves. The supposed equality of Whites was in counterpoint to the brutally unequal system that subjugated Black slaves. The economic prosperity that better access to credit made possible for White Americans rested in part on the increased suffering of enslaved Africans.

This book has described the evolution of laws governing credit in early America. The desire for increased credit was a thread running through British parliamentary legislation, colonial innovations in laws and institutions, and ultimately, the desire for independence. It led early colonial legislatures to adopt local title recording with transparency as a goal and led New England colonies to treat land as a "chattel" in the late seventeenth century. Parliament followed in 1732 with a law treating land, slaves, and other property as chattel in the context of creditors' claims. These policies reshaped the nature of inheritance, making land no longer a fundamental birthright of an heir. They promoted slavery, a form of servitude that expanded dramatically when slaves became the principal collateral for debts. The colonial legislatures enacted currency policies to expand liquidity and manage risk. When Parliament's Stamp Act taxed ground-level economic institutional services to generate revenue for the Crown, the colonists responded with the movement for independence. The lasting legacy of treating land like a commodity, the legacy of slavery, and the economic institutions created in colonial British America and still functioning today remain at the foundation of our economic and political life.

NOTES

Introduction

1. Max Farrand, ed., *The Records of the Federal Convention of 1787* (New Haven, CT: Yale University Press, 1937), vol. 1, 302.

2. See Robert J. Steinfeld, "Property and Suffrage in the Early American Republic," *Stanford Law Review* 41 (1989): 335–76, 339–40; Alexander Keyssar, *The Right to Vote: The Contested History of Democracy in the United States* (New York: Basic Books, 2000), ch. 1.

3. Philip S. Foner, ed., *The Complete Writings of Thomas Paine* (New York: Citadel Press, 1945), vol. 1, 203. Similarly, the historian Edmund S. Morgan has emphasized that "widespread ownership of property is perhaps the most important single fact about Americans of the Revolutionary period." Edmund S. Morgan, *The Birth of the Republic* (Chicago: University of Chicago Press, 1992), 8.

4. Daniel Webster, "A Discourse Delivered at Plymouth, December 22, 1820, in Commemoration of the First Settlement of New-England," Fourth edition. (Boston, MA: Wells and Lilly, 1826), 41.

5. Ibid., 43–44.

6. As A.W.B. Simpson has noted, in England through the late eighteenth century, land was acquired more frequently to gain "locally based political and social power" than for reasons of geographic mobility. A. W. B. Simpson, "Land Ownership and Economic Freedom," in *The State and Freedom of Contract*, ed. Harry N. Scheiber (Stanford: Stanford University Press, 1998), 13–43, 33. The House of Lords was constituted by the peers of the realm, a group of approximately two hundred landowners of large estates who held hereditary titles of nobility that passed by inheritance. See Gordon S. Wood, *The Radicalism of the American Revolution* (New York: Vintage Books, 1993), 25. In 1881, a study of English land ownership relying on *The New Domesday Book of 1871* estimated that "a landed aristocracy consisting of about 2,250 persons own together nearly half the enclosed land in England and Wales." George C. Brodrick, *English Land and English Landlords* (London: Cassel, Petter, Galpin & Co. 1881), 165.

7. See generally David Sugarman and Ronnie Warrington, "Land Law, citizenship, and the invention of 'Englishness.' The strange world of the equity of redemption," in *Early Modern Conceptions of Property*, ed. John Brewer and Susan Staves (New York: Routledge, 1996): 111–43, 121–25 (emphasizing English law's support for the landed class). This legal preference reflected a powerful social preference for cohesive estates. See John Habakkuk, *Marriage, Debt, and the Estates System, English Landownership,1650–1950* (New York: Oxford University Press, 1994), 55 ("The sense of obligation to keep the patrimony intact and in the family was so strong that the owner of an inherited estate of any reasonable size and antiquity, even when he was the last of his line and was free to dispose of the property, did not naturally consider selling it, unless his financial circumstances obliged him to do so. He sought among his friends or acquaintances for someone to continue the undivided ownership").

8. William Blackstone, *Commentaries on the Laws of England* (Chicago: University of Chicago Press, facsimile ed. 1979, 1765–69), vol. 2, 201.

9. Noah Webster, *An Examination into the Leading Principles of the Federal Constitution* (Philadelphia, PA: Prichard & Hall, 1787), 47.

10. See Paul Langford, *Public Life and the Propertied Englishman, 1689–1798* (Oxford: Clarendon Press; New York: Oxford University Press, 1991), 51.

11. James Kent, *Commentaries on American Law* (Buffalo, NY: Hein, 1984 repr.; New York: 1830), vol. 4, 450. Nathan Dane's *Digest of American Law* of the 1820s similarly states that English conveyancing law was a remnant of "the course of many centuries, and from the dangers and fears of confiscations in civil wars, the encroachment of the clergy, the numerous estates tail, and many other circumstances peculiar to those times, and to that country. . . . No simple, plain, valid, and intelligible form of conveyance by deed, was there introduced by the legislature, as it was here." Nathan Dane, *A General Abridgment and Digest of American Law: with Occasional Notes and Comments* (Boston: Cummings, Hilliard & Co., 1824), vol. 4, ch. 109, 88.

12. See the sources cited in Philip Hamburger, "The Conveyancing Purposes of the Statute of Frauds," *American Journal of Legal History* 27, no. 4 (1983): 354–85.

13. Joseph Story, *Commentaries on the Constitution of the United States* (Boston: Hilliard, Gray, & Co., 1833), book 1, §173, 160. Nathan Dane's legal treatise on Massachusetts in the 1820s concludes, "The English principles of law in regard to leases, are, on the whole, not much a subject of attention in this State; comparatively but few estates are leased." Dane, *Digest of American Law*, vol. 4, ch. 110, 127.

14. Story, *Commentaries*, book 1, §174, 160.

15. Ibid., 161.

16. Ibid, §182, 168.

17. Zephaniah Swift, *A System of the Laws of the State of Connecticut: In six books* (New York: Arno Press, 1972, repr.; Windham, CT: Printed by John Byrne, for the author, 1795), vol. 1, 313.

18. Webster, "A Discourse Delivered at Plymouth, December 22, 1820," 41.

19. Kent, *Commentaries*, vol. 4, 438.

20. The legal scholar Aziz Rana describes "the two faces of American freedom": that the settler society conception of US freedom was rooted in subordination of groups including Native American conquest and slavery. Aziz Rana, *The Two Faces of American Freedom* (Cambridge, MA: Harvard University Press, 2010). Both stories of conquest, over land and people, are foundational to the capitalist society we inherited from the past.

21. Gavin Wright, *Slavery and American Economic Development* (Baton Rouge: Louisiana State University Press, 2006), 62.

22. Bonnie Martin, "Neighbor to Neighbor Capitalism: Local Credit Networks and the Mortgaging of Slaves," in *Slavery's Capitalism: A New History of American Economic Development*, ed. Sven Beckert and Seth Rockman (Philadelphia: University of Pennsylvania Press, 2016): 107–21; Bonnie Martin, "Slavery's Invisible Engine: Mortgaging Human Property," *Journal of Southern History* 76, no. 4 (November 2010): 817–66; Bonnie Martin, "Silver Buckles and Slaves: *Borrowing, Lending, and the Commodification of Slaves in Virginia Communities*," in *New Directions in Slavery Studies: Commodification, Community, and Comparison*, ed. Jeff Forret and Christine E. Sears (Baton Rouge: Louisiana State University Press, 2015), 30–52; Edward E. Baptist, *The Half Has Never Been Told: Slavery and the Making of American Capitalism* (New York: Basic Books, 2014); Edward E. Baptist, "Toxic Debt, Liar Loans, Collateralized and Securitized Human Beings, and the Panic of 1837," in *Capitalism Takes Command: The Social Transformation of Nineteenth-Century America*, ed. Michael Zakim and Gary J. Kornblith (Chicago: University of Chicago Press, 2012), 69–92, 72, 89; Suresh Naidu, Felipe González, and Guillermo Marshall, "Start-Up Nation? Slave Wealth and Entrepreneurship in Civil War Maryland," *Journal of Economic History* 77, no. 2 (July 2017): 373–405; Carl Wennerlind, *Casualties of Credit: The English Financial Revolution,*

1620–1720 (Cambridge, MA: Harvard University Press, 2011), 230. An essential work is Richard Holcombe Kilbourne, Jr., *Debt, Investment, Slaves: Credit Relations in East Feliciana Parish, Louisiana, 1825–1885* (Tuscaloosa: University of Alabama Press, 1995). According to Kilbourne:

> Slaves represented a huge store of highly liquid wealth that ensured the financial stability and viability of planting operations even after a succession of bad harvests, years of low prices, or both. Slave property clearly collateralized a variety of credit instruments and was by far the most liquid asset in most planter portfolios. . . . [A]n investment in slaves was a rational choice, given the alternatives for storing savings in the middle of the [nineteenth] century. (5)

23. John J. McCusker and Russell R. Menard, *The Economy of British America, 1607–1789* (Chapel Hill: University of North Carolina Press, Institute for Early American History and Culture, 1985), 54 and table 3.1.

24. Alice Hanson Jones, *Wealth of a Nation to Be: The American Colonies on the Eve of the Revolution* (New York: Columbia University Press, 1980), 98 and table 4.5.

25. Petition of Several Merchants of the City of London (August 12, 1731), in *Calendar of State Papers Colonial, America and West Indies: Volume 38, 1731*, ed. Cecil Headlam and Arthur Percival Newton (London: His Majesty's Stationary Office, 1938), no. 367i, 224, 225, quoted in Board of Trade, *Representation of the Board of Trade Relating to the Laws Made, Manufacturers Set Up, and Trade Carried On, in His Majesty's Plantations in America* (n.p. 1734), 9; see also *Proceedings and Debates of the British Parliaments Respecting North America*, ed. Leo Francis Stock (Washington, DC: The Carnegie Institution of Washington, 1924–), vol. 4, 128 n.13, 130, 153–54 (referring to enactment of colonial statutes impeding the recovery of debts in parliamentary sessions of 1730 to 1732).

26. 5 Geo. 2, c. 7 (1732) (Eng.).

27. Story, *Commentaries*, book 1, §182, 168. For the Whig vision of colonial rule in the 1730s, see Steve Pincus, *The Heart of the Declaration: The Founders' Case for an Activist Government* (New Haven, CT: Yale University Press, 2016), 14–16.

28. Bryan Edwards, *The History of the British Colonies in the West Indies* (Philadelphia, PA: James Humphreys, 1806), vol. 2, 366. Thomas Russell, the modern scholar most knowledgeable about American slave auctions, identifies the Edwards essay as the earliest known writing on the frequency of slave auctions. See Thomas D. Russell, "A New Image of the Slave Auction: An Empirical Look at the Role of Law in Slave Sales and a Conceptual Reevaluation of Slave Property," *Cardozo Law Review* 18 (1996): 473–523, 481 (conducting an empirical analysis of slave auctions in antebellum South Carolina and finding that courts conducted or supervised a majority of slave auctions).

29. Edwards, *History of the British Colonies in the West Indies*, vol. 2, 366.

30. Ibid. 367–68.

31. 37 Geo. 3, c. 119 (1797) (Eng.).

32. William Knox, *The Interest of the Merchants and Manufacturers of Great Britain, in the Present Contest with the Colonies, Stated and Considered* (London, 1774) (London: University of London, Company of Goldsmiths, 1903), 35–36. See Jack P. Greene, "William Knox's Explanation for the American Revolution," *William and Mary Quarterly* 30, no. 2 (April 1973): 293–306, 293 ("[F]ew people in power in Britain thought more seriously or more deeply about the quarrel with the colonies at any stage of its development").

33. Knox, *Interest of the Merchants*, at 36, 38.

34. Alexander Hamilton, "Practical Proceedings in the Supreme Court of the State of New York" (circa. 1782), in *The Law Practice of Alexander Hamilton: Documents and Commentary*, ed. Julius Goebel, Jr. (New York: published under the auspices of the William Nelson Cromwell Foundation by Columbia University Press, 1964), vol. 1, 55–135, 97.

35. See, for example, Hernando de Soto, *The Mystery of Capital: Why Capitalism Triumphs in the West and Fails Everywhere Else* (New York: Basic Books, 2000); Katharina Pistor, *The Code of*

Capital: How Law Creates Wealth and Inequality (Princeton, NJ: Princeton University Press, 2019), 2; Rainer Haselmann, Katharina Pistor, and Vikrant Vig, "How Law Affects Lending," *Review of Financial Studies* 23 (February 2010): 549–80; Frederique Dahan and John Simpson, eds., *Secured Transactions Reform and Access to Credit* (Northampton, MA: Edward Elgar, 2008). A study in the 1990s estimated that barriers to secured transactions led to economic losses in Argentina and Bolivia amounting to 10–15% of their respective gross domestic products. Heywood Fleisig, "Secured Transactions: The Power of Collateral," *Finance & Development* (June 1996): 44–46; Heywood Fleisig, Mehnaz Safavian, and Nuria de la Peña, *Reforming Collateral Laws to Expand Access to Finance* (Washington, DC: World Bank, 2006).

36. Michael Zuckerman, *Peaceable Kingdoms: New England Towns in the Eighteenth Century* (US: W.W. Norton, 1978 (first published Toronto, Canada: George J. McLeod Ltd., 1970).

37. Examples are the field-defining work of Morton J. Horwitz, *The Transformation of American Law, 1780–1860* (Cambridge, MA: Harvard University Press, 1977) and James Willard Hurst, *Law and the Conditions of Freedom in the Nineteenth-Century United States* (Madison: University of Wisconsin Press, 1956).

38. Richard L. Bushman, *From Puritan to Yankee: Character and the Social Order in Connecticut, 1690–1765* (Cambridge, MA: Harvard University Press,1967); Christine Leigh Heyrman, *Commerce and Culture: The Maritime Communities of Colonial Massachusetts, 1690–1750* (New York: W.W. Norton, 1984); Winifred Barr Rothenberg, *From Market-Places to a Market Economy: The Transformation of Rural Massachusetts, 1750–1850* (Chicago: University of Chicago Press, 1992); Bernard Bailyn, *The New England Merchants in the Seventeenth Century* (Cambridge, MA: Harvard University Press, 1979), W. T. Baxter, *The House of Hancock: Business in Boston, 1724–1775* (Cambridge, MA: Harvard University Press, 1945); Virginia D. Harrington, *The New York Merchant on the Eve of the Revolution* (New York: Columbia University Press, 1935). On Virginia, see James H. Soltow, *The Economic Role of Williamsburg* (Williamsburg: University Press of Virginia, 1965). Scholars have emphasized the cultural aspects of early modern credit relations as well as the changing role of legal practices in local communities as the economy expanded in the eighteenth century. Margot C. Finn, *The Character of Credit: Personal Debt in English Culture, 1740–1914* (New York: Cambridge University Press, 2003); Craig Muldrew, *Economy of Obligation: The Culture of Credit and Social Relations in Early Modern England* (London: Palgrave Macmillan, 1998). On law and economic change in colonial New England, Cornelia Hughes Dayton, *Women Before the Bar: Gender, Law & Society in Connecticut, 1639–1789* (Chapel Hill: University of North Carolina Press, Omohundro Institute, 1995); Bruce H. Mann, *Neighbors and Strangers: Law and Community in Early Connecticut* (Chapel Hill: University of North Carolina Press, Studies in Legal History, 1987). See also Stanley L. Engerman and Robert E. Gallman, eds., *The Cambridge Economic History of the United States*, vol. 1 (Cambridge: Cambridge University Press, 1996). John J. McCusker and Russell R. Menard's account of the growth of the colonial economy by means of the movement of labor, management, and capital to the colonies remains a classic. John J. McCusker and Russell R. Menard, *The Economy of British America, 1607–1789* (Chapel Hill: University of North Carolina Press, Institute for Early American History and Culture, 1985). See also Edwin J. Perkins, *The Economy of Colonial America* (New York: Columbia University Press, 1980).

39. Bernard Bailyn, *The Ideological Origins of the American Revolution* (Cambridge, MA: Belknap Press, 1967); Gordon S. Wood, *The Creation of the American Republic, 1776–1787* (Chapel Hill: University of North Carolina Press, Institute of Early American Culture and History, 1969); Wood, *Radicalism of the American Revolution*. See also J.G.A. Pocock, *The Machiavellian Moment: Florentine Political Thought and the Atlantic Republican Tradition* (Princeton, NJ: Princeton University Press, 1975); Jack P. Greene, *The Constitutional Origins of the American Revolution* (New York: Cambridge University Press, 2011). Professor Jack P. Greene's early work, *The Quest for Power: The Lower Houses of Assembly in the Southern Royal Colonies, 1689–1776*, documented

in elaborate detail the colonial legislatures' efforts to gain power by building and controlling institutions and local political offices. According to Greene, "The rise of the representative assemblies was one of the most significant political and constitutional developments in the history of Britain's overseas empire before the American Revolution." Greene, *The Quest for Power: The Lower Houses of Assembly in the Southern Royal Colonies, 1689–1776* (Chapel Hill: University of North Carolina Press for the Institute of Early American History and Culture, 1963), 3. See also A. G. Roeber, *Faithful Magistrates and Republican Lawyers: Creators of Virginia Legal Culture, 1680–1810* (Chapel Hill: University of North Carolina Press, 1981). Similarly, an older generation of scholars offered sweeping histories of the British regulation of the colonies in the eighteenth century. See Charles M. Andrews, *The Colonial Period of American History* (New Haven, CT: Yale University Press, 1938). Sources cited in Claire Priest, "Law and Commerce, 1580–1815," in *The Cambridge History of Law in America*, ed. M. Grossberg and C. Tomlins (Cambridge: Cambridge University Press, 2008): 400–446.

40. Gregory S. Alexander, *Commodity and Propriety: Competing Visions of Property in American Legal Thought, 1776–1970* (Chicago: University of Chicago Press, 1997); Drew R. McCoy, *The Elusive Republic: Political Economy in Jeffersonian America* (Chapel Hill: University of North Carolina Press, 1980); Wood, *Radicalism of the American Revolution*; Holly Brewer, "Entailing Aristocracy in Colonial Virginia: 'Ancient Feudal Restraints' and Revolutionary Reform," *William and Mary Quarterly* 54, no. 2 (April 1997): 307–46; John F. Hart, "'A Less Proportion of Idle Proprietors': Madison, Property Rights, and the Abolition of the Fee Tail," *Washington and Lee Law Review* 58 (2001): 167–94; Stanley N. Katz, "Republicanism and the Law of Inheritance in the American Revolutionary Era," *Michigan Law Review* 76 (1977): 1–29, 3 ("In the study of revolution, the law of inheritance may serve as a touchstone measuring the depth of revolutionary transformation in a society"); Stanley N. Katz, "Thomas Jefferson and the Right to Property in Revolutionary America," *Journal of Law & Economics* 19 (1976): 467–88. Compare John V. Orth, "After the Revolution: 'Reform' of the Law of Inheritance," *Law & History Review* 10 (1992): 33–44 (emphasizing that the inheritance reforms of the Revolutionary Era could be evaded). Historians such as J.R.T. Hughes and Stuart Banner have focused on the transformation of property specifically, describing how property in the British American colonies shed many traditional English trappings as colonists adapted to the new environment. J.R.T. Hughes, *Social Control in the Colonial Economy* (Charlottesville: University Press of Virginia, 1976); Stuart Banner, *American Property: A History of How, Why, and What We Own* (Cambridge, MA: Harvard University Press, 2011).

41. Wood, *Radicalism of the American Revolution*, 269–70.

42. More recently, historians have shown that the Independence movement was driven by concerns that Lord Grenville's policies would suppress the colonial economy. Pincus, *The Heart of the Declaration: The Founders' Case for an Activist Government*. Pincus characterizes the Independence movement as a "a call to state formation": colonists wanted a strong state, capable of delivering Patriot policies "that would aim to promote prosperity for the largest number of people." Ibid., 92, 132. See also Justin DuRivage, *Revolution Against Empire: Taxes, Politics, and the Origins of American Independence* (New Haven, CT: Yale University Press, 2017), which situates the American Revolution in the context of Britain's contestation over theories of political economy. This work is consistent with the emphasis here: that the movement for independence was deeply concerned with matters relating to laws and legal institutions central to the economy.

43. Christine Desan asserts that the roots of capitalism lie in direct money creation by self-interested bankers as well as government banking institutions, when money became "a resource underwritten by public funds and endorsed for expansion by banks operating for profit." Christine Desan, *Making Money: Coin, Currency, and the Coming of Capitalism* (Oxford: Oxford University

Press, 2014), 5–6; P.G.M. Dickson, *The Financial Revolution in England: A Study in the Development of Public Credit, 1688–1756* (New York: Macmillan, 1967); Bray Hammond, *Banks and Politics in America: From the Revolution to the Civil War* (Princeton, NJ: Princeton University Press, 1957); Naomi R. Lamoreaux, *Insider Lending: Banks, Personal Connections and Economic Development in Industrial New England* (New York: Cambridge University Press, 1994); Claire Priest, "Currency Policy and Legal Development in Colonial New England," *Yale Law Journal* 110 (2001): 1303–1405.

44. Edmund S. Morgan, *American Slavery, American Freedom: The Ordeal of Colonial Virginia* (New York: W. W. Norton, 1975).

45. Eric Williams, *Capitalism and Slavery* (Chapel Hill: University of North Carolina Press, 1944). More recently, Carl Wennerlind revealed that the English slave trade provided the financial backing for the South Sea Company, which played an integral role in England's financial revolution but led to an early speculative bubble. Carl Wennerlind, *Casualties of Credit: The English Financial Revolution, 1620–1720* (Cambridge, MA: Harvard University Press, 2011); Barbara L. Solow and Stanley L. Engerman, eds., *British Capitalism and Caribbean Slavery: The Legacy of Eric Williams* (New York: Cambridge University Press, 1987). Robin L. Einhorn has shown how Southern slaveholding shaped tax-collecting capacity in colonial America and how the politics of slavery goes to the heart of how the US constitutional text should be interpreted. Robin L. Einhorn, *American Taxation, American Slavery* (Chicago: University of Chicago Press, 2006). See also Kenneth Morgan, *Slavery and Servitude in North America, 1607–1800* (Edinburgh: Edinburgh University Press, 2000). Christopher Tomlins's magisterial *Freedom Bound* offers a detailed description of the way that law structured power in labor relations, and in turn, the social and political context in which to understand colonial British America. According to Tomlins, "Law was the conceptual structure, the organizational discourse, by which their moves were enabled, the bridge that bore them across the ocean and planted them on the other side." Christopher Tomlins, *Freedom Bound: Law, Labor, and Civic Identity in Colonizing English America, 1580–1865* (Cambridge: Cambridge University Press, 2010), 69.

46. Seth Rockman, "What Makes the History of Capitalism Newsworthy?," *Journal of the Early Republic* 34, no. 3 (Fall 2014): 439–66.

Chapter 1. Colonial Land Distribution

1. See, e.g., Charter of Massachusetts Bay (March 4, 1629), www.avalon.law.yale.edu/subject_menus/17th. For a discussion of many colonial charters and proprietorships, see Christopher Tomlins, *Freedom Bound: Law, Labor, and Civic Identity in Colonizing English America, 1580–1865* (Cambridge: Cambridge University Press, 2010), 156–90.

2. See, e.g., Charter of Maryland (June 20, 1632), www.avalon.law.yale.edu/subject_menus/17th; Charter for the Province of Pennsylvania (February 28, 1681), www.avalon.law.yale.edu/subject_menus/17th.

3. At the time of the Revolution, Pennsylvania, Delaware, and Maryland remained as proprietary colonies, and New Hampshire, New York, New Jersey, Virginia, North Carolina, South Carolina, and Georgia were under direct royal rule. Marshall Harris, *The Origin of the Land Tenure System in America* (Ames: Iowa State College Press, 1953), 331–44. Connecticut, Massachusetts, and Rhode Island remained as corporate colonies. For further discussion of the classes of colonial administration, see Harris, 331–44, and also Viola Florence Barnes, "Land Tenure in English Colonial Charters of the Seventeenth Century," in *Essays in Colonial History Presented to Charles McLean Andrews* (New Haven, CT: Yale University Press, 1931), 4–40.

4. Colonial governors, according to the historian Mary Bilder, "symbolized the location of supreme authority in the settlement." Mary Sarah Bilder, "English Settlement and Local Governance," in *The Cambridge History of Law in America Volume 1: Early America (1580–1815)*, ed.

Michael Grossberg and Christopher Tomlins (New York: Cambridge University Press, 2008), 63–103, 84.

5. As Bilder notes, the council "advised the governor, sat as a court, composed the upper house in bicameral assemblies, and consulted in certain colonies on judicial and other appointments." Bilder, "English Settlement and Local Governance," 85.

6. See, e.g., Massachusetts Bay Charter of 1629.

7. See Mary Sarah Bilder, *The Transatlantic Constitution: Colonial Legal Culture and the Empire* (Cambridge, MA: Harvard University Press, 2004).

8. Edmund S. Morgan, *The Birth of the Republic, 1763–89*, 3rd ed. (Chicago: University of Chicago Press, 1992), 11.

9. As is clear from the vast body of surviving primary materials, and as Chris Tomlins has shown, an ethic of "improvement" of land pervaded property and immigration policy throughout the colonies. See Tomlins, *Freedom Bound.*

10. Robert Beverley, *The History and Present State of Virginia* (1705), reprint ed., introduction by Louis B. Wright (Chapel Hill: Published for the Institute of Early American History and Culture at Williamsburg, VA, by the University of North Carolina Press, 1947), 277. See Alan Taylor, *American Colonies* (New York: Penguin Group, 2001).

11. "An Act Concerning the Granting, Seating, and Planting, and for Settling the Titles and Bounds of Lands," (1705), *The Statutes at Large; Being a Collection of All the Laws of Virginia*, ed. William Waller Hening (Philadelphia, PA: Thomas Desilver, 1823), vol. 3, ch. 21, 304.

12. Ibid., 306.

13. Robert Beverley's notes that although indentured servants had the "Right to take up fifty Acres of Land" at the end of their term, "that is no great Privilege, for any one may have as good a right for a piece of Eight." Beverley, *The History and Present State of Virginia*, 277–78. I thank Al Sharp of the University of Virginia for the insight that his extensive work in the Virginia archives found only a small percentage of titles based on headrights, indicating the prevalence of direct purchases in land markets. The fact that British policy was to distribute land in small parcels was still of symbolic and practical importance for structuring colonial landownership.

14. Williams quoted in Edmund S. Morgan, *Roger Williams: The Church and the State* (New York: Harcourt, Brace & World, 1967), 122.

15. See Stuart Banner, *How the Indians Lost Their Land: Law and Power on the Frontier* (Cambridge, MA: Belknap Press, 2005), 15–16, 24.

16. Colin G. Calloway, *Pen and Ink Witchcraft: Treaties and Treaty-Making in American Indian History* (New York: Oxford University Press, 2013), 44.

17. Beverley, *The History and Present State of Virginia*, 278–79.

18. "Terms for Land Grants in New Colonies," in *Royal Instructions to British Colonial Governors, 1670–1776*, ed. Leonard Woods Labaree (New York, London: D. Appleton-Century, 1935), vol. 2, 528–29, §760.

19. See Edith M. Fox, *Land Speculation in the Mohawk Country* (Ithaca, NY: Cornell University Press, 1949), 3–4; Ray Allen Billington, "The Origin of the Land Speculator as a Frontier Type," *Agricultural History* 19, no. 4 (October 1945): 204–12.

20. Harris, *Origin of the Land Tenure System*, 76.

21. Lord Mansfield, Attorney General for the Governor (June 18, 1754), transcribed in Jack P. Greene, ed., "The Case of the Pistole Fee: The Report of a Hearing on the Pistole Fee Dispute Before the Privy Council, June 18, 1754," *Virginia Magazine of History and Biography* 66, no. 4 (1958): 399–422, 407–8.

22. George Clarke to Colden, September 22, 1731, Clarke Papers, cited in Edith M. Fox, *Land Speculation in the Mohawk Country.*

23. Gordon S. Wood, *The Radicalism of the American Revolution* (New York: Vintage Books, 1993), 77.

24. See, for e.g., John Frederick Martin, *Profits in the Wilderness: Entrepreneurship and the Founding of New England Towns in the Seventeenth Century* (Chapel Hill: Published for the Institute of Early American History and Culture, Williamsburg, Virginia, by the University of North Carolina Press, 1991), 25.

25. Joseph Dudley served on the Massachusetts Council in the 1680s, and the Council was heavily involved in confirming questionable titles to land that led to great profits for Dudley and the other members of the Council. Ibid., 90–91.

26. Ibid., 9.

27. Martin's examination of probate records revealed that town promoters held a median of 950 acres and an average of 2,910 acres at death, while the average landowner in early Connecticut held about 60–90 acres of land. Ibid., 30.

28. Charter of Massachusetts Bay (1629). www.avalon.law.yale.edu/subject_menus/17th. This is similar to the Charter of Carolina, March 24, 1663, which states that land will be held "as of our manner of East Greenwich in our county of Kent, in free and common soccage, and not in capite, or by knight service; yielding and paying yearly to us, our heirs and successors, for the same, the yearly rent of twenty marks of lawful money of England, at the feast of All Saints, yearly forever, the first payment thereof to begin and to be made on the feast of All Saints, which shall be in the year of our Lord one thousand six hundred and sixty-five, and also the fourth part of all gold or silver ore, which, within the limits aforesaid, shall from time to time happen to be found." Charter of Carolina, March 24 1663, www.avalon.law.yale.edu/subject_menus/17th. Similarly, the Pennsylvania Charter of 1691 states that land will be held "as of Our Castle of Windsor in Our County of Berks, in free and comon Socage, by fealty only for all Services, and not in Capite or by Knights Service: Yielding and paying therefore to Ifs, Our heires and Successors, Two Beaver Skins, to bee delivered at Our said Castle of Windsor on the First Day of January in every Year." Charter for the Province of Pennsylvania 1681, www.avalon.law.yale.edu/subject_menus/17th. All of the colonial charters granted land in "free and common socage" with a requirement that one-fifth of the precious minerals be paid to the Crown. Barnes, "Land Tenure in English Colonial Charters," 15.

29. William Blackstone, *Commentaries on the Laws of England* (Chicago: University of Chicago Press, facsimile ed. 1979, 1765–69), vol. 2, 59–60.

30. See Barnes, "Land Tenure in English Colonial Charters," 4–6.

31. Blackstone, *Commentaries*, vol. 2, 74–75.

32. Ibid., at 63–68, 78. In addition, feudal obligations included payments or "incidents" in the form of aids to support the knighting and marriage of the lord's eldest son and daughters, relief to take possession by inheritance, and wardship and marriage fines during the heir's infancy. Ibid. at 87. Payments or "aids" for knight service and socage were twenty shillings for every twenty pounds a year. 3 Edw. I, stat. 1, cap. 36, *Statutes of the Realm*, vol. 1, 35; 25 Edw. III, stat. 5, cap. 11, *Statutes of the Realm*, vol. 1, 322; Blackstone, *Commentaries*, vol. 2, 87. Tenants in chief paid a fine of one-third of the yearly value of the land for alienation. Barnes, "Land Tenure in English Colonial Charters," 7.

33. Blackstone, *Commentaries*, vol. 2, 80.

34. Land held by one of his manors, the tenant had to swear fealty and pay aids and relief but was not obliged to pay homage, pimer seisin, wardship, marriage, ouster le main, and fine on alienation. Barnes, "Land Tenure in the English Colonial Charters," 7. See also Sir James Ley, *A Learned Treatise Concerning Wards and Liveries* (London, UK: G. Bishop and R. White, 1642); William Noy, *The Compleat Lawyer; or A Treatise concerning Tenures and Estates in Lands of Inheritance for Life, etc.* (London, UK, 1661 ed.), 17–23.

35. Blackstone, *Commentaries*, vol. 2, 81. Blackstone states that "the tenure which prevails in Kent, called gavelkind, which is generally acknowledged to be a species of socage tenure; the preservation whereof inviolate from the innovations of the Norman conqueror is a fact universally known. And those who thus preserved their liberties were said to hold in *free* and *common* socage." Ibid.

36. Barnes, "Land Tenure in English Colonial Charters," 10–11; see also Harris, *Origins of the Land Tenure System*, 73; ed. Cecil T. Carr, *Select Charters of Trading Companies: 1530–1707* (London: B. Quaritch, 1913); William Dugdale, *The History of Imbanking and Draining of Divers Fens and Marshes* (London: W. Bowyer and J. Nichols, 1772).

37. See Barnes, "Land Tenure in English Colonial Charters," 11.

38. Ibid., 11–13.

39. Ibid., 22–34.

40. Charles W. McCurdy describes the resistance movements against feudal landholding practices in mid-nineteenth-century New York, in Charles W. McCurdy, *The Anti-Rent Era in New York Law and Politics, 1839–1865* (Chapel Hill: University of North Carolina Press, Studies in Legal History, 2001).

41. Factors typically earned a small percentage (such as 2.5–5%) of the gross sales of the goods. Factors remitted the proceeds of the sale (gross sales minus the commission, duties, and other expenses) either by purchasing bills of exchange or by providing a return cargo. See Jacob M. Price, *Capital and Credit in British Overseas Trade: The View from the Chesapeake, 1700–1776* (Cambridge, MA: Harvard University Press, 1980), 105 (2.5% charged by factorage firms selling wool and cloth on consignment in the Chesapeake region); Richard Pares, *Merchants and Planters* (New York: Cambridge University Press, Economic History Review Supplement, 1960), 31 (5% charged by French *commissionaires* in Martinique). The credit terms from England were generally twelve months. In order to pay their English debts on time, goods were offered locally on shorter credit terms, customarily the terms of credit ranged from six to twelve months, and possibly less. See, for example, Virginia D. Harrington, *The New York Merchant on the Eve of the Revolution* (New York, 1935), 103 (suggesting between 3 and 12 months as the customary terms for domestic credit); James H. Soltow, *The Economic Role of Williamsburg* (Williamsburg: University Press of Virginia, 1965), 133 (describing customary domestic credit terms as between 6 and 12 months).

42. Price, *Capital and Credit*. Merchants in the colonial era had diversified business practices. They were exporters, importers, wholesalers, retailers, purchasing agents, bankers, insurance underwriters, and attorneys. Arthur Louis Jensen, *The Maritime Commerce of Colonial Philadelphia* (Madison, WI: State Historical Society, 1963), 11.

43. Jacob Price found that factors selling wool and cloth in the Chesapeake charged an additional 2.5% to guarantee payments by purchasers. See Price, *Capital and Credit*, 105.

44. He continued, "[S]uch is the difference of character, of manners, of religion, of interest of the different colonies . . . [that] were they left to themselves, there would soon be a civil war, from one end of the continent to the other; while the Indians and Negroes would, with better reason, impatiently watch the opportunity of exterminating them all together." Andrew Burnaby, *Travels through the Middle Settlements in North America in the Years 1759 and 1760* (Dublin, Ireland: R. Marchbank, 1775), 202–3.

45. Soltow, *Economic Role of Williamsburg*, 41–44.

46. Adam Smith offers a classic account of the late-eighteenth-century "mercantile" view of colonies and their role in the British Empire. Adam Smith, *An Inquiry into the Nature and Causes of the Wealth of Nations*, ed. Edwin Cannan (1904) (Chicago: University of Chicago Press, 1976), vol. 2, 66–181. As Steve Pincus has emphasized, the Tory and Patriot Whig political parties had conflicting views of the role of colonies in the broader political economy of the time. See Steve Pincus, *The Heart of the Declaration: The Founders' Case for an Activist Government* (New Haven, CT: Yale University Press, 2016).

47. John J. McCusker and Russell R. Menard, *The Economy of British America, 1607–1789* (Chapel Hill: University of North Carolina Press, Institute for Early American History and Culture, 1985), at 108 table 5.2 and 199 table 9.3.

48. Curtis P. Nettels, *The Emergence of a National Economy, 1775–1815* (New York: Holt, Rinehart and Winston, 1962), 6.

49. Paul M. Kennedy, *The Rise and Fall of British Naval Mastery* (New York: Humanity Books, 1998), 21–22.

50. See, for example, Charter of Massachusetts Bay (March 4, 1629) (reserving for the Crown, "the fifte Parte of the Oare of Gould and Silver, which should from tyme to tyme, and at all Tymes then after happen to be found, gotten, had, and obteyned in, att, or within any of the saide Landes, Lymitts, Territories, and Precincts").

51. David W. Galenson, "The Settlement and Growth of the Colonies: Population, Labor, and Economic Development," in *The Cambridge Economic History of the United States, Volume 1, The Colonial Era*, ed. Stanley L. Engerman and Robert E. Gallman (Cambridge: Cambridge University Press, 1996): 135–207, 158. Galenson cites Abbot Emerson Smith, *Colonists in Bondage: White Servitude and Convict Labor in America, 1607–1776* (Chapel Hil: Published for the Institute of Early American History and Culture at Williamsburg, VA, by the University of North Carolina Press, 1947), 336.

52. The Trans-Atlantic and Intra-American Slave Trade Database estimates that 229,584 slaves landed in mainland North America via the Trans-Atlantic slave trade and that 35,175 slaves landed in mainland North America via the intra-American slave trade by 1776, https://www.slavevoyages.org/tast/index.faces.

53. See Edmund S. Morgan, *American Slavery, American Freedom: The Ordeal of Colonial Virginia* (New York: W. W. Norton, 1975), 71–107; Bernard Bailyn, *The New England Merchants in the Seventeenth Century* (Cambridge, MA: Harvard University Press, 1979), 2–15.

54. Kennedy, *Rise and Fall of British Naval Mastery*, 46.

55. An Act for the Encouragement of Trade, 15 Charles II, c. 7 (1663).

56. 12 Charles II, c. 18, sec. 18; see Henry Scobell, *A Collection of Acts and Ordinances of General Use*, (London: Henry Hills and John Field, 1658), vol. 2, 176–77. Prior to 1651, commercial statutes addressed particular colonies and particular products, such as a 1621 act requiring that all tobacco produced in Virginia be transported to England prior to being exported to foreign countries. For a more thorough discussion of mercantilism and British economic regulation of the colonies, see John J. McCusker, "British Mercantilist Policies and the American Colonies," in *The Cambridge Economic History of the United States, Volume 1, The Colonial Era*, ed. Stanley L. Engerman and Robert E. Gallman (Cambridge: Cambridge University Press, 1996), 337–62.

57. Robert Paul Thomas, "A Quantitative Approach to the Study of the Effects of British Imperial Policy upon Colonial Welfare: Some Preliminary Findings," *Journal of Economic History* 25, no. 4 (December 1965): 615–38, 619.

58. Harold E. Gillingham, *Marine Insurance Rates in Philadelphia, 1721–1800* (Philadelphia, PA: Patterson & White, 1933), 18, 64.

59. Adam Smith, *Wealth of Nations*, vol. 2, 91–92.

60. Thomas, "Effects of British Imperial Policy upon Colonial Welfare," 622.

61. Adam Smith, *The Wealth of Nations*, vol. 2, 109–44.

Chapter 2. The Backbone of Credit

1. Extract of a Letter from a Member of the Council in New Jersey to Mr. Dockwra relating to the Proceedings of some of the Council and of the Assembly of that Province, and to Colonel Hunters Administration (1711), Archives of the State of New Jersey, First Series, vol. 4, p 121. (The identity of the council member is unknown.)

2. The colony of New Jersey had experienced two major transitions in the previous eight years. From 1674 to 1702, the Province of New Jersey consisted of two political entities: East Jersey and West Jersey. In 1702, under Queen Anne, they were merged and became a royal colony, that is, directly ruled by the Crown. The royal colony's first governor, Edward Hyde, Lord Cornbury,

was found to be corruptly taking bribes and speculating on land and was recalled to England in 1708, leaving New Jersey to be governed by the colonial administration of New York. For the New York law, see An Act to prevent frauds in conveyancing of lands (November 3, 1683), *The Colonial Laws of New York* (Clark, NJ: The Lawbook Exchange, Ltd., 2006, repr.; Albany: James B. Lyon, 1894), vol. 1, ch. 15, 141–42.

3. Extract of a Letter from a Member of the Council (1711), 121.

4. An Act for Acknowledging and Recording of Deeds and Conveyances of Land within each Respective County of this Province (March 15, 1713/14), *Laws of the Royal Colony of New Jersey, 1703–1745* (Bernard Bush, compiled) (Trenton, NJ: Archives and History Bureau, New Jersey Archives, 3d. ser.), vol. 2, 160–161, 160.

5. An Act for Acknowledging and Recording of Deeds (1713/1714), 161.

6. Letter from Governor Burnet to the Lords of Trade (May 25, 1722), Archives of the State of New Jersey, First Series, vol. 5, 32.

7. An Act concerning the acknowledging and registering Deeds and Conveyances of Land, and declaring how the Estate or Right of a Feme Covert may be conveyed or extinguished (February 10, 1727/28), *Laws of the Royal Colony of New Jersey, 1703–1745* (Bernard Bush, compiled) (Trenton, NJ: Archives and History Bureau, New Jersey Archives, 3d. ser.), vol. 2, 388–91.

8. Memorial of James Smith, Secretary to the Province of New Jersey in relation to two Acts pass'd there in 1727 whereby he was prejudiced with respect to his Fees (November 14, 1728), Archives of the State of New Jersey, First Series, vol. 5, 199.

9. Ibid.

10. An Act concerning acknowledging Deeds in the Colony of New-Jersey, and declaring how the Estate or Right of a Feme Covert may be conveyed or extinguished (December 2, 1743), *Laws of the Royal Colony of New Jersey, 1703–1745* (Bernard Bush, compiled) (Trenton, NJ: Archives and History Bureau, New Jersey Archives, 3rd. ser.), vol. 2, 588–90.

Moreover, in a fifth effort in 1765, the Assembly enacted a law to prevent fraud by mortgages, which stated that "immediately" after the law was published, "each and of every the Clerks of the several Counties" shall "provide a fit and proper Book . . . for the registering of all Mortgages of Lands, Tenements and real Estate lying within their respective Counties." As with the previous law, the mortgage book would be publicly searchable: "all Persons whatsoever, at proper Seasons may have Recourse and Search." An Act for preventing Frauds by Mortgages which shall be made and executed after the First Day of January, 1766 (1765), *Laws of the Royal Colony of New Jersey, 1703–1745*, vol. 4 (Bernard Bush, compiled) (Trenton, NJ: Archives and History Bureau, New Jersey Archives, 3d. ser.), 334–36, 334.

11. See, e.g., William E. Nelson, *Dispute and Conflict Resolution in Plymouth County, Massachusetts, 1725–1825,* (Chapel Hill: University of North Carolina Press, 1981), 23–24; A. G. Roeber, *Faithful Magistrates and Republican Lawyers: Creators of Virginia Legal Culture, 1680–1810* (Chapel Hill: University of North Carolina Press, 1981), 39–43; Erwin C. Surrency, "The Courts in the American Colonies," *American Journal of Legal History* 11, no. 3 (July 1967): 253–76.

12. A vast number of such colonial records survive today, and several collections have been published. See, e.g., 1–10 *Plymouth Court Records, 1686–1859,* ed. David Thomas Konig (Wilmington, DE : M. Glazier, 1978–1980); Marsha Martin, *Lancaster County, Pennsylvania, Land Records, 1729–1750, and Land Warrants, 1710–1742* (Westminster, MD: Family Line Publications, 1998).

13. Roeber, *Faithful Magistrates and Republican Lawyers*, 73–95; E. Lee Shepard, "'This Being Court Day,' Courthouses and Community Life in Rural Virginia," *Virginia Magazine of History & Biography* 103, no. 4 (October 1995): 459–70.

14. Roeber, *Faithful Magistrates and Republican Lawyers*, 85.

15. See, e.g., Cornelia Hughes Dayton, *Women Before the Bar: Gender, Law & Society in Connecticut, 1639–1789* (Chapel Hill: University of North Carolina Press, 1995), 77–79; Bruce H. Mann,

Neighbors and Strangers: Law and Community in Early Connecticut (Chapel Hill : University of North Carolina Press, 1987), 11–46; Claire Priest, "Currency Policies and Legal Development in Colonial New England," *Yale Law Journal* 110 (2001): 1303–1405, 1327–31.

16. See Jacob M. Price, *Capital and Credit in British Overseas Trade: The View from the Chesapeake, 1700–1776* (Cambridge, MA: Harvard University Press, 1980); James H. Soltow, *The Economic Role of Williamsburg* (Williamsburg: University Press of Virginia, 1965), 128–55.

17. *Howland v. Hatch*, Common Pleas (June 1725), no. 25, 191–92; *Knowlton v. Donham*, Common Pleas (December 1725), no. 3, 196; *Holbroke v. Hyland*, Common Pleas (March 1733), no. 38, 436; *Little v. Browne*, Common Pleas (March 1718), no. 19, 78; *Foord v. White*, Common Pleas (July 1718), no. 13, 83; *Despard v. Little*, Common Pleas (July 1718), no. 1,82; *Cowing v. Clarke*, Common Pleas (Dec. 1725), No. 8, 196 in David Thomas Konig, ed., *Plymouth Court Records, 1686–1859* (Wilmington, DE: M. Glazier, 1978).

18. Alice Hanson Jones, *Wealth of a Nation to Be: The American Colonies on the Eve of the Revolution* (New York: Columbia University Press, 1980), 98 and table 4.5. See also Marc Egnal, *New World Economies: The Growth of the Thirteen Colonies and Early Canada* (New York : Oxford University Press, 1998), 15 and table 1.2.

19. Edward Countryman, "The Uses of Capital in Revolutionary America: The Case of the New York Loyalist Merchants," *William and Mary Quarterly* 49, no. 1 (January 1992): 3–28, 19 n.47; Russell R. Menard, "Financing the Lowcountry Export Boom: Capital and Growth in Early South Carolina," *William and Mary Quarterly* 51, no. 4 (October 1994): 659–76, 667; G. B. Warden, "The Distribution of Property in Boston, 1692–1775," *Perspectives in American History* 10 (1976): 81–128, 87–98.

20. Warden, "Distribution of Property in Boston," 81. Boston mortgages stated a one-year term, but Warden found that they were typically paid off in six to eight years. Ibid., 96.

21. Bonnie Martin, "Slavery's Invisible Engine: Mortgaging Human Property," *Journal of Southern History* 76, no. 4 (November 2010): 817–66, 821. See also Bonnie Martin, "Neighbor to Neighbor Capitalism: Local Credit Networks and the Mortgaging of Slaves," in *Slavery's Capitalism: A New History of American Economic Development*, ed. Sven Beckert and Seth Rockman (Philadelphia: University of Pennsylvania Press, 2016), 107–21; Bonnie Martin, "Silver Buckles and Slaves: *Borrowing, Lending, and the Commodification of Slaves in Virginia Communities*," in *New Directions in Slavery Studies: Commodification, Community, and Comparison*, ed. Jeff Forret and Christine E. Sears (Baton Rouge: Louisiana State University Press, 2015), 30–52.

22. Menard, "Financing the Lowcountry Export Boom," 670.

23. Claire Priest, "Colonial Courts and Secured Credit: Early American Commercial Litigation and Shays' Rebellion," *Yale Law Journal* 108 (1999): 2413–50, 2421.

24. Ibid., 2444.

25. George Athan Billias, "The Massachusetts Land Bankers of 1740" (Orons: University of Maine Studies, Second Series, No. 74) *University of Maine Bulletin* 61, no. 17 (April 1959): x–59, 5–6. See generally Andrew McFarland Davis, *Currency and Banking in the Province of the Massachusetts-Bay*, 1, no. 4 (New York: Macmillan Co. for the American Economic Association, December 1900), 66–69 (discussing the advocacy of private banks in the 1720s).

26. John Colman, "The Distressed State of the Town of Boston Considered" (Boston: Nicholas Boone, Benjamin Gray & John Edwards, 1720), reprinted in Andrew McFarland Davis, comp., *Colonial Currency Reprints* (Boston: Prince Society, 1910–11): vol. 1, 398–99.

27. John Adams, "Novanglus: Or, A History of the Dispute with America, from Its Origin, in 1754, to the Present Time," in *The Works of John Adams, Second President of the United States*, ed. Charles Francis Adams (Boston, MA, 1851): vol. 4, 3–177, 49 (italics added).

28. Thomas Hutchinson, *The History of the Colony and Province of Massachusetts-Bay* (1764), ed. Lawrence Shaw Mayo (Cambridge, MA: Harvard University Press, 1936), vol. 3, 212. One

biographer has argued that the currency crisis led Adams to write his 1743 master's thesis at Cambridge, entitled, "'Whether it be lawful to resist the Supreme Magistrate, if the Commonwealth cannot be otherwise preserved.' [Samuel Adams] fearlessly maintained the affirmative." William V. Wells, *The Life and Public Services of Samuel Adams* (New York: Books for Library Press, 2nd ed. 1865), vol. 1, 10 and fn.

29. The origins of institutions related to recording property titles and mortgages in the colonial era has been overlooked in scholarship on the period. Marshall Harris, *Origin of the Land Tenure System in the United States* (Ames: Iowa State College Press, 1953), 331–44, offers a useful, comprehensive, but essentially bibliographic account of colonial legislation relating to property, as does Amelia C. Ford, "Colonial Precedents of Our National Land System as it Existed in 1800" (PhD diss., University of Wisconsin, 1908). The other articles on land title registration examine in a very technical fashion how the system differed from English law; see Joseph H. Beale, "The Origin of the System of Recording Deeds in America," *Green Bag* 19 (1907): 335–39; George L. Haskins, "The Beginnings of the Recording System in Massachusetts," *Boston University Law Review* 21 (1941): 281–304; R. G. Patton, "Evolution of Legislation on Proof of Title to Land," *Washington Law Review & State Bar Journal* 30 (1955): 224–35; and S. G. Nissenson, "The Development of a Land Registration System in New York," *New York History* 20, no. 1 (1939): 16–43. Herbert Osgood's sweeping histories of the colonies entitled *The American Colonies in the Seventeenth Century*, 3 vols. (New York: Macmillan Co.; London: Macmillan & Co., 1904–07), and *The American Colonies of the Eighteenth Century*, 4 vols. (New York: Columbia University Press, 1924) detail the political undertones of the establishment of land title registration, but the discussion of the topic sporadically interspersed within the broader narrative of colonial political history.

30. William Blackstone, *Commentaries on the Laws of England* (Chicago: University of Chicago Press, facsimile ed. 1979, 1765–69), vol. 2, 346. Blackstone's sentence begins by stating that "These grants, whether of lands, honours, liberties, franchises, or ought besides, are contained in charters, or letters *patent*, that is, open letters, *literae patentes*. Ibid.

31. As will be described in chapter 6, the Pistole crisis was a famous conflict over royal seals in Virginia in the 1750s. See Jack P. Greene, ed., "The Case of the Pistole Fee: The Report of a Hearing on the Pistole Fee Dispute Before the Privy Council, June 18, 1754," *Virginia Magazine of History and Biography* 66, no. 4 (October 1958): 399–422, 407–8; Glenn Curtis Smith, "The Affair of the Pistole Fee, Virginia, 1752–55," *Virginia Magazine of History & Biography* 48, no. 3 (July 1940): 209–21, 209–10.

32. As S. G. Nissenson describes, the English Statute of Uses of 1535 and the Statute of Enrollments of 1536 were intended to create greater transparency by recording land titles, but the recording provisions were not widely complied with. In the early feudal system, transfers of rights were recorded in the minutes of the lords' courts. Copyhold transfers were a matter of public record. Land transfers were enrolled or registered in the borough courts. Centralized registration developed in the king's courts at Westminster. Nissenson, "Development of a Land Registration System," 16. Parliament enacted a national Land Registry Act for England and Wales in 1862.

33. See, for example, Nathan Dane, Nathan Dane, *A General Abridgment and Digest of American Law: With Occasional Notes and Comments* (Boston: Cummings, Hilliard & Co., 1824), vol. 4, ch. 109, 38 ("We have adopted the English deed substantially in the English form").

34. 27 Hen. 8, cap. 16.

35. J. H. Baker, *An Introduction to English Legal History*, 4th ed. (London: Butterworths LexisNexis, 2002), 305–6.

36. Under English law, a basic conveyance of land was referred to as a "feoffment" (as opposed to a gift, or a lease, for example).

37. Without the ceremony, the new owner was a tenant at the will of the former owner. See Blackstone, *Commentaries*, vol. 2, 311.

38. Ibid.

39. Ibid., 315.

40. Ibid. Alexander Hamilton's *Practice Manual* also views livery of seisin and acknowl-edgment of a deed in court as substitutes. See Alexander Hamilton, "Practical Proceedings in the Supreme Court of the State of New York" (circa. 1782), in *The Law Practice of Alexander Hamilton: Documents and Commentary*, ed. Julius Goebel, Jr. (New York: published under the auspices of the William Nelson Cromwell Foundation by Columbia University Press, 1964): vol. 1, 55–135, 55, 87.

41. An act to appoint public Registers, and to direct the method to be observed in convey-ing lands, goods, and chattels; and for preventing fraudulent deeds and mortgages, 1715 North Carolina Sess. Laws, ch. 38, 17–19, 18.

42. Zephaniah Swift, *A System of the Laws of the State of Connecticut: In six books* (New York: Arno Press, 1972, repr.; Windham, CT: Printed by John Byrne, for the author, 1795), vol. 1, 307–8 (italics added).

43. An Act in addition to an Act entitled "An Act for the More Safe Keeping the Registry of Deeds and Conveyances of Lands," (November 17, 1720) reprinted in *The Acts and Resolves Public and Private of the Province of Massachusetts Bay* (Boston: Wright & Potter, printers to the State, 1874), vol. 2, ch. 12, 187.

44. An Act to prevent Deceits by Double Mortgages and Conveyances of Lands, Negroes and Chattels (October 8, 1698), *The Statutes at Large of South Carolina* (Columbia, SC: A. S. Johnston, 1837), vol. 2, no. 161, 137–38.

45. An Act for Acknowledging and Recording of Deeds (1713/1714).

46. The 1766 statute stated that the clerk of each county was to maintain a book including a comprehensive account of all mortgages, which contained clear information about the property, the parties involved, and the amount mortgaged on the land and when the debt was payable. An Act for preventing Frauds by Mortgages (1765), 334–36.

47. An Act for preventing frauds by Mortgages (Dec. 12, 1753), *The Colonial Laws of New York* (Clark, NJ: The Lawbook Exchange, Ltd., 2006, repr.; Albany: James B. Lyon, 1894), vol. 3, ch. 945, 958.

48. For inrollment of bargains and sales (Statute of Enrollments), 27 Hen. 8, cap. 16.

49. According to the statute, "All Leases, Estates, Interests of Freehold or Term of Years . . . made or created by Livery of Seisin only or by Parole and not putt in Writeing and signed by the parties . . . shall have the force and effect of Leases or Estates at Will only." An Act for Prevention of Frauds and Perjuries, 29 Car. 2, c. 3, § 3 (1676); Philip Hamburger, "The Conveyancing Purposes of the Statute of Frauds," *American Journal of Legal History* 27 (1983): 354–85.

50. 2 & 3 Anne 4 (West Riding, 1703), *Statutes of the Realm*, vol. 8, 253; 6 Anne 62 (East Riding, 1707), *Statutes of the Realm*, vol. 8, 797; 7 Anne 20 (Middlesex, 1708), *Statutes of the Realm*, vol. 9, 89; 8 Geo. II 6 (North Riding, 1735), ed. Danby Pickering, *Statutes at Large* (London: Joseph Bentham, 1765), vol. 16, 489.

51. 2 & 3 Anne 4 (West Riding, 1703), *Statutes of the Realm*, vol. 8, 253.

52. Against Fraudulent Deeds, *The Statutes at Large; Being a Collection of All the Laws of Virginia*, ed. William Waller Hening (New York: R. & W. & G. Bartow, 1823), vol. 1, Act 4, 418.

53. An Act to prevent Deceits by Double Mortgages and Conveyances of Lands, Negroes and Chattels (October 8, 1698), *Statutes at Large of South Carolina*, vol. 2, no. 161, 137–38.

54. Harris, *Origin of the Land Tenure System in the United States*, 331.

55. "Minutes of the Council and General Court, 1622–1629," *Virginia Magazine of History & Biography* 26 (1918): 235, 242.

56. Act 38 (1632), Hening, *Statutes at Large*, vol. 1, 197. See also Act 13 (1624) in Hening, *Statutes at Large*, vol. 1, 125.

57. Ibid., vol. 1, 197.

58. "Concerning Fraudulent Deeds and Conveyances, Acts of General Assembly 1639–40," *William & Mary Quarterly* 4 (July 1924): 149–50; Act 16 (1639), Hening, *Statutes at Large*, vol. 1, 227. A 1642 Act repeated this language. Act 12 (1642), Hening, *Statutes at Large*, vol. 1, 248.

59. Act IV, Against fraudulent deeds in Hening, *Statutes at Large*, vol. 1, 417, 418.

60. Ibid., 418.

61. Act 73, Against fraudulent conveyances (1662), Hening, *Statutes at Large*, vol. 2, 98–99. The statute explained that it was enacted so that "noe person or persons whatsoever shall passe over by conveyance or otherwise any part of his estate whither lands, goods or cattle, whereby his creditors not having notice therefore might be defrauded of their just debts, unless such conveyances or other deeds be acknowledged before the governor and councell at the general court, or before the justices at the county courts, and there registered in a booke for the purpose within six months after such alienation." In December 1662, the assembly passed another act to address the issue that "dayly experience sheweth that" Virginians "defraud their creditors in this country of their debts" by conveying their land privately to people in England. The act required that with regard to any conveyance to a party in England, copies of the deed must be sent on the "next shipping" to be entered in the Virginia general court records or else they would be deemed fraudulent and not a bar to the claims of creditors in Virginia. Act 9, "Noe conveyances allowed which are made in England unless recorded the next shipping after in the secretaryes office," (1662) in Hening, *Statutes at Large*, vol. 2, 168.

62. Conveyances Fraudulent (1640, 1641) in *The Book of the General Lawes and Libertyes Concerning the Inhabitants of Massachusetts* (1648), ed. Thomas G. Barnes (San Marino, CA: Huntington Library facsimile edition, 1975), 13–14.

63. Herbert Osgood, *The American Colonies in the Seventeenth Century* (New York: Macmillan Co.; London: Macmillan & Co., 1904–07), vol. 2, 43.

64. An Act to prevent frauds in conveyancing of lands (November 3, 1683), *Colonial Laws of New York*, vol. 1, 141–42.

65. An act to appoint public Registers, and to direct the method to be observed in conveying lands, goods, and chattels; and for preventing fraudulent deeds and mortgages, 1715 North Carolina Sess. Laws., ch. 38, 17.

66. See ibid. (reference to later statute modifying act).

67. An Act for the Acknowledgment and Recording of Deeds, ch. 136 (January 12, 1706), *The Statutes at Large of Pennsylvania* (Clarence M. Busch, State Printer, 1896), vol. 2, 206–12; An Act for the Acknowledging and Recording of Deeds, ch. 170 (February 28, 1711), *The Statutes at Large of Pennsylvania* (Clarence M. Busch, State Printer, 1896), vol. 2, 349–55; An Act for Acknowledging and Recording of Deeds, ch. 208 (May 28, 1715), *The Statutes at Large of Pennsylvania* (Clarence M. Busch, State Printer, 1896), vol. 3, 53–58. In the 1819 case *Keller v. Nutz*, the Pennsylvania Surpeme Court refers to a 1775 act and states, "The only deeds, before that act, required to be recorded, were mortgages, or defeasible deeds in the nature of mortgages. These, if not recorded within six months, were void against subsequent purchasers; but no law previously to that act of assembly required, under the penalty of forfeiting the estate conveyed, the registry of an absolute deed." *Keller v. Nutz*, 5 Serg & Rawle 246, 252 (Pa.) (1819).

68. David Thomas Konig, "Community Custom and the Common Law: Social Change and the Development of Land Law in Seventeenth-Century Massachusetts," *American Journal of Legal History* 18 (1974): 137–77, 137–38; see also Maureen E. Brady, "The Forgotten History of Metes and Bounds," *Yale Law Journal* 128 (2019): 872–953.

69. See John Frederick Martin, *Profits in the Wilderness: Entrepreneurship and the Founding of New England Towns in the Seventeenth Century* (Chapel Hill: Published for the Institute of Early American History and Culture, Williamsburg, Virginia, by the University of North Carolina Press, 1991), 260–80; Richard R. Johnson, *Adjustment to Empire: The New England Colonies,*

1675–1715 (New Brunswick, NJ: Rutgers University Press, 1981); Viola F. Barnes, *The Dominion of New England: A Study in British Colonial Policy* (New Haven, CT: Yale University Press, 1923); Dror Goldberg, "Why Was America's First Bank Aborted?," *Journal of Economic History* 71, no. 1 (March 2011): 211–22.

70. Martin, *Profits in the Wilderness*, 263.

71. The prominent lawyer Samuel Sewall wrote on April 26, 1689:

> The Title we have to our Lands has been greatly defamed and undervalued: which has been greatly prejudicial to the Inhabitants, because their Lands, which were formerly the best part of their Estate, became of very little value, and consequently the Owners of very little Credit. Samuel Sewell, *Diary of Samuel Sewell, 1674–1729* (Boston: Massachusetts Historical Society, Fifth Series, 1878), vol. 5, 251.

72. A Narrative of the Proceedings of Sir Edmund Andros and his Complices, Who Acted by an Illegal and Arbitrary Commission from the Late King James during his Government in New England, By Several Gentlemen who were of his Council (1691), *The Andros Tracts* (New York: Burt Franklin, n.d.; first published Boston, MA: The Prince Society, 1868), vol. 1, 133–47, 143 (italics in original). Others wrote that the fees for obtaining new titles could reach 25% of the value of the underlying land. Volume 1 of *The Andros Tracts* includes the following testimonials: p. 98 (hearing his land was to be taken, one resident "caused his Writ to be entred in the Publick Records in Mr. *West's* Office, which he paid for the Recording of; notwithstanding Sir *E.A.* ordered Captain *Clements* (as he said) to survey the same, and he shewed me a Plat thereof, and said, if I had a Patent for it, I must pay three pence *per* Acre, it being 650 Acres. He was further informed, That if the said *Russell* would not take a Patent for it, Mr. *Usher* should have it."); p. 205 ("Whether Husbandmen do need to be put in mind of the blessed Priviledge to which they were advancing, of taking Patents for their Lands, at a rate which would have reduced them to a meaner Estate than the Famine once brought the Egyptians unto?").

73. William Johnson, an Assistant, for example, wrote that: "Had not an happy *Revolution* happened in England, and so in *New-England*, in all probability those few ill men would have squeezed more out of the poorer sort of people there, than half their Estates are worth, by *forcing them to take Patents*. Major *Smith* can tell them, that an Estate not worth 200l. had more than 50l. demanded for a Patent for it." Daniel Turel and Edward Willis, (January 30, 1689), *The Andros Tracts*, vol. 1, 98; Martin, *Profits in the Wilderness*, 263.

74. An Act to prevent frauds in conveyancing of lands (November 3, 1683), *Colonial Laws of New York*, vol. 1, 142.

75. *A Catalogue of Fees Established by the Governour and Council at the Humble Request of the Assembly, NY* (New York: Printed and sold by William Bradford, printer to Their Majesties, King William and Queen Mary, at the Bible in New-York, 1693), 1–11, 1.

76. Ibid., 2.

77. Ibid., 3.

78. Ibid., 4.

79. An Act for preventing frauds by Mortgages (December 12, 1753), *Colonial Laws of New York*, vol. 3, 957.

80. Ibid., 958.

81. An Act for the Acknowledgment and Recording of Deeds (January 12, 1706), *The Statutes at Large of Pennsylvania from 1682 to 1801* (Clarence M. Busch, State Printer of Pennsylvania, 1896), vol. 2, ch. 136, 206–12, notation of Privy Council repeal on 212.

82. An Act for the Acknowledging and Recording of Deeds (February 28, 1711), *Statutes at Large of Pennsylvania*, vol. 2, ch. 170, 349–55, notation of Privy Council repeal on 355.

83. The notation on the statute book says, "Allowed to become a law by lapse of time, in accordance with the proprietary charter, having been considered by the Lord Justices in Council,

July 21, 1719, and not acted upon." An Act for Acknowledging and Recording of Deeds (May 28, 1715), *Statutes at Large of Pennsylvania*, vol. 3, ch. 208, 53–58, notation on 58.

84. An Act to prevent Deceits by Double Mortgages and Conveyances of Lands, Negroes and Chattels (October 8, 1698), *Statutes at Large of South Carolina*, vol. 2, no. 161, 137–38.

85. An Act for Remission of Arrears of Quit-Rents . . . and for keeping the office of Publick Register of this Province from being united to other office or offices, appointed or to be appointed by his Majesty, for Registering, Enrolling, or Recording of Grants or Deeds (August 20, 1731), *The Statutes at Large of South Carolina* (Columbia, SC: A. S. Johnston, 1838), vol. 3, no. 532, 289–304, 296.

86. An Act for establishing County Courts and for regulating the Proceedings therein, *Acts, Ordinances, and Resolves of the General Assembly of the State of South Carolina; Passed in March, 1785* (Charleston, SC: A. Timothy, Printer to the State, 1785), 24.

87. Ibid., 25.

Chapter 3. English Property Law

1. L. B. Namier, *England in the Age of the American Revolution* (London: Macmillan and Co., 1930), 22–23. As later described by Alexis de Tocqueville, who was from a French aristocratic family:

> Among nations whose law of descent is founded upon the right of primogeniture landed estates often pass from generation to generation without undergoing division, the consequence of which is that family feeling is to a certain degree incorporated with the estate. The family represents the estate, the estate the family; whose name, together with its origin, its glory, its power, and its virtues, is thus perpetuated in an imperishable memorial of the past and a sure pledge of the future.

Alexis de Tocqueville, *Democracy in America* (New York: Bantam Dell, 2004), vol. 1, 54. For a description of more recent debates about the social implications of English settlements, see J. H. Baker, *An Introduction to English Legal History*, 4th ed. (London: Butterworths LexisNexis, 2002), 295.

2. John Locke, *Two Treatises of Government*, ed. Peter Laslett (New York: Cambridge University Press, 1988; first published 1690), §88, 206–7. In contrast, Blackstone, who described inheritance as the centerpiece of English real property law, was more skeptical about inheritance and justified it on the basis of convenience—relatives were more likely to be close to the deceased, and possibly in possession of the deceased's property at the time of death—rather than on the basis of natural law. See William Blackstone, *Commentaries on the Laws of England* (Chicago: University of Chicago Press, facsimile ed. 1979, 1765–69), vol. 2, 11–12; see also Stanley N. Katz, "Republicanism and the Law of Inheritance in the American Revolutionary Era," *Michigan Law Review* 76 (1977): 1–29, 4–9 (discussing theories of inheritance posited by Locke, Blackstone, and others).

3. See Administration of Estates Act, 1925, 15 Geo. 5, c. 23, § 45 (Eng.) (abolishing primogeniture in England); Blackstone, *Commentaries*, vol. 2, 214–16 (discussing primogeniture); James Kent, *Commentaries on American Law* (Buffalo, NY: Hein, 1984 repr.; New York: 1830), vol. 4, 377–80 (same); see also Holly Brewer, *By Birth or Consent: Children, Law, and the Anglo-American Revolution in Authority* (Chapel Hill: Published for the Omohundro Institute of Early American History and Culture, Williamsburg, Virginia, by the University of North Carolina Press, 2005), 17–44 (describing primogeniture as the centerpiece of a broader political and social order based on a patriarchal ideology).

4. For a description of a typical settlement on marriage, see Baker, *Introduction to English Legal History*, 293–94. The customary practice was for the family estate to be "resettled" in every

generation, to account for events such as deaths, births, and marriages. Ibid., 294. The resettlement process, however, was most often used to tighten a family's hold on its real property interests, rather than to remove impediments to alienation. According to Baker, "the widespread employment by the landed classes of the strict settlement, with resettlement in each generation, served to shackle much of the land in England to the same families until Victorian times and beyond." Ibid., 295. According to Simpson, under the strict settlement:

> [T]he land was managed by a succession of life tenants, the settlement being reconstituted each generation to ensure that no single individual ever acquired an unfettered power to appropriate the family capital for his individual purposes. It is remarkable that in spite of Blackstone's exaltation of private *individual* property rights, the landowning class in reality had little use for them.

A. W. Brian Simpson, "Introduction to Book II, William Blackstone," in Blackstone, *Commentaries*, vol. 2, xi; see also John H. Langbein, "The Contractarian Basis of the Law of Trusts," *Yale Law Journal* 105 (1995): 625–75, 632–33 (describing the use of trust devices to provide for wives, daughters, and younger sons).

5. In the extreme, the landowner might obtain a life estate with no powers of mortgaging or selling and with trustees appointed to preserve the contingent remainder on behalf of future generations. See Baker, *An Introduction to English Legal History*, 293–95.

6. "Real" property includes all possessory interests in land held for indeterminate periods, such as fee simple estates, defeasible fees, and life estates. "Chattel" property includes moveables, such as livestock and physical possessions, as well as possessory interests in land held for specifically determined periods, such as leases (referred to as "chattels real" as opposed to "chattels personal"). J. H. Baker describes the distinction between real and personal property as "[t]he most fundamental distinction in the English law of property." Baker, *An Introduction to English Legal History*, 223. Frederick Pollock and Frederic Maitland characterize the division of all material things into these two classes as "one of the main outlines of [English] medieval law." Frederick Pollock and Frederic William Maitland, *The History of English Law Before the Time of Edward I*, 2nd ed. (London: Cambridge University Press, 1968), vol. 2, 2.

7. See Baker, *An Introduction to English Legal History*, 66; Blackstone, *Commentaries*, vol. 3, 417.

8. See Blackstone, *Commentaries*, vol. 3, 417–18; Pollock and Maitland, *The History of English Law Before the Time of Edward I*, vol. 2, 596.

9. The Parliament introduced the writ of elegit in 1285 as part of Edward I's reform of feudal law. See Statute of Westminster II, 13 Edw., c. 18 (1285) (Eng.); see also Blackstone, *Commentaries*, vol. 3, 418 (describing the writ of elegit). The impact of this statute on the closing of the commons in England is an intriguing topic that no scholar has examined. Once creditors gained possessory rights to land (however partial) and became willing to offer credit on the basis of these rights, one would imagine that the incentives for individuals to own parcels in fee simple absolute would dramatically increase: only fee simple owners would have access to the additional credit.

10. Blackstone, *Commentaries*, vol. 4, 419.

11. See Blackstone, *Commentaries*, vol. 3, 418–19.

12. 13 Edw., c. 18.

13. See Statute of the Staple, 27 Edw. 3, c. 9 (1353); Statute of Merchants, 13 Edw., c. 1 (1285).

14. Creditors were limited only by the debtor's ability to sue under the waste doctrine, which prevented creditors from diminishing the underlying value of the property. Blackstone, *Commentaries*, vol. 3, 227–29.

15. See Blackstone, *Commentaries*, vol. 3, 414–15. Peers and other Members of Parliament, as well as executors of estates, were exempt from this remedy. Ibid., 414.

16. See ibid., 419–20 (explaining that it was possible "that body and goods may be taken in execution, or land and goods; but not body and land too, upon any judgment between subject and subject in the course of the common law").

17. See Joanna Innes, "The King's Bench Prison in the Later Eighteenth Century: Law, Authority and Order in a London Debtors' Prison," in *An Ungovernable People: The English and Their Law in the Seventeenth and Eighteenth Centuries*, ed. John Brewer and John Styles (New Brunswick, NJ: Rutgers University Press, 1980), 250, 254; Bruce H. Mann, *Neighbors and Strangers: Law and Community in Early Connecticut* (Chapel Hill: University of North Carolina Press, 1987), 25 (noting that in colonial America, the attachment of a debtor's body was often a tactic "to obtain security for the debt, either from the debtor or from sympathetic friends or relatives").

18. See Innes, "The King's Bench Prison," 256. Once the debtor left jail, if the debt remained unsatisfied, the creditor could then sue for a writ of elegit. Such principles did not apply in the merchant and staple courts.

19. Blackstone, *Commentaries*, vol. 2, 510–12.

20. For a discussion of what constituted chattel property over which the executors assumed control, see Baker, *An Introduction to English Legal History*, 380–81.

21. Ibid.

22. Pollock and Maitland, *The History of English Law Before the Time of Edward I*, vol. 2, 334.

23. Ibid., 336.

24. See John Habakkuk, *Marriage, Debt, and the Estates System, English Landowner-ship,1650–1950* (New York: Oxford University Press, 1994), 307–12.

25. See Blackstone, *Commentaries*, vol. 2, 340.

26. The identity of the actual person who would inherit, of course, was unknown until the time of death.

27. Blackstone, *Commentaries*, vol. 1, 134–35.

28. An Act for Relief of Creditors Against Fraudulent Devises (Statute of Fraudulent Devises), 3 and 4 *William and Mary*, c. 14 (1691).

29. In 1290, Parliament enacted the Statute Quia Emptores Terrarum ("Quia Emptores"), 18 Edw., c. 1 (1290), which was the first legal recognition of the right to alienate real property after the Norman Conquest. Historians have established that Quia Emptores reflected Edward I's response to the fact that landowners were already transferring their interests for the purpose of obtaining credit—either by leasing the property or by the process of "subinfeudation." See A.W.B. Simpson, *An Introduction to the History of the Land Law* (London: Oxford University Press, 1961), 22, 50–51. Subinfeudation was a process by which a tenant would sell his possessory interest in land to a third party. See ibid. Subinfeudation could be economically detrimental to the lord, particularly if the tenant subinfeuded to a religious corporation that, as an organizational form, would not give rise to the incidents (payments) linked to family-related events, such as a tenant's marriage (the lord could sell an heir in marriage) and death (wardship, relief, and escheat). See ibid. Quia Emptores was enacted to formalize the requirement that those in possession of land held the land by the same feudal obligations as their predecessors. See ibid. The Statute of Wills of 1540, 32 Hen. 8, c. 1, gave landowners the freedom to devise their lands to whomever they chose. See Baker, *An Introduction to English Legal History*, 256.

30. The Statute of Wills of 1540, § 2. The statute closed a loophole that had denied secured creditors a remedy against heirs when the heirs sold the land they had inherited before the creditor filed a claim in court against them. The Act states as one of the problems it seeks to remedy:

[S]everal persons being heirs at law, to avoid the payment of such just debts, as in regard of the lands, tenements, and hereditaments descending to them they have by law been liable to pay, have sold, aliened, or made over such lands . . . before any process was or could be issued out against them. (§ 5)

31. The early form of mortgage involved a conveyance of land to the creditor (the mortgagee) in return for a sum of money. The agreement typically provided that when the debtor repaid money plus interest, title to the land would revert back to the borrower. If the mortgagor did not repay the loan, he would forfeit the land. See Pollock and Maitland, *The History of English Law Before the Time of Edward I*, vol. 2, 122; Blackstone, *Commentaries*, vol. 2, 340, 465. In the common law courts, mortgage agreements were interpreted strictly. See Simpson, *An Introduction to the History of the Land Law*, 226–27. A delay of any sort in tendering payment under the mortgage could result in the loss of the entire property interest to the creditor, even when the value of the mortgage was less than the value of the land. See Simpson, *An Introduction to the History of the Land Law*. Bonds were structured similarly. If a creditor obtained a judgment against a debtor under a bond, the sheriff would be directed to first try to satisfy the debt out of the obligor's personal estate. If the personal estate was insufficient, then the debt would be discharged out of the land. See Blackstone, *Commentaries*, vol. 2, 340–41, 465.

32. See Simpson, *An Introduction to the History of the Land Law*, 227–29; R. W. Turner, *The Equity of Redemption: Its Nature, History and Connection with Equitable Estates Generally* (Cambridge [Cambridgeshire]: Cambridge University Press, 1931), 26–27; Taisu Zhang, *The Law and Economics of Confucianism: Kinship and Property in Preindustrial China and England* (New York: Cambridge University Press, 2017); David Sugarman and Ronnie Warrington, "Land Law, Citizenship, and the Invention of 'Englishness': The Strange World of the Equity of Redemption," *in Early Modern Conceptions of Property*, ed. John Brewer and Susan Staves (New York: Routledge, 1995), 113–14.

33. See Henry Horwitz, *Chancery Equity Records and Proceedings 1600–1800: A Guide to Documents in the Public Record Office* (London: HMSO, 1995), 4 and n.14, 31.

34. Baker, *An Introduction to English Legal History*, 99.

35. Ibid.

36. Ibid., 111.

37. The 1691 statute against fraudulent devises clarified that notwithstanding its provisions, family settlement agreements made in writing before marriage would continue to be recognized "in full force." 3 and 4 *William and Mary*, c. 14, § 4 (1691). Chancery court procedures are described in Horwitz, *Chancery Equity Records and Proceedings 1600–1800*, 9–26. See also Baker, *An Introduction to English Legal History*, 111–12 (describing the "defects" of chancery procedure).

38. 3 and 4 *William and Mary*, c. 14, § 4 (1691).

39. For anecdotal evidence of the difficulty even secured creditors faced getting landowners to pay their debts, see John Habakkuk, "Presidential Address: The Rise and Fall of English Landed Families, 1600–1800: II," *Transactions of the Royal Historical Society* 30 (1980): 199, 208–10. For a detailed discussion of foreclosure, see Sheldon Tefft, "The Myth of Strict Foreclosure," *University of Chicago Law Review* 4 (1937): 575–96, 576–82 (describing opportunities given to mortgagors to extend the right to redeem during and even after conclusion of the foreclosure process).

40. Robert W. Gordon, "Paradoxical Property," in *Early Modern Conceptions of Property*, 95, 104.

41. See Adam S. Hofri-Winogradow, "Protection of Family Property from Creditors in the Enlightenment-Era Court of Chancery" (March 9, 2008). Available at SSRN: https://ssrn.com /abstract=1104385 or http://dx.doi.org/10.2139/ssrn.1104385), 35–36.

42. Ibid., 49.

43. This practice was overturned by statute in England in 1854. See An Act to Amend the Law Relating to the Administration of the Estates of Deceased Persons, 17 and 18 Vict., c. 113 (1854) (Eng.); see also George C. Brodrick, *English Land and English Landlords: An Enquiry into the Origin and Character of the English Land System, with Proposals for Its Reform* (London; New York:

Published for the Cobden Club by Cassell, Petter, Galpin, 1881), 345 (describing the practice as a "monstrous perversion of justice").

44. The equity courts protected landed inheritance in one other way in the early modern era: to ensure the transmission to the heir of the entire estate in land, by common practice the heir was exempted from a rule that money advanced to sons during their father's lifetime should be deducted from the share they received at his death. See Brodrick, *English Land and English Landlords*, 345.

45. For an extended discussion of the occasions when English landowners, however reluctantly, sold their real property, see Christopher Clay, "Property Settlements, Financial Provision for the Family, and Sale of Land by the Greater Landowners, 1660–1790," *Journal of British Studies* 21, no. 1 (Autumn 1981): 18–38.

46. Clay found that "the prospect of inheriting a house stripped bare of furnishing, even bedding, let alone valuables, a home farm without livestock or implements, and possibly a park denuded of timber" left families with little alternative other than to agree to the barring of an entail or to request a private act of Parliament to allow the sale of real property held in life estate. Ibid., 25.

47. See Dan Bogart and Gary Richardson, "Property Rights and Parliament in Industrializing Britain," *Journal of Law & Economics* 54 (2011): 241–74.

48. The common recovery involved a conveyance of entailed land to an accomplice in fee simple, with a third party paid to provide a false warranty of title. Under the law, the remainder-man's only recourse was against the real property of the party who provided the false warranty of title, and the people who typically agreed to perform this function were people (usually petty officials) who owned no real property. The "barred issue" was therefore left without a meaningful remedy. See Baker, *An Introduction to English Legal History*, 282.

49. Daniel J. Hulsebosch, *Constituting Empire: New York and the Transformation of Constitutionalism in the Atlantic World, 1664–1830* (Chapel Hill: University of North Carolina Press, 2005), 44–45; see also Mary Sarah Bilder, *The Transatlantic Constitution: Colonial Legal Culture and the Empire* (Cambridge, MA: Harvard University Press, 2004), 40; Joseph Henry Smith, *Appeals to the Privy Council from the American Plantations* (New York: Columbia University Press, 1950), 525.

50. The Charter of Libertyes and Priviledges Granted by His Royall Highnesse to the Inhabitants of New Yorke and Its Dependencyes (1683), *The Colonial Laws of New York* (Clark, NJ: The Lawbook Exchange, Ltd., 2006, repr.; Albany: James B. Lyon, 1894), vol. 1, 114.

51. Ibid.

52. Code of Laws (1650), *Public Records of the Colony of Connecticut*, ed. J. Hammond Trumbull (Hartford: Brown & Parsons, 1850), 509, 518–20.

53. An Act Directing the Manner of Levying Executions, and for Relief of Poor Prisoners for Debt (1705), in *The Statutes at Large; Being a Collection of All the Laws of Virginia*, ed. William Waller Hening (Philadelphia, PA: Thomas Desilver, 1823), vol. 3, ch. 37, 385. The writ of elegit, allowing creditors a possessory interest in debtors' land, was not introduced in Virginia until 1726. See An Act To Declare the Law Concerning Executions (1726), Hening, *Statutes at Large*, vol. 4, ch. 3, § 3, 151, 152–56 (describing process of execution under writs of *fieri facias, capias ad satisfaciendum*, and *elegit*).

54. An Act Directing the Manner of Suing Out Attachments in This Province and Limiting the Extent of Them (1704), *All the Laws of Maryland Now in Force* (Annapolis, MD: Thomas Reading, 1707), 4; see also An Act Directing the Manner of Suing Out Attachments in This Province, and Limiting the Extent of Them (1715), *A Compleat Collection of the Laws of Maryland* (Annapolis, MD: William Parks, 1727), 81, 83.

55. An Act for Establishing Courts, and Directing the Marshal's Proceedings, Act 19 (1681), *Acts of Assembly, Passed in the Island of Jamaica* (Kingston: Alexander Aikman, 1787), vol. 1, 26, 29.

56. See Richard Pares, *Merchants and Planters* (Cambridge [Eng.]: Published for the Economic History Review at the University Press, 1960), 45, 87 n.50 (citing Minutes of Council Assembly [July 5, 1684], Public Records Office, Colonial Office Papers 1/57 no. 48). Similarly, freehold property owners of ten acres were exempt from arrest in Barbados until the marshal had attempted to satisfy the debt owed by means of seizing all of the chattel property and lands of the debtor. See ibid.; Jonathan Blumeau, *Remarks on Several Acts of Parliament Relating More Especially to the Colonies Abroad* (London: T. Cooper, 1742), 11–12.

57. "Get Act Making Jamaica Lands Extendable (1715)," in *Royal Instructions to British Colonial Governors, 1670–1776*, ed. Leonard Woods Labaree (New York, London: D. Appleton-Century, [1935]), vol. 1, 339.

58. See Letter from Robert Carter to John Carter (July 19, 1720), *Letters of Robert Carter, 1720–1727*, ed. Louis B. Wright (San Marino, CA: Huntington Library, 1940), 32.

59. Ibid., 33.

60. Ibid., 32.

61. Letter from John Dixon to Isaac Hobhouse et al. (May 2, 1723), in "The Virginia Letters of Isaac Hobhouse, Merchant of Bristol," ed. Walter E. Minchinton, *Virginia Magazine of History and Biography* 66 (1958): 278, 291.

62. Ibid.

63. See Claire Priest, "Law and Commerce, 1580–1815," in *The Cambridge History of Law in America Volume 1: Early America (1580–1815)*, ed. Michael Grossberg and Christopher Tomlins (New York: Cambridge University Press, 2008), 400–46 (examining English mercantilism and its rejection in founding-era America).

64. In her study of the transatlantic legal culture of Rhode Island, Mary Sarah Bilder notes that "[a]s an English colony, Rhode Island's laws and governmental structures were to reflect those of England. As a far-off English colony, however, these laws and structures were expected to be in some way divergent." Bilder, *The Transatlantic Constitution*, 3.

65. See Act of July 1, 1633, *The Compact with the Charter and Laws of the Colony of New Plymouth*, ed. William Brigham (Boston: Dutton & Wentworth, 1836), 31, 33.

66. Ibid.

67. See Penn's Charter of Liberties of 1682, Frame of Government of Pennsylvania, and Laws Agreed Upon in England, in *The Federal and State Constitutions, Colonial Charters, and Other Organic Laws, Seven Volumes*, ed. Francis Newton Thorpe (Washington, DC: Government Printing Office, 1909), vol. 5, 3047–63, § 14, 3061. The precise language of section 14 of the Laws Agreed Upon in England states that "all lands and goods shall be liable to pay debts, except where there is legal issue, and then all the goods, and one-third of the land only." Ibid.

68. See An Act for Taking Lands in Execution for the Payment of Debts, Where the Sheriff Cannot Come at Other Effects to Satisfy the Same (1700), *Laws of the Commonwealth of Pennsylvania* (Philadelphia, PA: John Bioren, 1810), vol. 1, ch. 48, pmbl., 7 ("[A]ll lands and houses whatsoever, within this government, shall be liable to sale, upon judgment and execution obtained against the defendant, the owner, his heirs, executors or administrators, where no sufficient personal estate is to be found"). The Act's stated purpose was "that no creditors may be defrauded of the just debts due to them by persons . . . who have sufficient real estates, if not personal, to satisfy the same." With respect to the debtor's house, it permitted a one-year right of redemption, but afterward it "shall be and remain a free and clear estate to the purchaser or creditor, . . . his heirs and assigns for ever, as fully and amply as ever they were to the debtor." Ibid.

69. The statute states that if yearly rents or profits of the lands would satisfy the debt within seven years, then the lands would be delivered to the plaintiff "until the debt or damages be levied by a reasonable extent, in the same manner and method as lands are delivered upon writs of elegits in England." An Act for Taking Lands in Execution for Payment of Debts (1705), *Laws of the Commonwealth of Pennsylvania*, vol. 1, ch. 152, § 2, 58.

70. See ibid. § 3, 58.

71. Ibid. § 6, 59.

72. Ibid. § 6, 60.

73. See ibid.; see also *Graff v. Smith's Admors.*, 1 U.S. (1 Dall.) 481, 481–82 (Pa. Ct. Com. Pl. 1789) (discussing the 1700 and 1705 statutes).

74. Stanley N. Katz, "The Politics of Law in Colonial America: Controversies over Chancery Courts and Equity Law in the Eighteenth Century," in *Law in American History*, ed. Donald Fleming and Bernard Bailyn (Boston: Little, Brown, [c1971]), 257, 263–64.

75. See Blumeau, *Remarks on Several Acts of Parliament*, 18–19 (noting the practice in Barbados of defining "all their Estates" as "in the nature of, and no more than, Chattels for the Payment of Debts," and noting that this doctrine was "probably set on foot in the Infancy of the Island, for the Encouragement of Trade to it"); Pares, *Merchants and Planters*, 89 n.59; *Turner v. Cox* (1853) 8 Moore 289, 301, 14 Eng. Rep. 111, 116 (referring to early practice in Barbados of selling land for unsecured debt and citing 1745 Barbados law that stated "all lands have ever been looked upon as chattels for the payment of debts, though what remains afterwards to descend to the heir-at-law, or go to the devisee" (quoting An Act To Quiet the Inhabitants of This Island in the Peaceable Possession of Their Estates (1745)), *Laws of Barbados* (London: William Clowes & Sons, 1875), vol. 1, no. 35, pmbl, 37, 37) [internal quotation mark omitted]).

76. See Pares, *Merchants and Planters*, 89 n.58; Jacob M. Price, "Credit in the Slave Trade and Plantation Economies," *Slavery and the Rise of the Atlantic System*, ed. Barbara L. Solow (Cambridge, MA: W.E.B. DuBois Institute for Afro-American Research, Harvard University; Cambridge [England]; New York: Cambridge University Press, 1991), 293, 306 n.26.

77. "Reenact Law for Sale by Outcry of Debtors' Lands," *Royal Instructions to British Colonial Governors, 1670–1776*, vol. 1, 338, 338–39.

78. Ibid. 339.

79. See Price, "Credit in the Slave Trade and Plantation Economies," 306 n.26. Professor Richard Pares describes the state of property exemption law in the Caribbean prior to 1732 as "a whirl of divergence between islands and of tergiversation in the same island, out of which one example at least of everything can be found sticking out." Pares, *Merchants and Planters*, 89 n.58.

80. See "The Acts and Laws of the General Free Assembly" (1682) (W. Jersey), *The Grants, Concessions, and Original Constitutions of the Province of New Jersey*, ed. Aaron Leaming and Jacob Spicer (Philadelphia, PA: Honeyman & Co., 1881), ch. 12, 442, 447 (The Act states that its purpose is to "prevent[] . . . fraud, deceit and collusions, between debtor and creditor, and that creditors may not be hindered from the recovery of their just debts." Ibid.

81. See "General Court Enactment of May 12, 1675," *Records of the Governor and Company of the Massachusetts Bay in New England*, ed. Nathaniel B. Shurtleff (New York: AMS Press, 1968 (1854)), vol. 5, 29 (stating that the recording of title of "houses & lands taken upon execution . . . shall be a legall assurance of such houses & lands to [the plaintiff] & his heires forever," meaning that the creditor would have a fee simple title). In 1647, Massachusetts's first code of law, The Book of General Laws and Liberties, provided that a writ of execution should permit an officer to levy on the goods and chattels of the debtor. In contrast to the law in England, the officer was permitted to break open the doors of the house if necessary. To satisfy criminal fines, the officer was permitted to "levie his land or person according to law" if personal property was insufficient. Massachusetts, and Max Farrand, *The Laws and Liberties of Massachusetts: Reprinted from the Copy of the 1648 edition in the Henry E. Huntington Library* (Cambridge, MA: Harvard University Press, 1929), 34.

82. An Act for Making of Lands and Tenements Liable to the Payment of Debts (1692), *The Acts and Resolves of the Province of the Massachusetts Bay* (Boston: Wright & Potter, 1869), vol.1, ch. 29, § 1, 68–69 [hereinafter *Acts and Resolves of Massachusetts*]. The statute then clarifies that it intends the conveyance of the entire fee simple interest to creditors. It provides that, after the transfer of title was recorded in the county registry, the creditor would have a "good title" to the

real property, for "his heirs and assigns forever." Ibid. § 1, 69. This Act was disallowed by the Privy Council in 1695 because it failed to provide for debts due to the Crown. See *Acts and Resolves of Massachusetts*, vol. 1, 69 (noting that the Act was repealed for this reason). The Act was then reenacted in 1696 with a provision specifying that debts due to the Crown had priority over all other debts. See An Act for Making of Lands and Tenements Liable to the Payment of Debts (1696), *Acts and Resolves of Massachusetts*, vol. 1, ch. 10, 254.

83. See Executions Act, *Acts and Laws of His Majesties Colony of Connecticut in New-England* (Boston, MA: Bartholomew Green & John Allen, 1702), 32.

84. See An Act for Making of Lands and Tenements Liable to the Payment of Debts, (1718) *Acts and Laws of His Majesty's Province of New Hampshire, in New-England* (Portsmouth: Daniel Fowle, 1761), 84.

85. See ibid.

86. An Act Prescribing the Forme of Writts for Possession, *Scire Facias*, and Replevin (1701), *Acts and Resolves of Massachusetts*, vol. 1, ch. 3, 461.

87. Thomas Hutchinson, *The History of the Colony and Province of Massachusetts-Bay*, ed. Lawrence Shaw Mayo (Cambridge, MA: Harvard University Press, 1936), vol. 1, 376.

88. *Phillips v. Dean*, No. 16 (Ct. C.P. June 1720), *Plymouth Court Records, 1686–1859*, ed. David Thomas Konig, vol. 5 (Wilmington, DE: M. Glazier, 1979), 113. Book accounts functioned like a tab and were a popular form of unsecured debt through the mid–nineteenth century largely because of a dearth of a cash currency. See Claire Priest, "Currency Policies and Legal Development in Colonial New England," *Yale Law Journal* 110 (2001): 1303–1405, at 1328–30. See also Executions Act, *Acts and Laws of His Majesties Colony of Connecticut in New-England*, 32 (calling for transfer of land to creditor after appraisal).

89. An Act for Making of Lands and Tenements Liable to the Payment of Debts (1692), *Acts and Resolves of Massachusetts*, vol. 1, ch. 29, 68.

90. The Board of Trade, for example, issued formal instructions to the colonial governors advising them on courses of action relating to local matters. Often these instructions related to the economic interests of English creditors. See, e.g., Instructions in *Royal Instructions to British Colonial Governors*, vol. 1, 338–39. To my knowledge, the first systematic accounting of colonial laws that conflicted with English economic interests was contained in a 1734 Board of Trade Report, the purpose of which was to describe all colonial laws conflicting with English "Trade, Navigation, and Manufactures." M. Bladen et al., *Representation of the Board of Trade Relating to the Laws Made, Manufacturers Set Up, and Trade Carried On, in His Majesty's Plantations in America* (n.p. 1734). For an overview of the mercantilist nature of English commercial regulations, see Priest, "Law and Commerce," 402–18.

91. See, e.g., *Meynell v. Moore* (1727) 4 Brown 103, 110, 2 Eng. Rep. 70, 74 (H.L.) (applying Antiguan law).

Chapter 4. Parliamentary Authority over Creditor's Claims

1. Their power to legislate in these areas was subject to legal regulation from London. A Parliamentary Act of 1696 enacted to improve the enforcement of mercantilist commercial regulations provided that colonial "laws, by-laws, usages or customs" that were "any ways repugnant to" parliamentary laws regulating the colonies "are illegal, null and void, to all intents and purposes." 7 & 8 Wm. III, c. 22, § 9 (1696) (Eng.).

2. See Jacob M. Price, "Credit in the Slave Trade and Plantation Economies," in *Slavery and the Rise of the Atlantic System*, ed. Barbara L. Solow (New York: Cambridge University Press, 1991), 306 (describing the "abysmally low prices in Europe for both sugar and tobacco").

3. Richard Pares, *Merchants and Planters* (Cambridge [Eng.]: Published for the Economic History Review at the University Press, 1960), 45.

4. Ibid., 46 (quoting John Ashley, The Fall of Barbados Since the French Edict in 1726, Public Records Office, Colonial Office Papers 28/25, A. a. 60) (internal quotation mark omitted). Professor Pares describes a plantation in Jamaica that in 1802 was valued for sale at £21,212 in its entirety and at £14,351 if the buildings, lands, slaves, and equipment were sold separately. Ibid. 88 n.55. One might ask, however, why Barbados and New England did not retain the English inheritance laws and other protections to land. Barbados is the principal exception to the general rule that colonies engaging primarily in staple crop production using slave labor maintained some version of English protections to land from creditors. By reforming their body of remedies, the Barbados planters signaled to creditors that the legal regime would protect creditors' interests. Barbados developed rapidly, but it was characterized by absenteeism because its landowners often lived in England. See John J. McCusker and Russell R. Menard, *The Economy of British America, 1607–1789* (Chapel Hill: University of North Carolina Press, Institute for Early American History and Culture, 1985), 154–55. These landowners relied on large numbers of imported slaves purchased on credit (the Barbados slave population did not reproduce itself until the end of the eighteenth century) and borrowed money to finance more capital-intensive sugar refining than the other sugar colonies. See ibid., 151–52, 164–67. Price and Menard speculate that Barbados's rapid development of the gang labor method of cultivation was related to its adoption of creditor-friendly remedies. See Jacob M. Price, "Credit in the Slave Trade and Plantation Economies," at 293; Russell R. Menard, "Law, Credit, the Supply of Labour, and the Organization of Sugar Production in the Colonial Greater Caribbean: A Comparison of Brazil and Barbados in the Seventeenth Century," in *The Early Modern Atlantic Economy*, ed. John J. McCusker and Kenneth Morgan (New York: Cambridge University Press, 2000), 154, 159–62. Why Barbados moved to this body of remedies so early is a complex question deserving further exploration.

5. For an economic analysis of variation in inheritance laws, see Lee J. Alston and Morton Owen Schapiro, "Inheritance Laws Across Colonies: Causes and Consequences," *Journal of Economic History* 44, no. 2 (June 1984): 277–87, 279–81.

6. See Claire Priest, "Currency Policies and Legal Development in Colonial New England," *Yale Law Journal* 110 (2001): 1303–1405, 1321–32.

7. As mentioned earlier, in the mid-Atlantic region, in 1774 land constituted 68.5% of wealth; in the South, land constituted only 48.6% of wealth, and slaves constituted 35.6%. Marc Egnal, *New World Economies* (New York: Oxford University Press, 1998), 15 and table 1.2; see also Alice Hanson Jones, *Wealth of a Nation to Be* (New York: Columbia University Press, 1980), 98 and table 4.5 (containing data underlying Egnal's table).

8. G. B. Warden's study of Massachusetts mortgage markets found that land transferred hands so rapidly that the mortgages themselves likely constituted a form of currency. See G. B. Warden, "The Distribution of Property in Boston, 1692–1775," *Perspectives in American History* 10 (1976): 81–128, 87–98; see generally Priest, "Currency Policies and Legal Development," 1317–34 (describing "money substitutes" in light of currency shortages in New England).

9. See Thomas D. Morris, *Southern Slavery and the Law, 1619–1860* (Chapel Hill: University of North Carolina Press, 1996), 66.

10. An Act to Explain and Amend the Act, for Declaring the Negro, Mulatto, and Indian Slaves, Within This Dominion, To Be Real Estate (1727), *The Statutes at Large; Being a Collection of All the Laws of Virginia*, ed. William Waller Hening (Richmond, VA: Franklin Press, 1820), vol. 4, ch. 11, § 14, 226.

11. Richard Kilbourne, for example, observes:

> Slaves represented a huge store of highly liquid wealth that ensured the financial stability and viability of planting operations even after a succession of bad harvests, years of low prices, or both. Slave property clearly collateralized a variety of credit instruments and was by far the most liquid asset in most planter portfolios. . . . [A]n investment in

slaves was a rational choice, given the alternatives for storing savings in the middle of the [nineteenth] century.

Richard Holcombe Kilbourne, Jr., *Debt, Investment, Slaves: Credit Relations in East Feliciana Parish, Louisiana, 1825–1885* (Tuscaloosa: University of Alabama Press, 1995), 5. Compare with Gavin Wright, *Old South, New South: Revolutions in the Southern Economy since the Civil War* (New York: Basic Books, 1986), 24–26, 30–31 (asserting that the large amount of wealth invested in slaves placed pressure on slaveholders to put slaves to their most productive use, which led to high rates of geographic mobility).

12. A 1705 Virginia act, for example, stated that:

> For the better settling and preservation of estates . . . all negro, mulatto, and Indian slaves, in all courts of judicature, . . . shall be held . . . to be real estate (and not chattels;) and shall descend unto the heirs and widows of persons departing this life, according to the manner and custom of land of inheritance, held in fee simple.

An Act Declaring the Negro, Mulatto, and Indian Slaves Within This Dominion, To Be Real Estate (1705), *The Statutes at Large; Being a Collection of All the Laws of Virginia*, ed. William Waller Hening (Philadelphia, PA: Thomas Desilver, 1823), vol. 3, ch. 23, pmbl., § 2, 333. A later section clarified that, notwithstanding the treatment of real property for the purpose of inheritance, "slaves shall be liable to the paiment of debts, and may be taken by execution, for that end, as other chattels or personal estate may be." Ibid., § 4, 334. Antiguan law was similar in that slaves, but not freehold estates, were liable to payment of unsecured debts. On the Antiguan legal regime, see *Meynell v. Moore* (1727) 4 Brown 103, 2 Eng. Rep. 70 (H.L.).

13. An Act To Explain and Amend the Act, for Declaring the Negro, Mulatto, and Indian Slaves, Within This Dominion, To Be Real Estate, Hening, *Statutes at Large*, vol. 4, ch. 11, § 14, 226.

14. Ibid., § 15, 226. The Act's primary purpose was "to preserve slaves for the use and benefit of such persons to whom lands and tenements shall descend . . . for the better improvement of the same." Ibid., § 11, 224; see also *Blackwell v. Wilkinson*, Jeff. 73, 77 (Va. Gen. Ct. 1768) (holding that the 1727 Act did not permit the entail of slaves when they were not annexed to lands).

15. Jeff. 5 (Va. Gen. Ct. 1731). As the historian Thomas Morris notes, the judge in this case overlooked the provision of the Virginia statute requiring the exhaustion of personal property before slaves were to be sold. See Morris, *Southern Slavery and the Law*, 70.

16. See ibid., 81–101.

17. See ibid., 308. The Instruction, which was given to most of the colonies, can be found in *Royal Instructions to British Colonial Governors, 1670–1776*, ed. Leonard Woods Labaree (New York, London: D. Appleton-Century [1935]), vol. 1, 338.

18. See Price, "Credit in the Slave Trade and Plantation Economies," 308; see also An Act Declaring How Long Judgments, Bonds, Obligations, and Accounts Shall Be in Force (1705), Hening, *Statutes at Large*, vol. 3, ch. 34, 377–81.

19. See Hening, *Statutes at Large*, vol. 3, 377 (noting repeal by proclamation in margin). The Board of Trade advised the Crown that the law conflicted with an English act that made rights created by judgment or by bond unlimited in time. See Price, "Credit in the Slave Trade and Plantation Economies," 308.

20. See An Act for Ascertaining the Damage upon Protested Bills of Exchange (1730), Hening, *Statutes at Large*, vol. 4, ch. 5, 273–75.

21. An Act Declaring How Long Judgments, Bonds, Obligations, and Accounts Shall Be in Force (1705), Hening, *Statutes at Large*, vol. 3, ch. 34, 380.

22. An Act for Regulating Fees (1711), *Acts of Assembly, Passed in the Island of Jamaica* (Kingston: Alexander Aikman, 1787), vol. 1, Act 56, § 122, 86, 90.

23. Ibid.

24. Letter from Governor Hunter to the Council of Trade and Plantations (August 3, 1728), in *Calendar of State Papers Colonial, America and West Indies: Volume 36, 1728–1729*, ed. Cecil

Headlam and Arthur Percival Newton (London: His Majesty's Stationary Office, 1937), No. 344, 167, 168 (discussing the Act of July 18, 1728).

25. Ibid. 167–68. A petition to the governor signed by thirty-five merchants and traders formally objected to the bill and explained "that it will injure the credit of the Island and ruin many of the inhabitants." Ibid., 169.

26. Petition of Several Merchants of the City of London (August 12, 1731), *Calendar of State Papers Colonial, America and West Indies: Volume 38, 1731*, ed. Cecil Headlam and Arthur Percival Newton (London: His Majesty's Stationary Office, 1938), No. 367i, 224, 225, quoted in Board of Trade, *Representation of the Board of Trade Relating to the Laws Made, Manufacturers Set Up, and Trade Carried On, in His Majesty's Plantations in America* (n.p. 1734), 9; see also *Proceedings and Debates of the British Parliaments Respecting North America*, ed. Leo Francis Stock (Washington, DC: The Carnegie Institution of Washington, 1924–), vol. 4, 89, 128 n.13, 130, 153–54 (referring to enactment of colonial statutes impeding the recovery of debts in parliamentary sessions of 1730 to 1732).

27. See Particular Facts and Instances in Support of the Merchants' Petition (August 12, 1731), *Calendar of State Papers*, vol. 38, No. 434i, 293.

28. Letter from John Tymms to Humfrey Morice (Sept. 13, 1731), *Calendar of State Papers*, vol. 38, No. 434ii, at 294, 294.

29. Ibid., 295.

30. Board of Trade, *Representation of the Board of Trade Relating to the Laws Made, Manufacturers Set Up, and Trade Carried On, in His Majesty's Plantations in America* (n.p. 1734), 9.

31. Ibid., 9–10.

32. 5 Geo. 2, c. 7 (1732) (Eng.), preamble.

33. Ibid., § 4. Parliament at times responded to generalized fears of colonial debt relief legislation with sweeping statutes that were not responsive to local conditions. See, e.g., An Act To Prevent Paper Bills of Credit, Hereafter To Be Issued in Any of His Majesty's Colonies or Plantations in America, from Being Declared To Be Legal Tender, 4 Geo. 3, c. 34 (1764).

34. 5 Geo. 2, c. 7, § 4 (emphasis omitted).

35. 5 Geo. 2, c. 7, § 4.

36. Colonists were incensed about this provision of the statute and believed it violated their right to defend themselves in court. See John M. Hemphill, II, *Virginia and the English Commercial System, 1689–1733* (New York: Garland, 1985) [1964], 188, 227–28.

37. 5 Geo. 2, c. 7, § 4 (mandating that such property would be liable to all debts "owing by any such Person to his Majesty, or any of his Subjects").

38. See 3 and 4 Will. 4, c. 104 (1833).

39. See Petition of Isham Randolph, Esq'r Agent for the Colony of Virginia (March 17, 1731), quoted in *Proceedings and Debates of the British Parliaments Respecting North America*, vol. 4, 153.

40. Ibid.

41. See, e.g., An Act for Rendering More Effectual the Laws Making Lands and Other Real Estates Liable to the Payment of Debts, *Session Laws of North Carolina* (Wilmington: Andrew Steuart, 1764), ch. 4 (stating that the Debt Recovery Act had been in effect and "many Lands and other real Estates . . . have accordingly been seized and sold . . . as well in the Lifetime of such Debtors, as after their Decease," and reaffirming that execution sales led to the transfer of the entire interest in the real property owned by the debtor); *Peckham's v. Fryers* (R.I. Eq. Ct. 1741) (holding that the Debt Recovery Act was in force in Rhode Island and applying the Act to disputes related to inheritance); *Peckham's v. Allen* (R.I. Eq. Ct. 1741) (same); Writ of Execution Against the Estate of William Harper, North Carolina State Archives (April 8, 1768) (on file with author) (authorizing sheriffs to seize all forms of personal and real property in the following order until the debt was satisfied: first, personal property; second, slaves; third, land); Writ of Execution Against the Estate of Joseph Jennett, North Carolina State Archives (June 4, 1767) (on file with author) (same).

42. See An Act for Making of Lands and Tenements Liable to the Payment of Debts (1718) *Acts and Laws of His Majesty's Province of New Hampshire, in New-England* (Portsmouth: Daniel Fowle, 1761), 84.

43. 5 Geo 2, c. 7, § 4. For evidence that the Debt Recovery Act was recognized as authoritative in New Hampshire, see *Acts and Laws of His Majesty's Province of New-Hampshire, In New-England* (Portsmouth: Daniel & Robert Fowle, 1771), iv, 233 (listing the Debt Recovery Act as one of the "perpetual laws" in operation in the colony and reprinting the law).

44. Governor Talcott of Connecticut responded to the enactment of the Debt Recovery Act by stating that Connecticut courts would be "blameless in reassuming our former Rules, in putting the Administrator . . . in the room and stead of the deceasd Debtor, to alienate his lands, for the payment of his just Debts." Letter from Governor Joseph Talcott to Francis Wilks (October 1732), *Collections of the Connecticut Historical Society* (Hartford, CT: Published for the Society, 1892), vol. 4, 260–61.

45. Letter from John Custis to Thomas Lloyd (1732), quoted in Hemphill, *Virginia and the English Commercial System*, 230.

46. Ibid.

47. Letter from John Custis to Thomas Lloyd (1732), quoted in Hemphill, *Virginia and the English Commercial System*, 230; see also Petition of Isham Randolph, Esq'r Agent for the Colony of Virginia.

48. Letter from Robert Carter to Micajah Perry (July 10, 1732), quoted in Hemphill, *Virginia and the English Commercial System*, 228.

49. Ibid.

50. *Harrison v. Halley*, Jeff. 58, 58 (Va. Gen. Ct. 1739).

51. Ibid.

52. The evidence is sparse regarding why Virginians decided to reject the Act internally. In 1748, however, a proposal was submitted in the House of Burgesses to make the Debt Recovery Act a force with respect to internal Virginia affairs, and the proposal was rejected without comment. *Journal of the House of Burgesses* (Williamsburg, VA: William Parks, 1748), 55–56 (reporting that the Committee of Propositions and Grievances rejected a proposition from the County of Richmond to make the Debt Recovery Act apply in Virginia). Yet also in 1748, the Virginia legislature enacted a statute that explicitly adopted the traditional English approach to remedies (limiting the remedies to *fieri facias* for "goods[] and chattels," *levari facias*, and *elegit*). This statute thereby officially rejected the Debt Recovery Act with respect to intracolonial debts. An Act Declaring the Law Concerning Executions; and for Relief of Insolvent Debtors, ch. 12 (1748), Hening, *Statutes at Large*, vol. 4, ch. 12, 526.

53. William Knox, *The Interest of the Merchants and Manufacturers of Great Britain, in the Present Contest with the Colonies, Stated and Considered* (London, 1774) (London: University of London, Company of Goldsmiths, 1903), 38.

54. Ibid. (emphases added). Writing in 1774, Knox noted that some colonists were calling for a repeal of the Act, by which the colonists would "ruin their trade and fortunes with their own hands." Ibid. For Knox, a repeal of the Act would not be nearly as damaging as what the colonists were also threatening: independence from all parliamentary authority. The patriots were the "assassins of the British merchant's security, and, by destroying their confidence in the Colonies, force them to withhold their credit, and thereby do the greatest injury to the Colonies themselves." Ibid., 42.

55. Joseph Story, *Commentaries on the Constitution of the United States* (Boston: Hilliard, Gray, & Co., 1833), book 1, §182, 168.

56. 5 Geo. 2, c. 7, § 4 (1732).

57. See James Kent, *Commentaries on American Law* (Buffalo, NY: Hein, 1984 repr.; New York: 1830), vol. 4, 428–31.

58. See *Peckham's v. Allen* (R.I. Eq. Ct. 1741) (same); Writ of Execution Against the Estate of William Harper, North Carolina State Archives (April 8, 1768) (on file with author) (authorizing sheriffs to seize all forms of personal and real property in the following order until the debt was satisfied: first, personal property; second, slaves; third, land); Writ of Execution Against the Estate of Joseph Jennett, North Carolina State Archives (June 4, 1767) (on file with author) (same).

59. Ibid.

60. As John Haywood, the prominent North Carolina lawyer, stated in his argument in *Baker v. Webb*:

> Before the passing of this act lands could not be sold for the payment of debts, and the heir was not liable to the simple contract, or other debts of the ancestor in which he was not named: since the passing of this act they are liable to be sold, and in the hands of the heir are liable to all debts justly owing from the ancestor. *Baker v. Webb*, 2 N.C. (1 Hayw.) 43, 69 (Sup. Ct. 1794) (Haywood arguing for the plaintiff).

61. Frederic William Maitland, *The History of English Law Before the Time of Edward I* (London: Cambridge University Press, 1968, 2nd ed.), vol. 2, 334.

62. 5 Geo. 2, c. 7, § 4 (1732).

63. As mentioned above, Blackstone described as an absolute right of property that no man shall be disinherited "unless he be duly brought to answer, and be forejudged by course of law." William Blackstone, *Commentaries on the Laws of England* (Chicago: University of Chicago Press, facsimile ed. 1979, 1765–69), vol. 1, 134–35.

64. *Waters v. Stewart*, 1 Cai. Cas. 47, 71 (N.Y. Sup. Ct. 1804); see also Kent, *Commentaries on American Law*, vol. 4, 429 (listing states that allowed land to be sold on a writ of fieri facias with no right of redemption).

65. 5 Geo. 2, c. 7, § 4 (emphasis added).

66. 2 N.C. (1 Hayw.) 72 (Super. Ct. 1794).

67. Ibid., 95; see also *Waters*, 1 Cai. Cas. at 70–71; Kent, *Commentaries on American Law*, vol. 4, 429.

68. This argument was made (unsuccessfully) by lawyers in an 1804 New York case heard by the New York Supreme Court. At the time of the Revolution, only Maryland, New Jersey, New York, Pennsylvania, and South Carolina had established separate equity courts. See Stanley N. Katz, "The Politics of Law in Colonial America: Controversies over Chancery Courts and Equity Law in the Eighteenth Century," in *Law in American History*, ed. Donald Fleming and Bernard Bailyn (Boston: Little, Brown, [1971]), 257, 263–64. After the American Revolution, several other states either established equity courts or granted full equity powers to common law courts. These included Alabama, Arkansas, Georgia, Kentucky, Maryland, Mississippi, North Carolina, South Carolina, Tennessee, and Virginia. See Marylynn Salmon, *Women and the Law of Property in Early America* (Chapel Hill: University of North Carolina Press, 1986), 82–83.

69. Bryan Edwards, *The History of the British Colonies in the West Indies* (Philadelphia, PA: James Humphreys, 1806), 366. Thomas Russell identifies the Edwards essay as the earliest known writing on the frequency of slave auctions. See Thomas D. Russell, "A New Image of the Slave Auction: An Empirical Look at the Role of Law in Slave Sales and a Conceptual Reevaluation of Slave Property," *Cardozo Law Review* 18 (1996): 473–523, 481 (finding empirically that courts conducted or supervised a majority of slave auctions in antebellum South Carolina).

70. Edwards, *The History of the British Colonies in the West Indies*, 366.

71. Ibid., 367–68. Parliament repealed the Debt Recovery Act with respect to slaves in the remaining British colonies in 1797. See 37 Geo. 3, c. 119 (1797) (Eng.).

72. The elimination of the risk of such colonial legislation likely affected all colonies, including those, such as Barbados and Massachusetts, that had voluntarily reformed their laws to make land available for debts prior to the Debt Recovery Act.

73. In two of the only works that have discussed potential economic implications of the Debt Recovery Act, Menard and Price emphasize the acceleration of legal relief as the most important effect. See Russell R. Menard, "Law, Credit, the Supply of Labour, and the Organization of Sugar Production in the Colonial Greater Caribbean: A Comparison of Brazil and Barbados in the Seventeenth Century," in *The Early Modern Atlantic Economy*, ed. John J. McCusker and Kenneth Morgan (New York: Cambridge University Press, 2000), 159–62; Price, "Credit in the Slave Trade and Plantation Economies," 294.

74. It is important to note that the Debt Recovery Act affected both secured and unsecured credit because the interplay between secured credit and unsecured credit is complex. A law permitting an unsecured creditor to seize real property has significance only if some value remains in the property beyond the amount owed on the mortgage. Conversely, if all property is mortgaged to the extent of its full value, a law permitting unsecured creditors to seize real property is irrelevant. Moreover, the exemption of real property from the claims of all unsecured creditors might benefit secured creditors by clarifying that only secured creditors have the right under law to seize that property. See Jeremy Berkowitz and Richard Hynes, "Bankruptcy Exemptions and the Market for Mortgage Loans," *Journal of Law and Economics* 42 (1999): 809–30 (demonstrating the importance of the distinction between secured and unsecured credit for bankruptcies that fund home mortgages). Thus, in America, both secured credit and unsecured credit were transformed during the colonial period. The total amount of credit extended in the society was therefore likely to have expanded, irrespective of the allocation between secured and unsecured credit.

75. Menard describes lower interest rates as an effect of the Debt Recovery Act. Menard, "Law, Credit, the Supply of Labour," 161. A 2004 study by Jeremy Berkowitz and Michelle J. White, for example, found that in states with unlimited homestead exemptions, interest rates on loans to small unincorporated firms were higher and these firms were more likely to be denied credit. Jeremy Berkowitz and Michelle J. White, "Bankruptcy and Small Firms' Access to Credit," *RAND Journal of Economics* 35, no. 1 (Spring 2004): 69–84, 78, 80–81. See Reint Gropp et al., "Personal Bankruptcy and Credit Supply and Demand," *Quarterly Journal of Economics* 112, no. 1 (February 1997): 217–51 (finding worse credit terms in states with higher property exemptions); Emily Y. Lin and Michelle J. White, "Bankruptcy and the Market for Mortgage and Home Improvement Loans," *Journal of Urban Economics* 50, no. 1 (July 2001): 138–62, 160–61 (finding that interest rates on mortgages are higher in jurisdictions offering exemptions on property from the claims of unsecured creditors).

76. An Act for the Reducing the Interest of Money on All Future Contracts, and for the Advancing the Credit of Bills of Exchange (1739), *Laws of Jamaica* (St. Jago de la Vega: Alexander Aikman, 1792), vol. 1, ch. 3, 262.

77. Ibid., pmbl., 262–63.

78. English creditors sold goods to colonial factors that the factors, in turn, sold to local colonial producers on credit for extended periods of time. See, e.g., Richard B. Sheridan, *Sugar and Slavery: An Economic History of the British West Indies, 1623–177* (Jamaica: Canoe Press, 1994 reprint), 284 (discussing the role of colonial factors).

79. See Marc Egnal, *New World Economies*, 93.

80. Ibid., 93 fig. 5.12.

81. Ibid. 93.

82. Bureau of the Census, *Historical Statistics of the United States: Colonial Times to 1970* (Washington, DC: US Department of Commerce, 1975), vol. 2, 1176; see also Egnal, *New World Economies*, 83 fig. 5.6 (graph of per capita imports).

83. *Historical Statistics of the United States*, vol. 2, 1176.

84. Sheridan, *Sugar and Slavery*, 290.

85. McCusker and Menard, *The Economy of British America, 1607–1789,* 68 ("The final thirty years of the colonial era were marked by a major improvement in the terms of trade as prices for American staples rose more rapidly than those for British manufactures").

86. T. H. Breen, *The Marketplace of Revolution* (New York: Oxford University Press, 2004), xv; see also Richard L. Bushman, *The Refinement of America: Persons, Houses, Cities* (New York: Knopf, 1992) (describing transformation of consumer culture and standard of living beginning in 1740s).

87. See Egnal, *New World Economies,* 100–101 (showing the increase in slave imports into Charleston, South Carolina).

88. *Historical Statistics of the United States,* vol. 2, 1172 tables 146–49.

89. Price notes that slave imports to Virginia were "buoyant" following the Debt Recovery Act. Price, "Credit in the Slave Trade and Plantation Economies," at 310 and n.36.

90. Colonial court fees were high. An empirical study of court fees and costs of court in litigation in 1740 in the Plymouth County, Massachusetts, Court of Common Pleas found that fees and costs totaled 79% of the underlying debt amount for the lowest quartile of debts, and averaged 32.6% of all debts. Claire Priest, "Colonial Courts and Secured Credit: Early American Commercial Litigation and Shays' Rebellion," *Yale Law Journal* 108 (1999): 2413–50, 2426 and table 1. The full impact of a law making real property available to satisfy unsecured debts will, therefore, not be reflected in the absolute number of judicially ordered foreclosure sales. Foreclosure sales are likely to represent only a small percentage of land sold to satisfy creditors' claims.

91. 5 Geo. 3, c. 12 (1765).

92. See William Knox, *The Claim of the Colonies to an Exception from Internal Taxes Imposed by Authority of Parliament* (London: W. Johnston, 1765). Knox owned large amounts of property in Georgia, a state directly affected by the Debt Recovery Act, so he had some practical basis for understanding the impact of the law.

93. Ibid., 10–11. Daniel Dulaney, a private citizen from Maryland, wrote a pamphlet attacking the Stamp Act in response to Knox's defense of it. See Daniel Dulaney, *Considerations on the Propriety of Imposing Taxes in the British Colonies, for the Purpose of Raising a Revenue by Act of Parliament* (Annapolis, MD: Jonas Green, 1765). In response to Knox, Dulaney minimized the impact of the Debt Recovery Act, stating that its principal effect was only to "subject Real Estates to the Payment of Debts *after* the Death of the Debtor," and to ensure that colonial legislatures did not characterize slaves as real property which "very considerably diminished the personal Fund, liable to *all* Debts." Ibid., 37. To Dulaney, "[t]his was, without Doubt, a Subject upon which the Superintendence of the Mother-Country might be justly exercised; it being relatie to her Trade and Navigation, upon which her Wealth and her Power depend." Dulaney's dismissal of the Act's importance, however, is contradictory. If the Act only affected inheritance proceedings, and if that change in the laws had as little impact as Dulaney suggests, then why did characterizing slaves as real property damage credit?

94. Alexander Hamilton, "Practical Proceedings in the Supreme Court of the State of New York" (circa. 1782), in *The Law Practice of Alexander Hamilton: Documents and Commentary,* ed. Julius Goebel, Jr. (New York: published under the auspices of the William Nelson Cromwell Foundation by Columbia University Press, 1964), vol. 1, 55–135, 97.

95. 7 Geo. 3, c. 56 (1767).

Chapter 5. Managing Risk through Property

1. Act for the More Easy Recovery of Debts in His Majesty's Plantations and Colonies in America, 5 Geo. 2, c. 7 (1732) (Eng.).

2. Gregory S. Alexander, *Commodity and Propriety: Competing Visions of Property in American Legal Thought, 1776–1970* (Chicago: University of Chicago Press, 1997); Drew R. McCoy, *The*

Elusive Republic: Political Economy in Jeffersonian America (Chapel Hill: University of North Carolina Press, 1980); Gordon S. Wood, *The Radicalism of the American Revolution* (New York: Vintage Books, 1993); Brewer, "Entailing Aristocracy," 307–46; John F. Hart, "'A Less Proportion of Idle Proprietors': Madison, Property Rights, and the Abolition of the Fee Tail," *Washington and Lee Law Review* 58 (2001): 167–94; Stanley N. Katz, "Republicanism and the Law of Inheritance in the American Revolutionary Era," *Michigan Law Review* 76 (1977): 1–29, 3 ("In the study of revolution, the law of inheritance may serve as a touchstone measuring the depth of revolutionary transformation in a society."); Stanley N. Katz, "Thomas Jefferson and the Right to Property in Revolutionary America," *Journal of Law & Economics* 19 (1976): 467–88. Compare John V. Orth, "After the Revolution: 'Reform' of the Law of Inheritance," *Law & History Review* 10 (1992): 33–44 (emphasizing that the inheritance reforms of the Revolutionary Era could be evaded).

3. To indicate a fee tail, the testator would convey to X and "the heirs of his body."

4. Sir Edward Coke, *The first part of the Institutes of the Lawes of England* (1628) (New York: Garland, 1979), sections 259–61; Brewer, "Entailing Aristocracy," 335.

5. In contrast to owners of a life estate, however, landowners in tail could not be sued in a waste action for reducing the value of the property. Primogeniture, in contrast, was an intestacy doctrine that passed all of the deceased's land to the eldest male heir. It allowed landed estates to be kept intact in the absence of a will to the contrary, but only to the benefit of the eldest son.

6. The historian Holly Brewer makes a convincing argument for its widespread use in Virginia in Holly Brewer, "Entailing Aristocracy in Colonial Virginia: 'Ancient Feudal Restraints' and Revolutionary Reform," *William and Mary Quarterly* 54, no. 2 (Apr. 1997): 307–46.

7. For a list of the 133 private acts of the Virginia legislature removing entails, see Claire Priest, "The End of Entail: Information, Institutions, and Slavery in the American Revolutionary Period," *Law and History Review* 33 (2015): 277–319, appendix.

8. A 1705 Virginia law provided that entails could be removed by legislative act only. "An Act . . . for Settling the Titles and Bounds of Lands," *The Statutes at Large; Being a Collection of All the Laws of Virginia*, ed. William Waller Hening (Philadelphia, PA: Thomas Desilver, 1823), vol. 3, 320.

9. Ch. 75, *The Statutes at Large; Being a Collection of All the Laws of Virginia*, ed. William Waller Hening (Richmond, VA: J. & G. Cochran, 1821), vol. 8, 452–53.

10. Ch. 17, Hening, *Statutes at Large*, vol. 8, 66.

11. Ibid., 67.

12. On the importance of skilled slaves to iron works, see Charles B. Dew, *Bond of Iron: Master and Slave at Buffalo Forge* (New York: W.W. Norton, 1994).

13. Ch. 12, Hening, *Statutes at Large*, vol. 8, 29.

14. Ch. 24, Hening, *Statutes at Large*, vol. 8, 225.

15. Ch. 29, *The Statutes at Large; Being a Collection of All the Laws of Virginia*, ed. William Waller Hening (Richmond, VA: Franklin Press, 1820), vol. 4, 463.

16. Ch. 7, *The Statutes at Large; Being a Collection of All the Laws of Virginia*, ed. William Waller Hening (Richmond, VA: Franklin Press, 1820), vol. 7, 514.

17. Ch. 42, Hening, *Statutes at Large*, vol. 8, 164.

18. Ch. 5, *The Statutes at Large; Being a Collection of All the Laws of Virginia*, ed. William Waller Hening (Richmond, VA: Franklin Press, 1819), vol. 6, 444.

19. Ch. 43, Hening, *Statutes at Large*, vol. 8, 166–67.

20. Ch. 60, Hening, *Statutes at Large*, vol. 8, 292.

21. Ch. 6, Hening, *Statutes at Large*, vol. 8, 302.

22. See, for example, ch. 5, Hening, *Statutes at Large*, vol. 4, 29 ("John Custis, and Frances, his wife, to sell a Mill, with certain Lands and Negros, which are entailed on the said Frances by the last will and testament of Daniel Parke, Esq. deceased, for paiment of the debts and legacies

of the said Daniel"); Ch. 71, Hening, *Statutes at Large*, vol. 8, 442 (petitioner "hath but few slaves to cultivate the lands").

23. An Act to enable tenants in taille to make leases of their lands (1765), ch. 51, Hening, *Statutes at Large*, vol. 8, 183.

24. "Mr. Fane to the Council of Trade and Plantations" (October 16, 1730), No. 488, in *Calendar of State Papers, Colonial Series, America and West Indies, 1730*, ed. Cecil Headlam (London: His Majesty's Stationery, 1937), 319–20.

25. An Act to Explain and Amend the Act, for Declaring the Negro, Mulatto, and Indian Slaves, Within This Dominion, To Be Real Estate (1727), Hening, *Statutes at Large*, vol. 4, ch. 11, § 14, 222–28, 224.

26. See Thomas D. Morris, *Southern Slavery and the Law, 1619–1860* (Chapel Hill: University of North Carolina Press, 1996), 81–101.

27. Report of Joint Committee of Council and House of Burgesses (1748), *The Statutes at Large; Being a Collection of All the Laws of Virginia*, ed. William Waller Hening (Richmond, VA: Franklin Press, 1819), vol. 5, 440 fn. (italics added).

28. Ibid. at 442 fn. As described in part II, the Report also notes that: "Besides the clause for subjecting intailed slaves to be taken in execution for the debts of the tenant in tail for the time being, in effect annuls the former provision; because an unthrifty or designing tenant, by running in debt or borrowing money, and then confessing judgment, and getting his creditors to sue out executions against the intailed slaves, might defeat their settlement." Ibid.

29. See J. H. Baker, *An Introduction to English Legal History*, 4th ed. (London: Butterworths LexisNexis, 2002), 282 ("[B]y the end of the fifteenth century the common recovery had made the fee tail freely convertible into a fee simple."). For Blackstone's discussion of how the common recovery became "looked upon as the legal mode of conveyance, by which a tenant in tail may dispose of his lands and tenements," see William Blackstone, *Commentaries on the Laws of England* (Chicago: University of Chicago Press, facsimile ed. 1979, 1765–69), vol. 2, 117. According to Blackstone, "no court will suffer them to be shaken or reflected on, and even acts of parliament have by a sidewind countenanced and established them." Ibid.

30. More specifically, the common recovery involved a conveyance of entailed land to an accomplice in fee simple, with a third party paid to provide a false warranty of title. Under the law, the remainderman's only recourse was against the real property of the party who provided the false warranty of title. The people who agreed to perform this function were usually petty officials who owned no real property. The "barred issue" was, therefore, left without meaningful remedies. Baker, *Introduction to English Legal History*, 282. For a thorough description of the common recovery and other early American conveyancing practices, see William Sheppard, *The Touchstone of Common Assurances* (New York: Isaac Riley, 1808), vol. 1, 37–50.

31. In England, conveyance lawyers prided themselves on the scrupulousness with which they handled the process because any error might put the new fee simple title in question. The cost of this scrupulousness, of course, was the price of the lawyers' time. Common recoveries were the "bread and butter" of English property lawyers. See J. Stuart Anderson, *Lawyers and the Making of English Land Law, 1832–1940* (New York: Oxford University Press, 1992). See also Katz, "Republicanism and the Law of Inheritance," 10 (The English "system of inheritance . . . could not operate without a large and sophisticated legal class.").

32. James Kent, *Commentaries on American Law* (1830) (Buffalo, NY: William S. Hein & Co., 1984), vol. 4, 13–14.

33. A strict settlement might involve a devise of the land to the chosen devisee (often the eldest son) in the form of a life estate with limited or no powers of conveyance and with trustees appointed to preserve the contingent remainder on behalf of future generations. Baker, *Introduction to English Legal History*, 293–95. According to Simpson, "[T]he land was managed by

a succession of life tenants, the settlement being reconstituted each generation to ensure that no single individual ever acquired an unfettered power to appropriate the family capital for his individual purposes. It is remarkable that in spite of Blackstone's exaltation of private *individual* property rights, the landowning class in reality had little use for them." A. W. Brian Simpson, "Introduction to Book II, William Blackstone," Blackstone, *Commentaries*, vol. 2, iii–xv, xi; P. S. Atiyah, *The Rise and Fall of Freedom of Contract* (Oxford: Oxford University Press, 1979), 88 ("The eighteenth century was the age of the strict settlement, that intricate piece of conveyancing designed to tie up property, provide for widows, younger sons, and daughters, and, above all, maintain the property intact—or preferably augmented—in the family."); Simpson, "Land Ownership and Economic Freedom," 19 ("The aim was to pass the complete estate as a unit down the family line, ideally to a succession of males. . . . Thus the family land was employed as a patrimony for the whole family, in which individuals performed distinct roles.").

34. In England, marriage settlements were administered by the Court of Chancery. In colonial America, marriage settlements were recognized in the colonies that established Chancery Courts—New York, Maryland, Virginia, and South Carolina—and in colonies where the common law courts adopted equitable rules, such as Pennsylvania. The current historical scholarship suggests, however, that marriage settlements were rare in colonial America. See Marylynn Salmon, *Women and the Law of Property in Early America* (Chapel Hill: University of North Carolina Press, 1986), 88 (Marriage settlements granting women separate estates "remained uncommon throughout the eighteenth and early nineteenth centuries."). See also, for example, Alexander, *Commodity and Propriety*, 38–39 ("In England, strict settlements were enforced by Courts of Equity, but since most of the colonies had not established separate equity courts, the strict settlement was generally unavailable to American testators in the seventeenth and early eighteenth centuries, leaving the entail to be the only testamentary device for maintaining family control of land."); and Bernard Bailyn, "Politics and Social Structure in Virginia," in *Seventeenth-Century America: Essays in Colonial History*, ed. James Morton Smith (Westport, CT: Greenwood Press, 1980), 90–115 ("The basic condition of aristocratic governance in England was never present in the American colonies, and not for lack of familiarity with legal forms. The economic necessity that had prompted the widespread adoption of the strict settlement in England was absent in the colonies.").

35. An Act for Barring Estates Tail (January 27, 1750), *The Statutes at Large of Pennsylvania* (WM Stanley Ray, State Printer, 1898), vol. 5, 100 (emphasis added).

36. James Sullivan, *The History of Land Titles in Massachusetts* (Boston, MA: I. Thomas & E. T. Andrews, 1801), 161.

37. An Act Concerning Estates Tail, *Laws of Maryland* (Annapolis, MD: Frederick Green, State Printer, 1783), pages not numbered.

38. An Act . . . to Limit Estates in Tail,"*Acts of the Eighth General Assembly of the State of New Jersey* (Trenton, NJ: Isaac Collins, State Printer, 1784), 97.

39. Julius Goebel and Joseph H. Smith, eds., *The Law Practice of Alexander Hamilton* (New York: Columbia University Press, 1980), vol. 3, 308–09.

40. These policies were likely modeled after the English private acts of Parliament that were available to free land from strict settlements, life estates, and other restraints on alienation for extraordinary reasons. See Christopher Clay, "Property Settlements, Financial Provision for the Family, and Sale of Land by the Greater Landowners, 1660–1790," *Journal of British Studies* 21, no. 1 (Autumn 1981): 18–38. In the colonies, however, the private legislative acts served as a *substitute* for common recoveries, rather than as a last resort for landowners who needed to sell land encumbered by stronger devices than an entail.

41. See Gerard W. Gawalt, *The Promise of Power: The Emergence of the Legal Profession in Massachusetts, 1760–1840* (Westport, CT: Greenwood Press, 1979), 14, table 1 (finding that Massachusetts had only 15 practicing lawyers in 1740, 1 per 10,108 people).

42. "Mr. Fane to the Council of Trade and Plantations" (November 12, 1727), *Calendar of State Papers, Colonial Series, America and West Indies, 1726–1727*, ed. Cecil Headlam (London: His Majesty's Stationery, 1936), No. 778, 392. The inadequacies of colonial lawyers and officials in executing common recoveries are also described in An Act for the Supplying the want of Fines and Recoveries in these Islands (Nevis, June 21, 1705), *Acts of Assembly passed in the Charibbee Leeward Islands, 1690–1730* (London: John Baskett, 1734), 20–22. The origins of Virginia's legislative approval requirement are more obscure. Virginia had a community of lawyers sophisticated enough to be able to perform common recoveries. The statute simply states that "it shall not be lawfull" for individuals to "to suffer any recovery to be had, whereby to cut off or defeat any estate in fee tail [or to use other means to bar an entail] except only by an act of the general assembly of this dominion." It then states that the use of law office procedures such as the common recovery to bar an entail "are hereby declared to be all intents and purposes, null and void." An Act for Settling the Titles and Bounds of Lands (1705), Hening, *Statutes at Large*, vol. 3, 320. This statute was reenacted in 1710. See ch. 13, Hening, *Statutes at Large*, vol. 3, 518–19. With regard to North Carolina, the historian John V. Orth speculates that "[t]he common recovery was apparently unknown in North Carolina, whether because colonial courts had not been up to its subtleties or because social conditions in the colony had lagged those along the Chesapeake." Orth, "After the Revolution," 41.

43. It is notable that these colonies were all under direct royal rule as opposed to having legal authority vested in the colonial legislatures by means of a charter or patent. Marshall Harris, *Origin of the Land Tenure System in the United States* (Ames: Iowa State College Press, 1953), 75.

44. "Journal of Assembly of Barbados" (February 20, 1677), in *Calendar of State Papers, Colonial Series, America and West Indies, 1677–1680*, ed. W. Noel Sainsbury and J. W. Fortescue (London: Her Majesty's Stationery, 1896), No. 74, 24.

45. An Act to Dock the Entail . . . and to vest the Fee-Simple thereof in Martha Lenoir (1717) *Acts of Assembly Passed in the Island of Barbadoes from 1648 to 1718* (London: John Baskett, 1721), 313.

46. Ibid., 314.

47. An Act to dock the Entail (1715), in *Acts of Assembly Passed in the Island of Barbadoes*, 306.

48. It is not unrelated that Barbados lacked a well-developed community of English colonists with a long-term interest in building a residential society on the island, and the economy of Barbados was entirely dominated by slave labor used to produce sugar. See, for example, Russell R. Menard, "Law, credit, the supply of labour, and the organization of sugar production in the colonial Greater Caribbean: a comparison of Brazil and Barbados in the seventeenth century," in *The Early Modern Atlantic Economy*, ed. John J. McCusker and Kenneth Morgan (New York: Cambridge University Press, 2000), 154–62.

49. See *Calendar of State Papers*.

50. According to Smith, "[Entails] are founded upon the most absurd of all suppositions, the supposition that every successive generation of men have not an equal right to the earth, and to all that it possesses; but that the property of the present generation should be restrained and regulated according to the fancy of those who died perhaps five hundred years ago. . . . The common law of England . . . is said to abhor perpetuities, and [entails] are accordingly more restricted there than in any other European monarchy; though even England is not altogether without them. In Scotland, more than one-fifth, perhaps more than one-third part of the whole lands of the country, are at present supposed to be under strict entail." Adam Smith, *An Inquiry Into the Nature and Causes of The Wealth of Nations* (1776), ed. Edwin Cannan (Chicago: University of Chicago Press, 1976), vol. 1, 409–10. Other scholars have analyzed the effects of Virginia's policy, but there has been no historical explanation provided for the adoption of the policy other than as an explicit effort to introduce a landed elite into Virginia. The best descriptions of Virginia's peculiar approach to

entails are Brewer, "Entailing Aristocracy," 326–28 (describing the difficulty of barring entails in Virginia); Hart, "Madison, Property Rights, and the Abolition of Fee Tail," 172–75; and Orth, "After the Revolution," 40–44.

51. Ch. 42, Hening *Statutes at Large*, vol. 8, 164.

52. Ch. 13, Hening, *Statutes at Large*, vol. 8, 34. For a list of representative acts, see, for example, Hening, *Statutes at Large*, vol. 4, 377–79. One states: "An Act for vesting certain entailed Lands . . . in *Thomas Turner*, in fee simple; and for settling other Lands and Negroes, of greater value, to the same uses." Ibid., 377.

53. "Report of Joint Committee of Council and House of Burgesses" (1748), in Hening, *Statutes at Large*, vol. 5, 442 fn.

54. The appendix in Priest, "The End of Entail," lists the private acts removing entails and whether the property at issue consisted of land, slaves, or both.

55. Ch. 72, Hening, *Statutes at Large*, vol. 8, 445.

56. John Cook, *Monarchy no Creature of God's Making* (Waterford, Ireland: Peter de Pienne, 1651), 26. See also Lloyd Bonfield, *Marriage Settlements, 1601–1740* (Cambridge: Cambridge University Press, 1983), 20 (discussing mid-seventeenth-century movement to lower costs of barring entails).

57. Matthew Hale, *A treatise shewing how usefull, safe, reasonable, and beneficial the inrolling & registring of all conveyances of lands may be* . . . (London: Mat. Wotton, 1694), 21.

58. See Dan Bogart and Gary Richardson, "Property Rights and Parliament in Industrializing Britain," *Journal of Law & Economics* 54, no. 2 (May 2011): 241–74.

59. An Act declaring tenants of lands or slaves in taille to hold the same in fee simple, Hening, *Statutes at Large*, vol. 9, 226.

60. An Act for amending the Act intitled . . . for Settling the Titles and Bounds of Lands, ch. 6, Hening, *Statutes at Large*, vol. 4, 399.

61. Ibid., 400.

62. The fee tail would be barred "in the same manner as the same estate might be barred, by fine, or recovery, according to the laws of England." Ibid., 400.

63. Ibid., 399–400.

64. An Act directing the Method for cutting or docking Intails of small Estates (1749) *The State Records of North Carolina*, ed. Walter Clark (Goldsboro, NC: Nash Brothers, 1904), vol. 23, 315–16.

65. Robert E. Brown and B. Katherine Brown, *Virginia 1705–1786: Democracy or Aristocracy?* (East Lansing: Michigan State University Press, 1964), 88. They conclude that, "In practice, whatever the intent, the *ad quod damnum* law helped both rich and poor to avoid the restraints of entail." Ibid., 85.

66. Landon Carter's diary mentions his effort to have the legislature insert a provision into each private act docking the entail on land that prohibited the entail on the new land from being subsequently removed according to the *ad quod damnum* process. Carter was not successful in getting the legislature to condition removal of the entail on this requirement. Brown and Brown, *Virginia 1705–1786*, 88. When entails were docked by legislative act, there is evidence that the tenants in tail evaded the requirement of entailing new land by pur- chasing multiple small parcels and, at a later time, removing the entails on the parcels through the *ad quod damnum* process.

67. Richard Henry Lee to William Lee (July 7, 1770), in *Letters of Richard Henry Lee* (1911), vol. 1, 50, quoted in Brown and Brown, *Virginia 1705–1786*, 85 n.39.

68. Matt. Kemp (June 10, 1737), *Virginia Gazette*, quoted in Brown and Brown, *Virginia 1705–1786*, 85 n.38.

69. There are clear advantages to protecting a family homestead from risk. As Gavin Wright has described, "The family farm provided a substantial measure of security—against starvation, unemployment, or old-age destitution. In an era of undeveloped and risky financial institutions,

the family farm provided a means of accumulating wealth in a reasonably safe form—the wealth being largely the product of the family's own labor in land clearing, fencing, drainage, etc.—and self-cultivation helped to ensure that the earnings from this wealth were continuous and fell into the proper hands. . . . Finally, the family farm gave the head of the household a convenient means for controlling and exploiting the labor of members of his own family." Wright, *Political Economy of the Cotton South*, 47.

70. C. Ray Keim, "Primogeniture and Entail in Colonial Virginia," *William and Mary Quarterly* 25 (1968): 545–86.

71. See Hening, *Statutes at Large*, Vols. 4–8. C. Ray Keim counted 125 Virginia Acts removing entails (11 fewer than reported here). Keim, "Primogeniture and Entail," 577. For clarity regarding what I counted, see the list of acts at Priest, *Law and History Review*, "The End of Entail," appendix. Some on my list were not located in Hening's Indices under "Fee Tail."

72. This is consistent with Stephanie Jones-Rogers's findings that women often owned slaves in antebellum America. Stephanie Jones-Rogers, *They Were Her Property: White Women as Slave Owners in the American South* (New Haven, CT: Yale University Press, 2019).

73. Ch. 6, Hening, *Statutes at Large*, vol. 6, 446.

74. Ibid.

75. Ch. 83, Hening, *Statutes at Large*, vol. 8, 474.

76. Ch. 29, Hening, *Statutes at Large*, vol. 7, 157–58.

77. Sir Edward Coke, *The first part of the Institutes of the Lawes of England* (1628), sections 259–61 (New York: Garland, 1979); and Brewer "Entailing Aristocracy," 335.

78. Ch. 52, Hening, *Statutes at Large*, vol. 6, 319.

79. Ibid.

80. See Linda L. Sturtz, *Within Her Power: Propertied Women in Colonial Virginia* (New York: Routledge, 2002), 19–41 (discussing the importance of legally separating property interests in the Chesapeake world of high mortality and the prevalence of blended stepfamilies); and Lois Green Carr, Russell R. Menard, and Lorena S. Walsh, *Robert Cole's World: Agriculture and Society in Early Maryland* (Chapel Hill: University of North Carolina Press, 1991), 142–50 (discussing late-seventeenth-century family structure in Maryland).

81. See Vivian Bruce Conger, *The Widows' Might: Widowhood and Gender in Early British America* (New York: New York University Press, 2009), 89–91 (finding that one-third of testate widows bequeathed real property, and discussing men's and women's propensity to bequeath to daughters).

82. Brown and Brown, *Virginia 1705–1786*, 86 (noting that some "entailed slaves to a male heir but devised other slaves to a female heir in fee simple. Others willed land to sons in fee simple but to daughters in fee tail").

83. James Ross McCain, *Georgia as a Proprietary Province* (Boston: Richard G. Badger, 1917), 263–72, describing requirements for obtaining different plot sizes, with five hundred acres as the maximum); and *An Account Shewing the Progress of the Colony of Georgia in American from its First Establishment* (London, 1741), 1–10.

84. *An Account Shewing the Progress of the Colony of Georgia*, 8–10.

85. Savannah Petition to the Trustees of Georgia (December 9, 1738), in *An Account Shewing the Progress of the Colony of Georgia*, 61.

86. Ibid., 60.

87. Ibid., 61–62.

88. Letter from the Trustees of Georgia to the Magistrates of Savannah (June 20, 1739), in ibid., 71.

89. Ibid., 70.

90. Betty Wood, *Slavery in Colonial Georgia, 1730–1775* (Athens: University of Georgia Press, 1984), 76.

91. Watson Jennison, *Cultivating Race: The Expansion of Slavery in Georgia, 1750–1860* (Lexington: University Press of Kentucky, 2012); Ben Marsh, "Planting families: Intent and outcome in the development of colonial Georgia," *The History of the Family* 12 (2007): 104–115.

92. Art. 51, *Georgia Constitution of 1777* ("Estates shall not be entailed . . ."); Art. IV, Sec. 6, *Georgia Constitution of 1789* (same).

93. See Alison D. Morantz, "There's No Place Like Home: Homestead Exemption and Judicial Constructions of Family in Nineteenth-Century America," *Law & History Review* 24 (2006): 245–95; and Paul Goodman, "The Emergence of Homestead Exemption in the United States: Accommodation and Resistance to the Market Revolution, 1840–1880," *Journal of American History* 80 (1993): 470–98.

94. See, for example, Richard H. Chused, "Married Women's Property Law: 1800–1850," *Georgetown Law Journal* 71 (1983): 1359–1426.

95. Ibid.; and Norma Basch, *In the Eyes of the Law: Women, Marriage, and Property in Nineteenth-Century New York* (Ithaca, NY: Cornell University Press, 1982), 125–26 ("Much of the early support for a married women's statute focused on the economic dislocations of men; considerations of women were often secondary. Just as debtor exemption laws for household items and tools eased the lot of farmers, artisans, and some wage earners and petty traders, so might a statute separating the wife's property from that of the husband have a similar effect.").

Chapter 6. The Stamp Act and Legal and Economic Institutions

1. Jared Ingersoll to Thomas Fitch, February 11, 1765, ed. Edmund S. Morgan, *Prologue to Revolution: Sources and Documents on the Stamp Act Crisis, 1764–1766* (Chapel Hill: Published for the Omohundro Institute of Early American History and Culture, Williamsburg, Virginia, by the University of North Carolina Press, 1959), 29–34, 34. [hereinafter *Prologue to Revolution: Sources and Documents*].

2. Ibid.

3. See, e.g., Brendan McConville, *The King's Three Faces: The Rise & Fall of Royal America, 1688–1776* (Chapel Hill: University of North Carolina Press, 2006), 249; Edmund S. Morgan, *The Birth of the Republic, 1763–89*, 3rd ed. (Chicago: University of Chicago Press, 1992), 18–28; Gordon S. Wood, *The American Revolution: A History* (New York: Random House, 2003).

4. Morgan, *The Birth of the Republic*, 23–28; Wood, *The American Revolution*, 38–44; Bernard Bailyn, *The Ideological Origins of the American Revolution* (Cambridge: President and Fellows of Harvard College, 1967), 94–104; Edmund S. Morgan and Helen M. Morgan, *The Stamp Act Crisis: Prologue to Revolution* (Chapel Hill: University of North Carolina Press, 1995), 54–121. The most prominent colonial responses to the Stamp Act, of course, followed this line of argument. The Virginia House of Burgesses, for example, published a set of resolutions in response to the Stamp Act, which stated, "That the Taxation of the People by themselves, or by Persons chosen by themselves to represent them . . . is the only Security against a burthensome Taxation, and the distinguishing Characteristick of *British* Freedom, without which the ancient Constitution cannot exist." The Resolutions as Printed in *The Journal of the House of Burgesses*, in Morgan, *Prologue to Revolution: Sources and Documents*, at 48. Similarly, The Pennsylvania Resolves of 1765 stated, "That it is the inherent Birth-right, and indubitable Privilege, of every *British* Subject, to be taxed only by his own Consent, or that of his legal Representatives, in Conjunction with his Majesty, or his Substitutes." The Pennsylvania Resolves, September 21, 1765, reprinted in Morgan, *Prologue to Revolution: Sources and Documents*, at 51. The Stamp Act Congress similarly stated in its declaration of October 1765: "That it is inseparably essential to the Freedom of a People, and the undoubted Right of *Englishmen*, that no Taxes be imposed on them, but with their own

Consent, given personally, or by their Representatives." The Declaration of the Stamp Act Congress, reprinted in *Morgan, Prologue to Revolution: Sources and Documents*, at 62–63. For other central historical works emphasizing the constitutional origins of the Stamp Act and the American Revolution, see H. T. Dickinson, "Britain's Imperial Sovereignty: The Ideological Case Against the American Colonists," in *Britain and the American Revolution*, ed. H. T. Dickinson (London: Longman, 1998) 65–81; Jack P. Greene, *Peripheries and Center: Constitutional Development in the Extended Polities of the British Empire and the United States, 1607–1788* (Athens: University of Georgia Press, 1986), 80–81; J.G.A. Pocock, *Virtue, Commerce, and History: Essays on Political Thought and History, Chiefly in the Eighteenth Century*, in ed. Richard Rorty, J. B. Schneewind, and Quentin Skinner (Cambridge: Press Syndicate of the University of Cambridge, 1985), 80–86; John Phillip Reid, *Constitutional History of the American Revolution*, Abridged edition (Madison: University of Wisconsin Press, 1995), xv–xvi, 26–30; and P.D.G. Thomas, *British Politics and the Stamp Act Crisis: The First Phase of the American Revolution 1763–1767* (Oxford: Clarendon Press, 1975), 33.

5. See Jack P. Greene, *The Quest for Power: The Lower Houses of Assembly in the Southern Royal Colonies*, 1689–1776 (Chapel Hill: Published for the Institute of Early American History and Culture at Williamsburg, VA, by the University of North Carolina Press, 1963).

6. The First Laws made by the Assembly in Virginia (1623) in *The Statutes at Large; Being a Collection of All the Laws of Virginia*, ed. William Waller Hening (New York: R. & W. & G. Bartow, 1823), vol. 1, no. 8, 124.

7. Greene, *The Quest for Power*, 148.

8. Ibid.

9. The fee laws of Massachusetts illustrate colonial legislatures' assertion of control over fee levels. See, e.g., *The Acts and Resolves, Public and Private, of the Province of Massachusetts Bay* (Boston: Wright & Potter, 1869) (1692 fee schedule), vol. 1, 84–88; *The Acts and Resolves, Public and Private, of the Province of Massachusetts Bay* (Boston: Wright, 1878), vol. 3, 13–18; *Acts and Resolves of Massachusetts*, vol. 3, 101–7 (1743 fee schedule); *Acts and Resolves of Massachusetts*, vol. 3, 176–81 (1744 fee schedule); *Acts and Resolves of Massachusetts*, vol. 3, 328–33 (1747 fee schedule); *Acts and Resolves of Massachusetts*, vol. 3, 525–31 (1751 fee schedule); *Acts and Resolves of Massachusetts*, vol. 3, 656–66 (1753 fee schedule); *Acts and Resolves of Massachusetts*, vol. 3, 1032–38 (1757 fee schedule); *The Acts and Resolves, Public and Private, of the Province of Massachusetts Bay* (Boston: Wright & Potter, 1886), vol. 5, 486–95 (1776 fee schedule); *Acts and Resolves of Massachusetts*, vol. 5, 761–70 (1778 fee schedule); 1782–1783 Mass. Acts, 10–24 (1782 fee schedule); 1784–1785 Mass. Acts, 458–62 (1785 fee schedule); 1786–1787 Mass. Acts, 226–38 (1786 fee schedule). See also Robert J. Taylor, *Western Massachusetts in the Revolution* (Providence, RI: Brown University Press, 1954), 31 (describing fee schedule revisions).

10. Act 64 (1632), See Hening, *Statutes at Large*, vol. 1, 176; Act 47 (1643), Hening, *Statutes at Large*, vol. 1, 266; Act 139 (1662), Hening, *Statutes at Large*, vol. 2, 143; Act 16 (1680), Hening, *Statutes at Large*, vol. 2, 485; Act 12 (1696), Hening, *Statutes at Large*, vol. 3, 153; Act 1 (1718), Hening, *Statutes at Large*, vol. 4, 59; Act 10 (1732), Hening, *Statutes at Large*, vol. 4, 340; Act 10 (1734), Hening, *Statutes at Large*, vol. 4, 409; Act 10 (1738), Hening, *Statutes at Large*, vol. 5, 38; Act 6 (1745), Hening, *Statutes at Large*, vol. 5, 326.

11. Claire Priest, "Colonial Courts and Secured Credit: Early American Commercial Litigation and Shays' Rebellion," *Yale Law Journal* 108 (1999): 2413–50, 2444–47.

12. See Greene, *The Quest for Power*, 158–59; Glenn Curtis Smith, "The Affair of the Pistole Fee, Virginia, 1752–55," *Virginia Magazine of History & Biography* 48, no. 3 (July 1940): 209–21, 209–10.

13. Greene, *Quest for Power*, 159.

14. Ibid.; *Acts of the Privy Council of England, Colonial Series, Volume 2, 1680–1720*, ed. W. L. Grant, James Munro (London: His Majesty's Stationary Office, 1910), 142–43.

15. Jack P. Greene, "The Case of the Pistole Fee: The Report of a Hearing on the Pistole Fee Dispute Before the Privy Council, June 18, 1754," *Virginia Magazine of History and Biography* 66, no. 4 (1958): 401 (quoting a letter from William Stith to the Bishop of London).

16. Ibid., 400. William Stith, president of the College of William and Mary and chaplain of the House of Burgesses, introduced this slogan while toasting the group of Burgesses members opposing the fee. Ibid.

17. Ibid., 400 n.13.

18. Transcripts of the hearing before the Privy Council are reprinted in their entirety in *The Case of the Pistole Fee*, 406–22.

19. "Alexander Hume Campbell, for the Governor, Transcript of Hearing before the Privy Council," (June 18, 1754) in *The Case of the Pistole Fee*, 409, 410 (discussing the differences between the pistole fee and Howard's fee).

20. "William Murray (Lord Mansfield), Attorney General for the Governor, Transcript of Hearing before the Privy Council," in *The Case of the Pistole Fee*, 409. Murray's testimony is reprinted in ibid., 406–09.

21. Ibid., 409.

22. Murray changed his interpretation in 1765: he defended the Stamp Act as a purely discretionary tax.

23. "Alexander Hume Campbell, for the Governor, Transcript of Hearing before the Privy Council" (June 18, 1754) in *The Case of the Pistole Fee*, 410.

24. Ibid. Lord Mansfield similarly emphasized:

> It has long been the Custom in that Colony to make Application to the proper Officer, to take up great quantities of Land, more than the Takers up ever intended to Cultivate; merely, with a design to keep out other Tenants; Which your Lordships must be convinced to be the Case, when you are informed, that in one Day, there were granted out no less than One Million four hundred thousand acres. William Murray (Lord Mansfield), Attorney General for the Governor, Transcript of Hearing before the Privy Council, in *The Case of the Pistole Fee*, 407.

25. *The Case of the Pistole Fee*, 401 (alteration in original) (internal quotation marks omitted).

26. "Robert Henley, for the Assembly, Transcript of Hearing before the Privy Council" (June 18, 1754) in *The Case of the Pistole Fee*, 412, 414. Henley also emphasized:

> This demand of the Governor is made in a very extraordinary Manner, in Contempt of the Authority of this Board, and is an Infringement of an Order made by your Lordships' Predecessors. It is not to be wondered at that a free People, living in a remote Country under so mild a Government, as that of his present Majesty's, should be alarmed at such an unusual, such an oppressive Demand. (412)

27. Duties in America (Stamp) Act § 58. Justin DuRivage, *Revolution Against Empire: Taxes, Politics, and the Origins of American Independence* (New Haven, CT: Yale University Press, 2017), 113.

28. Currency Act, 4 Geo. 3, c. 34, § 1 (1764). At the time of its passage, 160 Virginia pounds equaled about 100 pounds sterling. John J. McCusker, *Money and Exchange in Europe and America, 1600–1775* (Chapel Hill: Published for the Institute of Early American History and Culture, Williamsburg, VA, by the University of North Carolina Press, 1978), 211.

29. See Justin duRivage and Claire Priest, "The Stamp Act and the Political Origins of American Legal and Economic Institutions," *Southern California Law Review* 88 (2015): 875–912.

30. Duties in America (Stamp) Act § 1.

31. Ibid.

32. Ibid. duRivage, *Revolution Against Empire*, 108.

33. Duties in America (Stamp) Act, 5 Geo. 3, c. 12, § 1 (1765). See also duRivage, *Revolution Against Empire*, 113.

34. Duties in America (Stamp) Act, 5 Geo. 3, c. 12, § 1 (1765). Robert Taylor reports that, in 1781, Northampton paid master tradesmen forty-five pence (33.74 pence sterling) per day for summer labor and, in 1782, paid twenty-eight pence (20.99 pence sterling) and twenty-one pence (15.75 pence sterling) per day for unskilled labor in the summer and fall, respectively. See Robert J. Taylor, *Western Massachusetts in the Revolution* (Providence, RI: Brown University Press, 1954), 195 n.56. According to Taylor, these wages are similar to those paid by other towns. Ibid. In the 1780s, sterling values were calculated according to the par exchange rate: £133 7s. 6.d Massachusetts money equals £100 English Sterling. McCusker, *Money and Exchange*, 120.

35. The Petition to the House of Commons, reprinted in *Prologue to Revolution: Sources and Documents*, 66–69, 68.

36. See Steve Pincus, *The Heart of the Declaration: The Founders' Case for an Activist Government* (New Haven, CT: Yale University Press, 2016); duRivage, *Revolution Against Empire*.

37. B. R. Mitchell, *British Historical Statistics* (New York : Cambridge University Press, 1988), 601.

38. See DuRivage and Priest, "The Stamp Act."

39. Ibid.

40. Grenville's economic vision is elaborated in duRivage, *Revolution Against Empire*.

41. Francis Bernard, "Principles of Law and Policy Applied to the British Colonies in America" (1764) (unpublished manuscript, on file with British Library, Liverpool Papers, Additional Manuscript 38,342), 195; William Knox, "Hints Respecting the Civil Establishments in the American Colonies" (February 25, 1763) (on file with British Library, Liverpool Papers, Additional Manuscript 38,335), 21, 23. On Knox, his views on imperial reform, and his political career, Jack P. Greene, "William Knox's Explanation for the American Revolution," *William and Mary Quarterly* 30, no. 2 (Apr. 1973): 293–306.

42. Letter from George Grenville, Member of Parliament, to William Knox, Provost Marshall of Ga. (August 15, 1768) (on file with Huntington Library, Stowe Papers 7, George Grenville Letterbook, vol. 2) [hereinafter: Letter from George Grenville to William Knox].

43. Letter from Thomas Whately, Junior Sec'y of Treasury, to John Temple, Surveyor Gen. of the Customs of the N. Dist. in Bos. 12 (February 9, 1765) (on file with Huntington Library, Stowe Grenville Papers, Stamp Act letter book, box 13, folder 6).

44. Letter I: From T[homas] W[hately], Junior Sec'y of Treasury to J.I. (Spring 1764), in Mr. Ingersoll's Letters Relating to the Stamp-Act 1, 4 (New Haven: Samuel Green, 1766) [hereinafter Letter from Thomas Whately to Jared Ingersoll].

45. Letter from George Grenville to William Knox.

46. Ibid.

47. Letter from Thomas Whately to Jared Ingersoll, 4. See duRivage and Priest, "The Stamp Act."

48. Daniel Dulany, *Considerations on the Propriety of Imposing Taxes in the British Colonies* (New York: John Holt, 1765), 24–25.

49. See duRivage, *Revolution Against Empire*; Copy of Mr. Secretary Whately's General Plan, 312–13; Duties in America (Stamp) Act, 5 Geo. 3, c. 12, § 1 (1765).

50. John Adams, "A Dissertation on the Canon and the Feudal Law (1765)," in *Papers of John Adams*, ed. Robert J. Taylor (Cambridge, MA: Belknap Press of Harvard University Press, 1977), vol. 1, 123, 128.

51. John Adams, Instructions Adopted by the Braintree Town Meeting (September 24, 1765), in *Papers of John Adams*, vol. 1, 137.

52. Ibid., 138.

53. Thomas Fitch, *Reasons Why The British Colonies, In America, Should Not Be Charged With Internal Taxes, By Authority Of Parliament; Humbly Offered, For Consideration, In Behalf Of The Colony Of Connecticut* (New Haven, CT: B. Mecom 1764), 22.

54. Ibid.

55. Dulany, *Considerations on the Propriety of Imposing Taxes in the British Colonies*, 24.

56. James Otis, *Considerations on Behalf of the Colonists. In a Letter to a Noble Lord* (London: J. Almon, 1765), 32.

57. The Examination of Doctor Benjamin Franklin, Before an August Assembly, Relating to the Repeal of the Stamp-Act, &c 10 (Philadelphia, PA: Hall & Sellers, 1766).

58. Ibid.

59. Dulany, *Considerations on the Propriety of Imposing Taxes in the British Colonies*, 24.

Chapter 7. Property Exemptions and the Abolition of the Fee Tail

1. See Robert J. Steinfeld, "Property and Suffrage in the Early American Republic," *Stanford Law Review* 41 (1989): 335–76, 339–40; Alexander Keyssar, *The Right to Vote: The Contested History of Democracy in the United States* (New York: Basic Books, 2000), ch. 1; Gregory S. Alexander, *Commodity and Propriety: Competing Visions of Property in American Legal Thought, 1776–1970* (Chicago: University of Chicago Press, 1997), 66–69.

2. Gordon S. Wood, *The Radicalism of the American Revolution* (New York: Vintage Books, 1993), 234 (quoting *Pa. Packet*, Nov. 26, 1776; *S.C. & Am. Gazette*, Nov. 6, 1777) (internal quotation marks omitted).

3. *Pritchard v. Brown*, 4 N.H. 397, 404 (1828). The Act also remained enacted law in the parts of Washington, DC that Maryland had ceded to create the territory. See Suckley's *Adm'r v. Rotchford*, 53 Va. (12 Gratt.) 60, 67 (1855) ("It . . . is fully shown by numerous adjudged cases in the Court of appeals of Maryland, that the statute 5 George 2, ch. 7, § 4, was in force in that state February 27th, 1801, when their laws were extended by act of congress to Washington county; and was in force in Washington county June 24th, 1812, when the law of that county was extended to Alexandria county.").

4. An Act for Establishing Courts of Law, and for Regulating the Proceedings Therein (November 15, 1777) *The Acts of Assembly of the State of North Carolina*. 1777, Second Session (Newbern, NC: James Davis, 1778), ch. 2, § 29, 16; see also Act of Feb. 15, 1791, 1791 N.H. Laws 122 (establishing a regime whereby lands would be transferred to creditors in kind, with a one-year statutory redemption period, when a debtor's personal property was deficient).

5. Letter from Thomas Jefferson to James Madison (September 6, 1789), *The Papers of Thomas Jefferson*, ed. Julian P. Boyd (Princeton, NJ: Princeton University Press, 1950-), vol. 15, 392 (internal quotation mark omitted).

6. Ibid., 393 (footnotes omitted).

7. James Kent, *Commentaries on American Law* (Buffalo, NY: Hein, 1984 repr.; New York: 1830), vol. 4, 18.

8. Ibid., 27.

9. "Thomas Jefferson, Autobiography, 1743–1790," *The Writings of Thomas Jefferson*, ed. Paul Leicester Ford (New York: G.P. Putnam's Sons, 1892–99), vol. 1, 68; see also "A Bill Concerning Wills; the Distribution of Intestate's Estates; and the Duty of Executors and Administrators," *The Papers of Thomas Jefferson*, vol. 2, 394 (describing the process for settling the estates of the deceased); "A Bill Directing the Course of Descents," *The Papers of Thomas Jefferson*, vol. 2, 391 (abolishing primogeniture).

10. A less controversial issue involved whether the personal property had to be exhausted before the sheriff seized the debtor's real property. Most states, either by statute or court decision, determined that, in the ordinary course of debt collection, the sheriff could seize land only when the debtor's personal property could not satisfy the debt. Maryland was exceptional in allowing

creditors to choose whether to take the debtor's personal property or real property. See *Hanson v. Barnes' Lessee*, 3 G. & J. 359, 367 (Md. 1831) (noting that the Debt Recovery Act "stripped lands in the Plantations, of the sanctity with which they had been guarded, and by subjecting them to sale, no longer considered them as a secondary fund for the payment of debts in the hands of a debtor, but rendered them equally liable with his personalty. It is at the election of the plaintiff, whether he will seize lands or goods, and this has always been the construction of the statute."). Statutes passed in New York in 1787 and 1801 were more typical: they required courts to treat land exactly like personal property for the satisfaction of debts, but added the requirement that the personal property be exhausted first.

11. 3 S.C.L. (1 Brev.) 289 (S.C. Const. Ct. 1803).

12. Ibid., 290.

13. Ibid., 291.

14. Ibid.

15. Ibid., 292.

16. Ibid.

17. *Telfair v. Stead's Executors*, 6 U.S. (2 Cranch) 407, 418 (1805). Kent notes that the same policy existed in Pennsylvania. Kent, *Commentaries on American Law*, vol. 4, 417.

18. James Kent's treatise of 1830 states that the policy of affording no right of redemption was still in force in New Jersey, Maryland, North Carolina, Tennessee, South Carolina, Georgia, Alabama, and Mississippi when he wrote. Kent, *Commentaries on American Law*, vol. 4, 426. New York followed the same policy until 1821, when the legislature adopted a fifteen-month redemption period for land sold in execution sales. Ibid., 427. Kent overlooked New Hampshire, where in 1828 the state's highest court held that the Debt Recovery Act—which was still in force— was properly interpreted as requiring the sale of the equity-of-redemption interest with the real property at foreclosure sales. *Pritchard v. Brown*, 4 N.H. 397, 404 (1828). The court questioned whether the Debt Recovery Act necessarily implied that the equity of redemption should be sold but concluded that "this practice is of too long standing, and is the foundation of too many titles to be now questioned." Ibid.

19. 1 Cai. Cas. 47 (N.Y. 1804); See *The Law Practice of Alexander Hamilton*, ed. Julius Goebel, Jr. and Joseph H. Smith (New York: Published under the auspices of the William Nelson Cromwell Foundation by Columbia University Press, 1980), vol. 3, 638–44.

20. *Waters v. Stewart*, 1 Cai. Cas. 49–50.

21. See ibid., 68.

22. Act of Mar. 19, 1787, ch. 56, 1787 N.Y. Laws 108; see also Act of Mar. 31 1801, ch. 105, 1801 N.Y. Laws 388 (reenacting 1787 law).

23. *Waters v. Stewart*, 1 Cai. Cas. 52.

24. Ibid.

25. Ibid.

26. Ibid.

27. See ibid., 54–55.

28. See ibid., 68–69.

29. Ibid., 69.

30. Ibid., 71.

31. Ibid.

32. Ibid., 70.

33. Ibid.,73.

34. Ibid., 70.

35. See, e.g., *Ford v. Philpot*, 5 H. & J. 312 (Md. 1821) (holding, under the Debt Recovery Act and Maryland statutory law, that when a fee simple interest is sold at auction, the mortgagor

retains no right to redeem); *Ingersoll v. Sawyer*, 19 Mass. (2 Pick.) 276 (1824) (holding that if a mortgagor does not redeem property sold at auction within the one-year statutory period, he loses his freehold); *Bell v. Hill*, 2 N.C. (1 Hayw.) 72 (1794) (holding that whole interest may be sold at auction); see generally Kent, *Commentaries on American Law*, vol. 4, 426–27.

36. Daniel Webster, "A Discourse Delivered at Plymouth, December 22, 1820, in Commemoration of the First Settlement of New-England," 4th ed. (Boston, MA: Wells and Lilly, 1826), 41.

37. Daniel Webster would likely have approved of the reform movement that developed in the 1820s and 1830s that condemned the English regime as epitomizing the brutal injustice and aristocratic nature of England's criminal law, which protected landowners while imprisoning and impoverishing merchants and debtors who did not own land. According to Jeremy Bentham:

> [N]oble lords have been heard to say . . . that for small debts . . . there ought to be no remedy. . . . In pursuance of this same policy, property, in a shape which noble lords and honourable gentlemen have more of their property than in all other shapes put together, is exempted from the obligation of affording the satisfactive remedy—in a word, from the obligation of paying debts, while property in these other shapes is left subject to it. Noble lords or honourable gentlemen contract debts, and instead of paying them, lay out the money in the purchase of land: land being exempted from the obligation of being sold for payment, creditors are thus cheated. Noble lord's son is too noble, honourable gentlemen's son too honourable to pay the money, but not so to keep the land. Jeremy Bentham, *Justice and Codification Petitions* (London: R. Heward, 1829), Part 4, Abridged Petition for Justice, 84–85.

38. Noah Webster, *An Examination into the Leading Principles of the Federal Constitution* (Philadelphia, PA: Prichard & Hall, 1787), 47.

39. See Robert J. Taylor, *Western Massachusetts in the Revolution* (Providence, RI: Brown University Press, 1954), 105–20; Charles Warren, *Bankruptcy in United States History* (Cambridge, MA: Harvard University Press, 1935), 147. For the economic context of Shays's Rebellion, see Claire Priest, "Colonial Courts and Secured Credit: Early American Commercial Litigation and Shays' Rebellion," *Yale Law Journal* 108 (1999): 2413–50, 2440–44.

40. Bruce H. Mann, *Republic of Debtors* (Cambridge, MA: Harvard University Press, 2002), 174–75; Warren, *Bankruptcy in United States History*,147. These debt relief laws were typically either stay laws or legal tender laws. Stay laws literally "stayed" the process of execution for a period of time, such as for a year. Warren, at 146–48. Legal tender laws allowed debtors to satisfy their debts with either real property or chattel property of a lesser value than was explicitly contracted for.

41. 2 N.C. (1 Hayw.) 43 (Super. Ct. 1794).

42. Ibid., 71 (Macay, J.).

43. See ibid.

44. Judge Macay, for example, stated that:

> [The Debt Recovery Act] meant to provide for two things, the sale of lands for debts, and the making them liable to all just debts in the hands of the heir: and I am of opinion, that since the act of Geo. II. the same distinctions between real and personal property is [sic] to be kept up as before—and that lands, upon the death of an ancestor, descend to the heir, and personal chattels go to the executor as before; and lands in the hands of an heir, are no more to be affected by an action or judgment against the executor, than the personal estate in the hands of an executor, are to be affected by a judgment against the heir: their interests are totally distinct and separate. Ibid., 71.

45. *Baker v. Webb*, 2 N.C. at 54–55 (Haywood, J.). Haywood said further:

> That property which is deemed the most sacred, and is the best secured by law, becomes more than any other the object of attention, because it is the most permanent, and it is

good policy to make that property most the object of attention, which the most effectually attaches its proprietor to the country he lives in, and real property possesses this quality more than any other. An industrious man, who by his labour has collected wherewithal to purchase him a little property, naturally fixes his attention on that which in all probability will continue the longest with his posterity, and which the law has rendered the most difficult to be taken from him—a freehold becomes his object, as well for the reasons above mentioned, as because the Constitution of the country has annexed to it certain privileges that advance him in the rank of citizenship; and as the freehold, when acquired, is incapable of being moved away like personal property when the danger threatens or the State has occasion to call for personal or pecuniary aid, he is always ready to be called on, and to supply the emergencies of the commonwealth; when at the same time the holder of personal property, apprised of the services which the State needs, hath withdrawn both himself and his effects from the country, and possibly throw them into the scale of the enemy. Ibid.

46. See Va. Code ch. 186, § 9 (1849); Stefan A. Riesenfeld, "Enforcement of Money Judgments in Early American History," *Michigan Law Review* 71 (1973): 691–728, 712.

47. *Smith v. Ford*, 161 A. 214 (Del. 1932), describes the history of Delaware and Pennsylvania laws making lands available to satisfy unsecured debts. See ibid., 216–17. The first statute in Pennsylvania to substantially modify the regime enacted in 1705 was an 1836 statute allowing a landowner to waive his right to have his property subject to the writ of elegit and to allow it to be sold for debts worth less than seven years of earnings. Act of June 16, 1836, No. 191, 1836 Pa. Laws 755; see also *Levy v. Spitz*, 146 A. 548, 549 (Pa. 1929); Kent, *Commentaries on American Law*, vol. 4, 428.

48. In a case heard by the Delaware Court of Chancery, for example, a tenant by elegit failed to rotate crops according to customary practice. See *Wilds v. Layton*, 1 Del. Ch. 226 (1822). The court relied on the waste doctrine to enjoin him from using any method other than the rotating three-fields system of tilling the land. Ibid., 229.

49. See A True Friend, To the Inhabitants of Virginia, *Virginia Independent Chronicle*, Nov. 14, 1787, reprinted in *The Documentary History of the Ratification of the Constitution Digital Edition*, ed. John P. Kaminski et al. (Charlottesville: University of Virginia Press, 2009; print edition, vol. 8, 1988), 159.

50. Ibid., 161–64.

51. Ibid., 160.

52. Ibid., 161.

53. It was possible, of course, to value freehold property ownership as a prerequisite to political participation and to defend laws subjecting real property to the claims of all unsecured creditors. For example, in the 1820s, Daniel Webster simultaneously attacked the English laws exempting property from creditors' claims and defended the proposition that government representation should be structured so that property owners exercised political power in proportion to the amount of property they owned. See Daniel Webster, "Speech at the Massachusetts Constitutional Convention of 1820–1821" (Dec. 15, 1820) in *Democracy, Liberty, And Property: The State Constitutional Conventions of the 1820's*, ed. Merrill D. Peterson (Online edition, Liberty Fund, 2012 repr.; Indianapolis: Bobbs-Merrill Co., 1966), 83–96.

54. See *Journal of the House of Delegates of Virginia* (October 7–December 21, 1776) (Williamsburg, VA: Alexander Purdie, 1776), 13, 24 (reporting Jefferson's introduction of the bill to abolish the fee tail). For the text of the 1776 bill, see *The Papers of Thomas Jefferson*, vol. 1, 560–61. For the 1776 Act, see An Act declaring tenants of lands or slaves in taille to hold the same in fee simple (1776), in *The Statutes at Large; Being a Collection of All the Laws of Virginia*, ed. William Waller Hening (Richmond: J & G Cochran, 1821), vol. 9, 226. It was discovered that the statute

could be avoided by placing a remainder in tail after a fee tail, because the act stated that it applied to remainders after life estates or "any lesser estate" (and fee tails were greater on the hierarchy of estates than life estates). The 1785 act stated that "Every estate in lands or slaves, which on [October 7, 1776] was an estate in fee tail, shall be deemed . . . an estate in fee simple." "An act for regulating conveyances," Hening, *Statutes at Large*, vol. 12, 156–57.

55. Thomas Jefferson, "Autobiography," *The Writings of Thomas Jefferson*, vol. 1, 49, 68.

56. The principal works on the significance of the reform of property and inheritance law in founding era political ideology are Alexander, *Commodity and Propriety*, 37–42 (examining abolition of the entail on both anti-aristocratic and functional grounds); Drew R. McCoy, *The Elusive Republic: Political Economy in Jeffersonian America* (Chapel Hill: University of North Carolina Press, 1980); Wood, *Radicalism*, 182–84; Holly Brewer, "Entailing Aristocracy in Colonial Virginia: 'Ancient Feudal Restraints' and Revolutionary Reform," *William and Mary Quarterly* 54, no. 2 (April 1997): 307–46; Richard L. Bushman, "'This New Man': Dependence and Independence, 1776," in *Uprooted Americans: Essays to Honor Oscar Handlin*, ed. Richard L. Bushman et al. (Boston, MA: Little Brown & Co., 1979), 77–96; John F. Hart, "'A Less Proportion of Idle Proprietors': Madison, Property Rights, and the Abolition of the Fee Tail," *Washington and Lee Law Review* 58 (2001): 167–94; Stanley N. Katz, "Republicanism and the Law of Inheritance in the American Revolutionary Era," *Michigan Law Review* 76 (1977): 1–29, 3 ("In the study of revolution, the law of inheritance may serve as a touchstone measuring the depth of revolutionary transformation in a society."); Stanley N. Katz, "Thomas Jefferson and the Right to Property in Revolutionary America," *Journal of Law & Economics* 19 (1976): 467–88; and David Thomas Konig, "Jurisprudence and Social Policy in the New Republic," in *Devising Liberty: Preserving and Creating Freedom in the New American Republic*, ed. David Thomas Konig (Stanford: Stanford University Press, 1995), 178–216, 191–96. Compare John V. Orth, "After the Revolution: 'Reform' of the Law of Inheritance," *Law & History Review* 10 (1992): 33–44 (emphasizing that the inheritance reforms of the Revolutionary Era could be evaded).

57. C. Ray Keim, "Primogeniture and Entail in Colonial Virginia," *William & Mary Quarterly* 25, no. 4 (October 1968): 545–86, 557–61. Following Keim, scholars such as Stanley N. Katz emphasized the symbolism of abolishing the entail, often grouping it with the abolition of primogeniture. According to Katz, "History showed that primogeniture and entail were feudal remains that had no place in a republican scheme of things and that represented the dead hand of an aristocractic corporatism they rejected." Katz, "Republicanism and the Law of Inheritance," 29. Similarly, to Gregory Alexander, primogeniture and the entail "were the principal symbols of the social hierarchy that American republicans associated with 'feudal' corruptions of the common law of property. . . . The release of land from these feudal constraints meant a release of individuals from dependency and inequality." Alexander, *Commodity and Propriety*, 40.

58. Bernard Bailyn, "Politics and Social Structure in Virginia," in *Seventeenth-Century America: Essays in Colonial History*, ed. James Morton Smith (Westport, CT: Greenwood Press, 1980): 90–115, 111.

59. Brewer estimates that 50–75% of all privately owned land was entailed in Virginia. Brewer, "Entailing Aristocracy," 311, 319, fig. 3, 345.

60. Ibid., 341–43. Brewer infers that "the Virginia legislators consciously sought to introduce into Virginia a type of feudalism." Ibid., 339.

61. Ibid., 337.

62. Gordon S. Wood, *The Creation of the American Republic, 1776–1787* (Chapel Hill: University of North Carolina Press, 1998), 88; Gordon S. Wood, *The American Revolution: A History* (New York: Modern Library, 2003), 67 (describing the Pennsylvania Constitution as "the most radical constitution of all the states").

63. See, for example, *Goodright v. Morningstar*, 1 Yeates 313 (1793), holding that entailed lands descend according to common law rules in the state, and distinguishing entail from primogeniture

on the grounds that primogeniture was against the "true spirit of the laws and constitution of this commonwealth" because "[w]e have nothing further to do with the pride of family in the character of an elder son." The entail was abolished in An Act . . . for the more Just and Safe Transmission and Secure Enjoyment of Real and Personal Estate, No. 387 (1855), in *Laws of the General Assembly of the State of Pennsylvania* (Harrisburg, PA: A. Boyd Hamilton, 1855), 368 ("[W]henever hereafter by any gift, conveyance, or devise, an estate in fee tail would be created according to the existing laws of this state, it shall be taken and construed to be an estate in fee simple, and as such shall be inheritable and freely alienable.").

64. Wood, *Radicalism*, 181–89.

65. An Act . . . to do away entails (1784), *Laws of North Carolina* (Newbern, NC: Thomas Davis, 1784), ch. 22, 33–34.

66. An Act declaring tenants of lands or slaves in taille to hold the same in fee simple (1776), Hening, *Statutes at Large*, vol. 9, 226.

67. Kent, *Commentaries on American Law*, vol. 4, 20 ("Entailments are recommended in monarchical governments, as a protection to the power and influence of the landed aristocracy; but such a policy has no application to republican establishments, where wealth does not form a permanent distinction, and under which every individual of every family has his equal rights, and is equally invited, by the genius of the institutions, to depend upon his own merit and exertions."); St. George Tucker, *Blackstone's Commentaries: with Notes of Reference, to the Constitution and Laws, of the Federal Government of the United States; and of the Commonwealth of Virginia* (1803) (Union, NJ: The Lawbook Exchange, 1996), vol. 3, 119, n.14. ("[W]hen the revolution took place, a different mode of thinking succeeded; it was found that entails would be the means of accumulating and preserving great estates in certain families, which would . . . be utterly incompatible with the genius and spirit of our constitution and government.")

68. Edmund S. Morgan, *American Slavery, American Freedom: The Ordeal of Colonial Virginia* (New York: W. W. Norton, 1975).

69. The problem of information costs imposed by restraints on alienation is emphasized in Thomas W. Merrill and Henry E. Smith, "Optimal Standardization in the Law of Property: The Numerus Clausus Principle," *Yale Law Journal* 110 (2000): 1–70; Henry Hansmann and Reinier Kraakman, "Property, Contract, and Verification: The Numerus Clausus Problem and the Divisibility of Rights," *Journal of Legal Studies* 31 (2002): 373–420; and Michael A. Heller, "The Boundaries of Private Property," *Yale Law Journal* 108 (1999): 1163–1223.

70. Blackstone, *Commentaries*, vol. 2, 115–16.

71. An Act declaring tenants of lands or slaves in taille to hold the same in fee simple (1776), Hening, *Statutes at Large*, vol. 9, 226.

72. An Act . . . to Limit Estates in Tail, 98 ("that no Entailment of any Lands or other Real Estate shall continue to entail the same in any Case whatever, longer than the Life of the Person to whom the same hath been or shall be first given or devised by such Entailment"); and "An Act relating to the Age, Ability and Capacity of Persons," *Acts and Laws of the State of Connecticut, in America* (Hartford, CT: Elisha Babcock, 1786), 3 ("*[I]n order to avoid Perpetuities . . .* all Estates given in Tail, shall be and remain an absolute Estate in Fee-Simple, to the Issue of the first Donee in Tail.").

73. An Act Providing a More Easy and Simple Method than is Now in Use of Barring Estates Tail in Lands (1792), *Acts and Laws of the Commonwealth of Massachusetts, 1790–91* (Massachusetts, 1889): 359–60 (Massachusetts Act allowing entails to be barred by deed); "An Act to Facilitate the Barring of Entails" (January 16, 1799), *The Statutes at Large of Pennsylvania* (Harrisburg, PA: C. E. Aughinbaugh, State Printer, 1911), vol. 16, 149–50 (Pennsylvania Act allowing entails to be barred by deed); and An Act Concerning Estates Tail, *Laws of Maryland* (Annapolis, MD: Frederick Green, State Printer, 1783), pages not numbered. (Maryland Act allowing entails to be barred by deed.)

74. An Act . . . to Limit Estates in Tail,"*Acts of the Eighth General Assembly of the State of New Jersey* (Trenton, NJ: Isaac Collins, State Printer, 1784), 97.

75. An Act Concerning Estates Tail, *Laws of Maryland* (Annapolis: Frederick Green, State Printer, 1783), pages not numbered.

76. An Act declaring tenants of lands or slaves in taille to hold the same in fee simple (1776), Hening, *Statutes at Large*, vol. 9, 226; An act for regulating conveyances, Hening, *Statutes at Large*, vol. 12, 156–57.

77. Art. 51, *Georgia Constitution of 1777* ("Estates shall not be entailed . . ."); Art. IV, Sec. 6, *Georgia Constitution of 1789* (same), in *Sources and Documents of United States Constitutions*, vol. 2, ed. William F. Swindler (Dobbs Ferry, NY: Oceana Publications, 1973), 449, 454.

78. An Act to Abolish Entails (July 12, 1782), *Laws of the State of New York* (Poughkeepsie, NY: John Holt, State Printer, 1782), ("[I]n all Cases wherein any Person . . . would, if this Law had not been made, have been seized in Fee-Tail . . . such Person . . . shall, in future, be deemed to be seized of the same in Fee-Simple"); and An Act to Abolish Entails (February 23, 1786), in *Laws of the State of New York* (New York: Samuel Loudon & John Loudon, 1786), 14 "[A]ll Estates Tail shall be, and are hereby abolished . . .").

79. An Act . . . to do away entails (1784), *Laws of North Carolina* (Newbern, NC: Thomas Davis, 1784), ch. 22, 33–34.

80. Act of December 19, 1796 ("Every estate in lands or slaves, which on [October 7, 1776] was an estate in fee-tail, shall be deemed from that time to have been, and from thenceforth to continue an estate in fee simple . . ."), in *Acts Passed at the First Session of the Fifth General Assembly for the Commonwealth of Kentucky* (Lexington, KY: James H. Stewart, 1796), 75.

81. "An Act to amend an Act, respecting Conveyances" (December 22, 1812) in *Acts Passed at the Second Session of the Seventh General Assembly of the Mississippi Territory* (Natchez, MS: Peter Isler, 1812), 87 ("every estate in lands, or slaves, which now is or shall hereafter be created an estate in fee-tail, shall from henceforth be an estate in fee-simple . . .").

82. "An Act Declaring what laws shall be in force in this territory" (January 19, 1816) in *Acts Passed by the General Assembly of the Territory of Missouri* (St. Louis, MO: Joseph Charless, 1816), 32–33 ("The doctrine of entails shall never be allowed . . .").

83. Ch. 11, Hening, *Statutes at Large*, vol. 4, 226.

84. James H. Soltow, *The Economic Role of Williamsburg* (Williamsburg: University Press of Virginia, 1965), 24.

85. Harry J. Carman, ed., *American Husbandry* (1775) (New York: Columbia University Press, 1939), 164.

86. William Tatham, *An Historical and Practical Essay on the Culture and Commerce of Tobacco* (London: T. Bensley, 1800), 6.

87. Ch. 31, Hening, *Statutes at Large*, vol. 7, 460.

88. This analysis of the abolition of the entail is consistent with the eighteenth-century perception of the South held by residents of regions with fewer slaves. According to the historian David Brion Davis, "As early as the mid-eighteenth century, . . . slave societies were acquiring the image of social and cultural wastelands blighted by an obsessive pursuit of private profit." David Brion Davis, *Slavery and Human Progress* (New York: Oxford University Press, 1984), 80.

89. An Act declaring tenants of lands or slaves in taille to hold the same in fee simple, Hening, *Statutes at Large*, vol. 9, 226.

90. David F. Weiman, "Peopling the Land by Lottery? The Market in Public Lands and the Regional Differentiation of Territory on the Georgia Frontier," *Journal of Economic History* 51, no. 4 (December 1991): 835–60. Weiman discusses inequities that emerged in the market for public lands in frontier areas. The profitability of slavery, however, was likely to have led to a similar dynamic in more settled regions.

Chapter 8. Property and Credit in the Early Republic

1. Madison to Washington, April 16, 1787, *The Papers of James Madison,*ed. W. T. Hutchinson, William M. E. Rachal, and R. A. Rutland (Chicago: University of Chicago Press, 1962–), vol. 9, 383–84. See also Alison L. LaCroix, *The Ideological Origins of American Federalism* (Cambridge, MA: Harvard University Press, 2010), 145–53.

2. See Act of Sept. 29, 1789, ch. 21, 1 Stat. 93; Charles Warren, "Federal Process and State Legislation," *Virginia Law Review* 16 (1929–1930): 421–50, 426–30.

3. 2 Annals of Cong. 1730 (1790).

4. See Warren, "Federal Process and State Legislation" (describing the use of state remedies in the federal courts through the first half of the nineteenth century).

5. See "A Law Subjecting Real Estate to Execution for Debt" (1795) in *The Laws of the Northwest Territory, 1788–1800*, ed. Theodore Calvin Pease (Springfield: Trustees of the Illinois State Historical Library, 1925), 131.

6. "Letter from Thomas Jefferson to Thomas Mann Randolph, Jr." (Dec. 21, 1792) in *The Papers of Thomas Jefferson*, ed. John Catanzariti (Princeton, NJ: Princeton University Press,1990), vol. 24, 775.

7. "Thoughts on the Bankruptcy Bill" (circa Dec. 10, 1792) in *The Papers of Thomas Jefferson*, vol. 24, 722. For a more detailed discussion of Jefferson's views on bankruptcy legislation, see Bruce H. Mann, *Republic of Debtors* (Cambridge, MA: Harvard University Press, 2002), 196–98.

8. 9 Annals of Cong. (1799), 2660.

9. Ibid.

10. Ibid., 2651.

11. 1 Annals of Cong., ed. Joseph Gales (1851), 533–34; Charles Warren, *Bankruptcy in United States History* (Cambridge, MA: Harvard University Press, 1935), 19–20.

12. See G. Marcus Cole, "The Federalist Cost of Bankruptcy Exemption Reform," *American Bankruptcy Law Journal* 74 (2000): 227–74, 242–46 (describing variation in property exemption laws in colonial and founding era America, recognized under nineteenth-century bankruptcy statutes, as evidence of the "federalist character" of early bankruptcy policy).

13. See William T. Vukowich, "Debtors' Exemption Rights," *Georgetown Law Journal* 62 (1974): 779–878, 783.

14. See, e.g., Act of June 16, 1807, 1807 N.H. Laws 19. Colonial legislation typically exempted only "tools of the trade."

15. Charles Warren, *Bankruptcy in United States History* (Cambridge, MA: Harvard University Press, 1935), 26–27.

16. See ibid.; Edward J. Balleisen, *Navigating Failure: Bankruptcy and Commercial Society in Antebellum America* (Chapel Hill: University of North Carolina Press, 2001), 12.

17. See Balleisen, *Navigating Failure*, 12; see also *Annual Law Register of the United States* (William Griffith, ed., 1822), vols. 3-4 (listing state property exemptions). In response to the proliferation of educational institutions, many of the new state laws exempted "bibles and school books," "books of professional men," or "books of a student" from creditors' claims. See Morton J. Horwitz, "Conceptualizing the Right of Access to Technology," *Washington Law Review* 79 (2004): 105–18, 113 and n.37.

18. James Kent, *Commentaries on American Law* (Buffalo, NY: Hein, 1984 reprint) (New York: 1830), vol. 4, 427 ("[A]ll . . . redemptions must be within the fifteen months from the time of the sheriff's sale; for the sheriff is then to execute a deed to the person entitled, and the title so acquired becomes absolute in law." [citing *Revised Statutes of the State of New York* (Albany: Packard & Van BenThuysen, 1829), vol. 2, 370–74)].

19. Ibid., 426.

20. See Richard H. Chused, "Married Women's Property Law: 1800–1850," *Georgetown Law Journal* 71 (1983):1359–1426, 1400–1404.

21. See ibid., 1398–99 and nn.207–09 (citing laws enacted in Mississippi in 1839; Maryland in 1842 and 1843; Florida, Maine, Massachusetts, Michigan, and Vermont in 1845; Connecticut in 1845 and 1849; Alabama, Arkansas, Iowa, Kentucky, New Hampshire, and Ohio in 1846; Indiana in 1847; New York and Pennsylvania in 1848; Missouri and North Carolina in 1849; Tennessee and Wisconsin in 1850; and New Jersey in 1852).

22. The homestead exemption laws typically required that homeowners preregister their property as exempt—by signing a certificate that was then attached to the title recorded by the county—prior to obtaining the benefits of the law. See Paul Goodman, "The Emergence of Homestead Exemption in the United States: Accommodation and Resistance to the Market Revolution, 1840–1880," *Journal of American History* 80, no. 2 (September 1993): 470–98, 470–72; see also Alison D. Morantz, "There's No Place Like Home: Homestead Exemption and Judicial Construction of Family in Nineteenth-Century America," *Law & History Review* 24 (2006): 245–95, 252–54 (describing by region the spread of homestead exemption laws); Vukowich, "Debtors' Exemption Rights," 783 (discussing economic depressions and other factors as impetuses for homestead exemption laws in Southern and Western states).

23. Joseph Story, *Commentaries on the Constitution of the United States* (Boston: Hilliard, Gray, & Co., 1833), book 1, §182.

24. An Act To Prevent the Committing of Frauds by Bankrupts, 5 Geo. 2, c. 30 (1732).

25. An Act for More Effectually Securing the Payment of the Debts of Traders, 47 Geo. 3, c. 74 (1807). As mentioned, in 1833, Parliament repealed all protections to land from the claims of unsecured creditors as part of a broad reform of English property law.

Chapter 9. Property, Institutions, and Economic Growth in Colonial America

1. For a nuanced description of both political and economic justifications of property, see Carol M. Rose, "Property as the Keystone Right?" *Notre Dame Law Review* 71 (1995): 329–70.

2. Gary D. Libecap, "Property Rights," *The Oxford Encyclopedia of Economic History*, ed. Joel Mokyr (Oxford: Oxford University Press, 2003).

3. These incentives emanate in part from what J. E. Penner has called the "exclusion thesis" that the right to property is "a right to exclude others from things which is grounded by the interest we have in the use of things." J. E. Penner, *The Idea of Property in Law* (New York: Oxford University Press, 1997), 71.

4. Thrainn Eggertsson, "Open Access versus Common Property," *Property Rights: Cooperation, Conflict, and Law*, ed. Terry L. Anderson and Fred S. McChesney (Princeton, NJ: Princeton University Press, 2003), 73–89.

5. Thomas W. Merrill and Henry E. Smith, "Optimal Standardization in the Law of Property: The Numerus Clausus Principle," 110 *Yale Law Journal* (2000), 1–70. Similarly, Carol Rose emphasizes that government supports property regimes by providing "off-the-rack" property forms. Carol M. Rose, "What Government Can Do for Property (and Vice Versa)," in *The Fundamental Interrelationships Between Government and Property*, ed. Nicholas Mercuro and Warren J. Samuels (Stamford, CT: JAI Press, 1999), 209.

6. Merrill and Smith, "Optimal Standardization." In a similar vein, Gary Libecap and Dean Lueck used a natural experiment in nineteenth-century Ohio to empirically analyze the economic effects of two dominant systems of demarcating land boundaries: metes and bounds, where land boundaries are marked by natural or other local features and are often irregular; and the rectangular system, that is, the grid system adopted as part of the Northwest Ordinance. Consistent

with Merrill's and Smith's prediction that lowering information costs improves market conditions, Libecap and Lueck found that prices of the standardized parcels, those demarcated according to the rectangular system, had economic benefits that kept increasing over time: There were lower costs of enforcing boundaries, lower trading costs in land markets, lower coordination costs in building infrastructure like roads and fences, and the land parcels had higher prices per acre that grew over time in relation to the metes and bounds parcels. Gary D. Libecap and Dean Lueck, "The Demarcation of Land and the Role of Coordinating Property Institutions, *Journal of Political Economy* 119, no. 3 (June 2011): 426–67. Maureen Brady examines the advantages of metes and bounds in small communities, such as colonial New Haven, in Maureen E. Brady, "The Forgotten History of Metes and Bounds," *Yale Law Journal* 128 (2018): 872–953.

7. Henry Hansmann and Reinier Kraakman, "Property, Contract, and Verification: The Numerus Clausus Problem and the Divisibility of Rights," *Journal of Legal Studies* 31 (2002): 373–420.

8. North defines institutions broadly as the "humanly devised constraints that . . . structure incentives in humam exchange, whether political, social, or economic." Institutions consist of both "formal constraints—such as rules that human beings devise—and . . . informal constraints—such as conventions and codes of behavior." Douglass C. North, *Institutions, Institutional Change, and Economic Performance* (New York: Cambridge University Press, 1990), 3, 4. See also Douglass C. North, *Structure and Change in Economic History* (New York: W.W. Norton, 1981); Douglass C. North, John Joseph Wallis, and Barry R. Weingast, *Violence and Social Orders: A Conceptual Framework for Interpreting Recorded Human History* (Cambridge: Cambridge University Press, 2013). North's earlier work often described "property rights" in relation to central government confiscation of property and representative bodies that enact laws binding all political actors in the society. In their influential article of 1989, for example, Douglass North and Barry Weingast explain the growth of English capital markets as deriving, in part, from the Glorious Revolution of 1688, which empowered Parliament to impose restraints on the monarchy and to credibly commit to upholding property rights. Douglass C. North and Barry R. Weingast, "Constitutions and Commitment: The Evolution of Institutions Governing Public Choice in Seventeenth-Century England,"*Journal of Economic History* 49, no. 4 (December 1989): 803–32.

9. Daron Acemoglu, Simon Johnson, and James A. Robinson, "The Colonial Origins of Comparative Development: An Empirical Investigation," *American Economic Review* 91, no. 5 (December 2001): 1369–1401, 1369 (linking economic growth to the effect of mortality rates on institutional development). In a separate article, the authors define institutions of private property as "a cluster of (political, economic, and social) institutions ensuring that a broad cross section of society has effective property rights." Daron Acemoglu, Simon Johnson, and James A. Robinson, "Reversal of Fortune: Geography and Institutions in the Making of the Modern World Income Distribution," *Quarterly Journal of Economics* 117, no. 4 (November 2002): 1231–1294, 1262.

10. Rafael La Porta, Florencio Lopez-de-Silanes, and Andrei Shleifer, "The Economic Consequences of Legal Origins," *Journal of Economic Literature* 46, no. 2 (June 2008): 285–332. For a nuanced analysis comparing legal origins with the national identity of the colonizer, see Daniel M. Klerman et al., "Legal Origin or Colonial History?" *Journal of Legal Analysis* 3 (2011): 379–409.

11. Acemoglu, Johnson, and Robinson, "Colonial Origins of Comparative Development," 1369. As the legal scholar Christian Burset has described, however, the settler mortality theory overlooks that British colonial officials decided as a policy matter in eighteenth-century that Bengal and other colonies were to adopt a more extractive model of colonial rule. Christian Burset, "Why Didn't the Common Law Follow the Flag?," *Virginia Law Review* 105 (2019): 483–542.

12. Acemoglu, Johnson, and Robinson, "Reversal of Fortune." See also Kenneth L. Sokoloff and Stanley L. Engerman, "History Lessons: Institutions, Factor Endowments, and Paths of Development in the New World," *Journal of Economic Perspectives* 14, no. 3 (Summer 2000): 217–32.

13. Joel Mokyr, *The Enlightened Economy: An Economic History of Britain, 1700–1850* (New Haven, CT: Yale University Press, 2009), 413.

14. Ibid., 26.

15. Joseph H. Smith, *Appeals to the Privy Council from the American Plantations* (New York: Columbia University Press, 1950).

16. Katharina Pistor, *The Code of Capital: How Law Creates Wealth and Inequality* (Princeton, NJ: Princeton University Press 2019), 2.

17. Hernando de Soto, *The Other Path: The Economic Answer to Terrorism* (New York: Basic Books, 1989).

18. Hernando de Soto, *The Mystery of Capital: Why Capitalism Triumphs in the West and Fails Everywhere Else* (New York: Basic Books, 2000).

19. De Soto cites the historian Amelia C. Ford, who described a 1779 Virginia law as "a legal expression of a widespread sentiment . . . that the squatter was really a benefactor to the state, and not a trespasser." Amelia C. Ford, *Colonial Precedents for Our National Land System as It Existed in 1800* (Madison: University of Wisconsin Press, 1910), 132. An Act for Adjusting and Settling the Titles of Claimers to Unpatented Land Under the Present and Former Government, Previous to the Establishment of the Commonwealth's Land Office, (May 3, 1779) *The Statutes at Large; Being a Collection of All the Laws of Virginia*, ed. William Waller Hening (Richmond, VA: George Cochran, 1822), vol. 10, ch. 12, 40; De Soto, *Mystery of Capital*, 120. De Soto's chapter examines the history of the battle between squatters who wanted recognition of their title and politicians who wanted to sell plots of public land to pay down the federal debt throughout the first half of the nineteenth century. Building on the work of Terry Anderson, P. J. Hill, Gary Libecap, and others, he draws upon numerous and wide-ranging examples from the seventeenth century through the nineteenth century where high-level government actors recognized property rights in settlers who had improved land or staked mining claims. Terry L. Anderson and P. J. Hill, "The Evolution of Property Rights: A Study of the American West," *Journal of Law and Economics* 18 (1975), 163–79; Gary D. Libecap, "Economic Variables and the Development of the Law: The Case of Western Mineral Rights," *Journal of Economic History* 38, no. 2 (June 1978), 338–62.

20. De Soto, *Mystery of Capital*, 39–67. Similarly, the World Bank's researchers advance the view that formalizing property titles improves individuals' chances of obtaining credit and increases property values. For World Bank data on the number of procedures, time, and cost of registering title in 185 countries, see http://www.doingbusiness.org/data/exploretopics/registering-property. The World Bank has implemented many title registration programs as part of its long-standing economic development program.

21. See Christopher Woodruff, "Review of de Soto's *The Mystery of Capital*," *Journal of Economic Literature* 39 (December 2001): 1215–23, 1222 ("[L]and titling by itself is not likely to have much effect. . . . Improving the efficiency of judicial systems, re-writing bankruptcy codes, restructuring financial market regulations and similar reforms will involve much more difficult choices for policy makers."; Edesio Fernandes, "The Influence of de Soto's 'The Mystery of Capital,'" *Land Lines* (Lincoln Institute of Land Policy, January 2002): 5–8, https://www.lincolninst.edu/publications/articles/influence-sotos-mystery-capital.

22. The development of colonial legal institutions is described in chapter 2.

23. The historian Bonnie Martin empirically examined mortgages in three colonies and found that, although only 39% of the mortgages used slaves as some or all of collateral, the mortgages that used slaves as collateral account for two-thirds of the funds extended. Bonnie Martin, "Slavery's Invisible Engine: Mortgaging Human Property," *Journal of Southern History* 76, no. 4 (November 2010): 817–66, 821.

24. An Act to prevent Deceits by Double Mortgages and Conveyances of Lands, Negroes and Chattels (October 8, 1698), *The Statutes at Large of South Carolina* (Columbia, SC: A. S.

Johnston, 1837), vol. 2, no. 161, 66–67. The economic historian Jenny Wahl has analyzed how slavery led to introduction of implied warranty law in the nineteenth century. Jenny Bourne Wahl, *The Bondsman's Burden: An Economic Analysis of the Common Law of Southern Slavery* (New York: Cambridge University Press, 1998), 34–42.

25. Gavin Wright, *Slavery and American Economic Development* (Baton Rouge: Louisiana State University Press, 2006), 29.

26. Gavin Wright, *Old South, New South: Revolutions in the Southern Economy since the Civil War* (New York: Basic Books, 1986), 24–26, 30–31 (asserting that the large amount of wealth invested in slaves placed pressure on slaveholders to put slaves to their most productive use, which led to high rates of geographic mobility).

27. Wright, *Slavery and American Economic Development*, 60 and table 2.4 (regional wealth in 1850 and 1860).

28. Ibid., 62, 73.

29. An Act for the Reducing the Interest of Money on All Future Contracts, and for the Advancing the Credit of Bills of Exchange (1739), in *Laws of Jamaica* (St. Jago de la Vega, Alexander Aikman 1792), vol. 1, ch. 3, 262.

30. Ibid., pmbl., 262–63.

31. An Act for Establishing Courts of Law, and for Regulating the Proceedings Therein (1777) in *Acts of Assembly of the State of North Carolina* (Newbern, James Davis 1778), ch. 2, § 29, 8, 16; see also Act of Feb. 15, 1791, 1791 N.H. Laws 122 (establishing a regime whereby lands would be transferred to creditors in kind, with a one-year statutory redemption period, when a debtor's personal property was deficient).

32. Story, *Commentaries*, book 1, §182, p. 168.

33. Jacob M. Price, "Credit in the Slave Trade and Plantation Economies," in *Slavery and the Rise of the Atlantic System*, ed. Barbara L. Solow (New York: Cambridge University Press, 1991), 296, 298 (internal quotation marks omitted); Russell R. Menard, "Law, Credit, the Supply of Labour, and the Organization of Sugar Production in the Colonial Greater Caribbean: A Comparison of Brazil and Barbados in the Seventeenth Century," in *Early Modern Atlantic Economy*, ed. John J. McCusker and Kenneth Morgan (New York: Cambridge University Press, 2000), 161.

34. Menard, "Law, Credit," 161; see also Richard B. Sheridan, *Sugar and Slavery: An Economic History of the British West Indies, 1623–1775* (Kingston, Jamaica: Canoe Press, 1994), 288–90 (describing briefly the Debt Recovery Act in the context of the slave trade in the West Indies).

35. Alice Hanson Jones, "Wealth Estimates for the American Middle Colonies, 1774," *Economic Development and Cultural Change* 18, no. 4 (July 1970): 1–172, 130; John J. McCusker and Russell R. Menard, *The Economy of British America, 1607–1789* (Chapel Hill: University of North Carolina Press, Institute for Early American History and Culture, 1985), 55.

36. Robert C. Allen, Tommy E. Murphy, and Eric B. Schneider, "The Colonial Origins of the Divergence in the Americas: A Labor Market Approach," *Journal of Economic History* 72, no. 4 (December 2012): 863–94.

37. Peter H. Lindert and Jeffrey G. Williamson, *Unequal Gains: American Growth and Inequality since 1700* (Princeton, NJ: Princeton University Press, 2016), ch. 2.

38. Joshua L. Rosenbloom, "The Colonial American Economy," Iowa State University Digital Repository, Economics Working Papers (02-27-2018), 3. James A. Henretta's review of an earlier literature found that the growth rate in per capita income in the New England colonies averaged no more than 0.2–0.5% per year. James A. Henretta, "Wealth and Social Structure," *The Origins of American Capitalism: Collected Essays* (Boston, MA: Northeastern University Press, 1991), at 148, 167 (finding that, although there is variation between economists' studies, all current scholarship places per capita growth rates in the New England colonies within the range of 0.2–0.5%). Gloria L. Main's and Jackson T. Main's study of probate inventories in southern New England over the

period 1640 to 1774 found that wealth was growing in land and buildings, but found a little growth in other categories of wealth. Based on their evaluation of Massachusetts and Connecticut probate records, Gloria L. Main and Jackson T. Main argue that total estate value in pounds constant per free White male had an average annual growth rate of 0.35–0.5% in the period from 1650 to 1774. Gloria L. Main and Jackson T. Main, "Economic Growth and the Standard of Living in Southern New England, 1640–1774," *Journal of Economic History* 48, no. 1 (March 1988): 27–46, at 35; Alice Hanson Jones argues that the colonies' per capita nonhuman wealth increased 0.3% per year during the period from 1650 to 1725, 0.4% during the period from 1725 to 1750, and 0.5% during the period from 1750 to 1774. Alice Hanson Jones, *Wealth of a Nation to Be: The American Colonies on the Eve of the Revolution* (New York: Columbia University Press, 1980), 305.

39. To what do they attribute the source of the second growth spurt? To McCusker and Menard, "the second period of growth can be attributed to burgeoning metropolitan demand for American products, although more-strictly internal processes that reflected a widening domestic market also played a role." McCusker and Menard, *Economy of British America*, 60.

40. Ibid., 280, table 13.1. The authors note that the data are compiled and printed in the Bureau of the Census, *Historical Statistics of the United States: Colonial Times to 1970* (Washington, DC: US Department of Commerce, 1975), vol. 2, 1176–78 (for population data, 1168).

41. Peter C. Mancall and Thomas Weiss, "Was Economic Growth Likely in Colonial British North America?" *Journal of Economic History* 59, no. 1 (March 1999): 17–40.

42. Peter C. Mancall, Joshua L. Rosenbloom, and Thomas Weiss, "Commodity Export, Invisible Exports, and Terms of Trade for the Middle Colonies, 1720 to 1775" (September 2008), NBER Working Paper.

43. McCusker and Menard estimate that the total population of the continental colonies grew 3% per year from 1660 to 1780. They state that the mainland colonies show diversity, with New England growing at an annual average rate of 2.4%, and the Lower South growing at 4.3%. McCusker and Menard, *Economy of British America*, 217. The economic historian Nick Crafts found lower growth rates for England during the eighteenth and early nineteenth centuries. Nick Crafts, "The Industrial Revolution," *Economic History of Britain since 1700*, ed. Roderick Floud and D. N. McCloskey (New York: Cambridge University Press, 1994), vol. 1, 44–59, 47 and table 3.3 (finding growth rates of 0.6–1.9% during the period from 1700 to 1831); see also Robert Allen, "Agriculture During the Industrial Revolution," *Economic History of Britain since 1700*, vol. 1, 96–122, 100–103 and fig. 5.1 (reviewing literature on growth rates during England's agricultural and industrial revolutions).

44. Ran Abramitzky and Fabio Braggion, "Migration and Human Capital: Self-Selection of Indentured Servants to the Americas, *Journal of Economic History* 66 (2006): 882–905.

45. Rachel E. Kranton and Anand V. Swamy, "The Hazards of Piecemeal Reform: British Civil Courts and the Credit Market in Colonial India," *Journal of Development Economics* 58 (1999): 1–24.

INDEX

The Princeton Economic History of the Western World
Joel Mokyr, Series Editor

Recent titles

A NOTE ON THE TYPE

This book has been composed in Adobe Text and Gotham.
Adobe Text, designed by Robert Slimbach for Adobe,
bridges the gap between fifteenth- and sixteenth-century
calligraphic and eighteenth-century Modern styles.
Gotham, inspired by New York street signs, was designed
by Tobias Frere-Jones for Hoefler & Co.